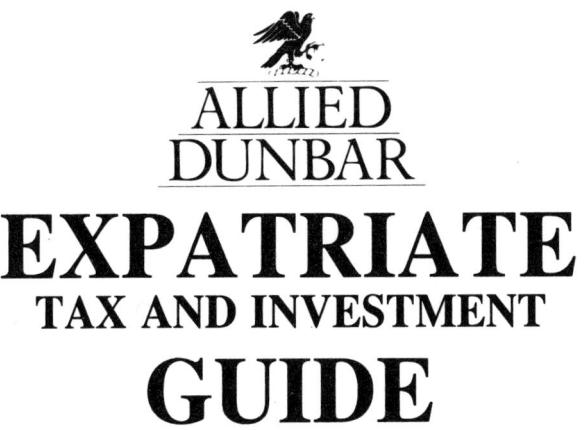

EXPATRIATE
TAX AND INVESTMENT
GUIDE

ALLIED DUNBAR
EXPATRIATE TAX AND INVESTMENT GUIDE

Third Edition

by

Nigel Eastaway, FCA, FCCA, FCMA,
FCIS, FTII, FHKSA, FTIHK
of Moores & Rowland, Chartered Accountants
Jonathan Miller
International Marketing
Allied Dunbar
and
David Phillips
publisher
Resident Abroad, a Financial Times publication

©Allied Dunbar Financial Services Ltd 1989

ISBN 0 85121 468 1

Published by

Longman Professional and Business Communications Division
Longman Group UK Limited
21–27 Lamb's Conduit Street, London WC1N 3NJ

Associated Offices

Australia Longman Cheshire Pty Ltd, Longman House, Kings Gardens, 91–97 Coventry Street, South Melbourne, Victoria 3205

Hong Kong Longman Group (Far East) Limited
Cornwall House, 18th Floor, Taikoo Trading Estate, Tong Chong Street, Quarry Bay

Malaysia Longman Malaysia Sdn Bhd
No 3 Jalan Kilang A, Off Jalan Penchala, Petaling Jaya, Selangor, Malaysia

Singapore Longman Singapore Publishers (Pte) Ltd
25 First Lok Yang Road, Singapore 2262

USA Longman Group (USA) Inc
500 North Dearborn Street, Chicago, Illinois 60610

All rights reserved.
No part of this publication may be reproduced, stored in a retrieval system, or transmitted, in any form or by any means, electronic, mechanical, photocopying, recording or otherwise, without either the prior written permission of the copyright holder for which application should be addressed in the first instance to the publishers, or a licence permitting restricted copying issued by the Copyright Licensing Agency Limited, 33–34 Alfred Place, London, WC1E 7DP.

British Library Cataloguing-in-Publication Data
A CIP catalogue record for this book is available from the British Library.

Printed in Great Britain by Biddles Ltd, Guildford, Surrey

Acknowledgement

We would like to thank for their assistance in the preparation of this new edition, John Jeffrey-Cook, FCA, FCIS, FTII, Colin Rhead, FCA, Richard H Parry, FCA, ATII of *Moores & Rowland*, V J Jerrard, LLB, ACII, Stuart G Reynolds, LLB, M D Davies, BA, S R C Arnot BA, LLB, and S M Redman, LLB all of *Allied Dunbar Assurance plc*, and Bill Glover of *Personal Financial Consultants Ltd*. Two new chapters have been specially written for this edition: on investment and floating exchange rates, by Howard Flight, MA, managing director, *Guinness Flight Global Asset Management Ltd*; and on the tax aspects of UK property income, by P A Goodman, MA, ACA, ATII of *Wilkins Kennedy*. The chapter on investment has been re-written by Richard Sayer, senior consultant International Investment Marketing *Allied Dunbar Assurance plc*.

Finally, general editorial advice on the preparation of this edition has been given by David Phillips, MA, DPhil, of *Resident Abroad* and *Financial Times Business Information*.

Nigel Eastaway
Jonathan Miller
December 1988

Introduction

The word 'expatriate' means simply a person living away from his or her native country: it in no way refers (as is often mistakenly implied) to a person's former situation or state. In this book, two broad categories of expatriate are considered: British citizens living overseas, whether in employment or in retirement; and foreign nationals living in the UK, or, at least, visiting it for a considerable period. In both cases, we have tried to explain the individual's liability to UK taxation, with a view to enabling him or her to plan his or her financial affairs and investments in a tax-efficient way. In any form of tax planning it is essential to bear in mind that it is the net return after taxation that is important, and that reducing tax payments should never be an end in itself. Since 1981, moreover, a number of legal judgments have nullified complicated tax avoidance schemes of one sort or another; and it is now established that if a pre-ordained series of transactions contains steps inserted with no business purpose other than the avoidance of tax, the inserted steps will be ignored for tax purposes : *Craven* v *White* 1988 STC 476.

For some purposes in this book, for example in explaining UK capital gains tax or UK inheritance tax, it has been necessary to consider both categories of expatriate, the Briton overseas, and the non-Briton in the UK, in one and the same chapter. But a separate chapter has been devoted to overseas visitors to the UK (Chapter 8). Similarly, a separate chapter has been devoted to Britons who retire overseas or emigrate for good (Chapter 3), because as the law stands at present their liability to UK tax is in some areas different from that of working British expatriates. The special concerns of British expatriates returning to the UK are the subject of Chapter 4.

As the expatriate Briton may be residing anywhere in the world, it is clearly impractical to deal with his taxation liabilities in the country of residence but these are, of course, of considerable importance and may well require local professional advice. Nor is it possible in a book of this length to deal with matters in great depth and we have tried to concentrate on those areas which we feel are of prime importance to the expatriate. For a more detailed explanation of the UK tax legislation, the reader is referred in the first instance to the *Allied Dunbar Tax Guide*, the *Allied Dunbar Pensions Guide* and the *Allied Dunbar Capital Taxes and Estate Planning Guide*, and in the field of investment to the *Allied Dunbar Investment Guide* and the *Expatriates Guide to Savings and Investment* published by the Financial Times. Taxation is a complicated subject and in many cases competent professional advice will be required.

This book goes to press at a time when fundamental and far-reaching changes in, firstly, the law of domicile in the UK, and secondly, the system of UK taxation based on the (not statutorily defined) concepts of 'residence' and 'ordinary residence' are under review by the authorities concerned. The Law Commission and the Scottish Law Commission have drawn up a report on the Law of Domicile, that was presented to Parliament in September 1987. The report (Cm 200) contains the draft of a Bill intituled an Act to make new provision for determining the domicile of individuals, and also a summary of the recommendations made in the report. The report identifies seven areas where domicile is relevant to UK tax, and states that no clear case had been put to its authors for abandoning the use of domicile in the context of taxation. But the report also recommends that the legislation to implement its proposals should come into effect, not two or three months after Royal Assent, but on an identified date which could be fixed at a date some months after Royal Assent in order to give taxpayers and their advisers full opportunity to consider how changes in the law of domicile might affect their individual taxation circumstances.

The second set of proposed changes referred to in the preceding paragraph is contained in the Inland Revenue's consultative document *Residence in the United Kingdom: the scope of UK taxation for individuals*, published in July 1988. This document looks at two main issues: the existing rules for determining UK tax residence; and the unique UK 'remittance basis' of taxation which, for many years, has been a major tax advantage for foreigners in the UK. As regards domicile, the document considers two possible approaches: to retain the concept of domicile, but to introduce a rule that, purely for tax purposes, a person who had been resident in the UK for a number of years should be regarded as sufficiently 'fiscally connected' with the UK to be liable to tax in the UK on his worldwide income and gains; or to drop the concept of domicile altogether (in the context of tax) and replace it by a concept of 'fiscal connection' based purely on years of residence. With some qualifications, the authors of the document seem to favour the latter of these two approaches. What in effect is being proposed by the Inland Revenue is a statutory test of residence under which an individual who is present in the UK for 30 days or fewer than 30 days in any tax year would not be tax resident, but an individual who is present in the UK for 183 days or more in any tax year would be tax resident in the UK in that year. If an individual is present in the UK between 30 and 183 days in any tax year, his residence status for tax purposes will be determined by including not only the days spent in the UK during the year in question, but also one-third of those in the preceding tax year and one-sixth of those in the tax year before that. The effect would be that an individual would be able to spend up to 120 days every year in the UK without ever becoming resident for tax purposes. To overcome the possible abuse of the proposed system by individuals leaving the UK for short absences, it is suggested in the consultative document that the concept of 'fiscal connection' be applied, so that if an individual ceases to be resident in the UK for less than four years, capital gains and certain UK source income would continue to be taxed.

The Revenue believe that the remittance basis of taxation for non-domiciled individuals produces unfair results and is difficult to enforce. For many years wealthy individuals have been able to come to the UK and structure their affairs so that all their income arises outside the UK except so much as they need to live on. Because foreign income that is not remitted to the UK has not been taxable in the UK, a non-domiciled individual's tax liability has been based more on what that individual is prepared to pay than on his ability to pay. Because of the complexity of the law of domicile and the difficulties of changing a domicile, particularly a domicile of origin, it has been possible for individuals from abroad to live on this basis for many years in the UK. In determining their liability it is necessary to establish whether amounts remitted to the UK are capital, income or capital gains. The problem of identifying the source of remittances has thrown a burden on the Revenue which they consider to be unacceptable. They therefore propose that the concept of 'fiscal connection' will apply to these individuals also.

An individual who is not resident in the UK under the rules described above will be liable to tax only on UK income, but there would be an intermediate basis of taxation which would apply to residents of the UK who have not been resident here for at least seven out of the previous 14 years. The basis of this intermediate taxation would be that an individual would pay the greater of (a) tax on his UK source income or (b) a proportion of the tax on his world wide income. This proportion would increase with each additional year of residence so that after seven years residence out of 14, worldwide income would be fully taxable.

These changes would not have significant effects for a foreign executive working in the UK if the majority of his income consists of his salary for UK duties. Such an individual would both at present and in the future be fully taxable on his remuneration. A wealthy individual however who keeps the majority of his wealth and income outside the UK would be very considerably affected by this change. There are many connected issues which the Revenue have not yet addressed in their consultative document. For instance, it is not possible to say what the tax consequences would be upon offshore trusts or offshore companies controlled by a taxpayer who falls into this category; and there has been no attempt to deal with the international double taxation issues and reporting issues which arise.

The Inland Revenue consultative document, touching as it does on matters of law (such as the law of domicile) that extend beyond the field of taxation, is necessarily expressed in cautious, not to say tentative terms; but the Board of Inland Revenue, on the basis of the document, seems to believe that changes along the lines set out above ought to be made. There is a passing reference in the document to the Finance Act 1989, with the implication that some changes in the law will be made at that time. But even if radical changes are made in the rules of residence, detailed knowlege of the present rules will obviously be still required, and indeed for some years to come. In the meantime, this new edition of the *Allied Dunbar Expatriate Tax and Investment Guide* refers in the appropriate contexts to some of the detailed changes adumbrated in the Inland Revenue consultative document.

Contents

	Page
Acknowledgement	v
Introduction	vi
1 Domicile and residence	1
The concept of domicile	1
The concept of fiscal residence	5
The 'rules' of residence	7
The six-month rule	7
The three-month rule	8
The accommodation rule	9
Residence summary	11
The concept of ordinary residence	11
Residence and ordinary residence in the year of departure	12
Residence in the year of return	13
2 The expatriate who remains UK resident	**15**
Long absences	16
Example: Qualifying periods	17
Foreign emoluments	19
Other reliefs for resident expatriates	20
The resident self-employed expatriate	23
Claims for relief	24
Overseas earnings of the non-resident	24
Crown servants	25
Armed forces	26
Seafarers and airmen	26
Oil rig workers	27
The expatriate family	27
Non-UK investment income	29

National insurance contributions	30
Occupational pension schemes	31

3 Retiring abroad and the permanent emigrant 33

Immediate considerations	33
Capital gains tax	35
Inheritance tax	35
Coming home again	36

4 The returning expatriate 39

Tax liabilities on return	39
Example: Capitalisation of investments	42
Capital gains tax	44
Dangers of evasion	45
Miscellaneous investments	46
Unremittable overseas income	46
National Insurance	47
Other matters	47

5 UK income of British expatriates 49

Interest from bank and building society deposits	49
Interest from Government, local authority and corporate stocks	52
Life assurance policies	54
National Savings	56
Pensions	56
Employments	57
Trades and professions	58
Royalties and patents	59
Maintenance payments	59
Trust and estate income	61
Avoidance of higher rate liability	61
Lloyd's Underwriters	62
Non-resident's entitlement to UK personal allowances	63

6 Tax aspects of UK property by P A Goodman 67

Rental income	67
Administration and collection of tax	68
Furnished holiday lettings	70
Mortgage interest relief at source (MIRAS)	70
Capital gains tax: principal private residence	72

Contents xiii

7 Double taxation agreements 75

Fiscal residence	75
Dividends	76
Interest	77
Royalties	77
Income from real property	78
Businesses	78
Capital gains	79
Independent personal services	79
Dependent personal services	79
Artistes and athletes	80
Pensions	80
Students and teachers	82
Other income	82
Non-discrimination	82
Mutual agreement procedure	82
Exchange of information	83
Inheritance tax	83
Unilateral relief	84
Treaty shopping	84

8 Overseas visitors to the UK 85

Short visits	85
Long stays	85
Non UK-domiciled visitor	86
Remittance basis	86
Maintenance	88
Remuneration	89
Ordinary residence	91
National Insurance	92
Unremittable income	92
Foreign diplomats and members of the armed forces	92
Teaching and other academic exchange programmes	93

9 Capital gains tax 95

Residence	95
Husband and wife	95
Emigration	96
Immigration	96
Property	96
Business gains	97
Foreign taxes	100

xiv *Contents*

Non-UK domiciled 101
Trusts 101
Offshore funds 101
Gifts from non-residents 102
Non-sterling bank accounts 102

10 Inheritance tax **103**

Chargeable transfers 104
Exemptions and reliefs 104
Potentially exempt transfers 105
Transfers between spouses 105
Annual allowances 105
    Example: Inheritance tax—annual allowance 106
Normal expenditure out of income 106
Gifts in consideration of marriage 106
Dispositions for maintenance of family 107
Other exempt transfers 107
Business property relief 107
Agricultural property relief 108
Potentially exempt lifetime transfers of agricultural and
   business property 108
Persons not domiciled in the UK 109
Location of assets 109
The non-UK domiciled spouse 110
Settled property 111
Inheritance tax planning 112
    Example: Inheritance tax—estate planning 113
Insurance policies 113
The family home 114
    Example: Inheritance tax—the family home 114
Wills 115
Will trusts 116
Incidence of IHT 116
Written variations 117
    Example: Inheritance tax—written variation 118

11 Trusts **119**

The residence of trusts 119
Resident trusts 120
Trusts created *inter vivos* 121
Income tax 121
Capital gains tax 124
Inheritance tax 125

Contents xv

Non-resident trusts 127

12 Companies 131

Residence 131
Trading in the UK 132
Investing in the UK 133
Property development in the UK 133
Treaty shopping 134
Anti-avoidance provisions 135
Offshore funds 135
Controlled foreign companies 136
Pre-return planning 137
Non-resident Irish companies 137

13 Other taxes 139

Value added tax 139
VAT exemptions and zero-rating 139
Property 140
Car tax 141
Excise duties 141
Personal belongings 141
Stamp duty 142

14 Investment by Richard Sayer 145

Introduction 145
Establishing the objective 146
Constructing a portfolio 147
Principal investment media 150
Banking and deposits 150
Building society deposit 151
National Savings (UK) 152
British Government Stocks 153
Overseas Government Securities and Eurobonds 154
Collective investment media 155
UK unit trusts and investment trusts 157
Offshore funds 158
Life assurance policies 160
Pensions 163
Miscellaneous investments 167
Exchange controls 167
Methods of holding an investment 168
Making the choice 169

15 Investment and floating exchange rates by Howard Flight — 171

Introduction	171
Factors driving exchange rate movements	171
Exchange rates and equity investment	173
Exchange rates and bonds	174
Exchange rates and cash	175

16 Checklists of do's and don'ts — 177

Going abroad	177
While overseas	178
Coming home	178

Appendix I Inland Revenue booklet IR20: Residents' and non-residents' liability to tax in the UK — 181

Appendix II Tax tables — 209

Appendix III Extra-statutory concessions and Revenue statements (IR1-1985) — 213

Appendix IV Text of the 1977 OECD Model Agreement — 223

Appendix V Guide to domicile and residence — 245

Index — 262

1 Domicile and residence

Under the law in the UK, citizenship and nationality are irrelevant in determining an individual's liability to tax. Instead, the key terms are 'domicile', 'residence' and 'ordinary residence'. As explained in the Preface and mentioned elsewhere in this book, all three terms are under official review. But it is essential to grasp their meaning if one is to understand how UK taxation applies to expatriates, whether Britons overseas, or foreign nationals living in the UK; and this will still be the case when present law and practice are changed.

There is a fundamental difference between domicile on the one hand, and residence and ordinary residence on the other, which must be made clear at the outset: **domicile** is a long-established concept of law in the UK, and is a well-defined, basic concept that determines an individual's legal rights and duties; while **residence** and **ordinary residence** are terms derived essentially from Inland Revenue practice. They have no statutory definition, although they have been commented on and interpreted from time to time in judgments delivered in English courts. Some of these judgments are quoted below. We begin our explanation of these terms, however, with domicile, as it is more fundamental and of wider legal application than residence. Our explanation goes into some detail, but a simpler treatment of the subject is to be found in Appendix V, which includes step-by-step charts as a practical guide to determining domicile and residence in individual cases.

The concept of domicile

Domicile is a concept of the common law, and is relevant to marriage and divorce, besides tax. Although the Taxes Acts and the Civil Jurisdiction and Judgments Act 1982 make reference to domicile in the United Kingdom, there is, strictly speaking, no such thing. What is meant is domicile in England and Wales, Scotland, or Northern Ireland. Domicile is that legal relationship between a person and a territory subject to a distinctive legal system which invokes the system as his or her personal law. Put more practically, if somewhat less accurately, domicile refers to the country to which a person 'belongs', the country which is his or her 'natural home'. Important as it is in UK law, domicile is not a universal concept of private international law. Outside the British Commonwealth, only the United States, Denmark, Norway and Brazil use domicile as the connecting link between a person and the system of law and the courts to which he or she is subject.

Domicile takes three forms in the general law: domicile of origin, domicile of choice, and domicile of dependence. For certain inheritance tax (IHT) purposes (and for those alone) there is what might be described as a fourth form: deemed domicile. Domicile is of particular importance in regard to inheritance tax but can also have important consequences for a person's liability for income tax and capital gains tax.

Domicile of origin

While it is perfectly possible for an individual to be without a fiscal residence at any time, he cannot be without a domicile. A domicile of origin is established at birth. For legitimate children this is the domicile of the father. An illegitimate child, or a legitimate child whose father dies before his birth, takes the domicile of the mother at the time of birth. The parent's domicile will prevail regardless of where the child is born, despite any effect the place of birth may have on the child's nationality or citizenship. A child will retain this domicile of origin until he can establish an independent domicile of choice or until his father (or mother in the case of illegitimate children) himself acquires a new domicile of choice. In the latter case the child will also acquire the new domicile but this will be a domicile of dependence, not a domicile of choice.

Domicile of dependence

Dependency on the domicile of the parent will continue until the child reaches the age of 16 or marries, whichever is earlier (Domicile and Matrimonial Proceedings Act 1973). This does not, however, apply in Scotland where a boy can acquire an independent domicile at age 14 and a girl at age 12. Where the parents of a child under 16 (or the respective ages in Scotland) are living apart, the child's dependent domicile is that of his mother if he lives with her and does not have a home with his father.

Until 1973, a woman acquired her husband's domicile on marriage. Any woman married before 1 January 1974 will therefore have had a domicile of dependence, but she will now (following DMPA 1973) be considered to have that domicile as one of choice if it is not also her domicile of origin. Since the beginning of 1974, a married woman has been treated as an independent person in matters of domicile and will retain her domicile of origin unless she establishes her own new domicile of choice.

Domicile of choice

The third form of domicile, the domicile of choice, is the one which can be of greatest interest to expatriates and which can cause the most problems. It can be very difficult to convince the courts that a new domicile has been acquired. The basic requirements are that the person should reside in the new country and that he should intend to stay there for an unlimited period. The residence part can be simply established; the length of that residence is not necessarily material, so that if, for example, a person dies shortly after arrival, he may nonetheless have satisfied the test of residence. Providing evidence of the intention to remain is more complex.

Some of the indicators of intent which will be considered on the advancement of any claim to a change of domicile include the following:

(a) a period of residence in the new country;
(b) purchase of a home there;
(c) disposal of property in the old country;
(d) development of business, social, religious and political interests in the new country;
(e) burial arrangements there;
(f) local education of children;
(g) the making of a new will according to local laws;
(h) application for citizenship of the new country;
(i) severance of all formal ties with the old country.

It is invariably impossible to prove an intention; the best that can be hoped for is that the circumstantial evidence will be sufficient for the authorities to be convinced.

If a domicile of choice is abandoned then the domicile of origin revives until such time as a new domicile of choice is acquired. It would be open to the authorities to claim that on the facts of the abandonment of a purported new domicile, it did not exist. This can have serious effects for inheritance tax if the revived domicile of origin is considered as never having been lost.

Deemed domicile

The 'deemed domicile' provisions contained in IHTA 1984, s 267 have no counterpart in the income tax or capital gains tax legislation. The effect of this section is to treat as UK-domiciled, anyone who emigrates from the UK having been previously domiciled there or who had been a long-term resident. This deeming provision endures for a period of at least three years following departure.

The section treats an individual as domiciled in the UK if:

(a) he was domiciled in the UK within the three years immediately preceding the relevant time; or
(b) he was resident in the UK in not less than 17 out of the 20 income tax years ending with the income tax year in which the relevant time falls.

The 'relevant time' referred to above is the time at which a transfer of value takes place.

For the person domiciled initially within the UK, item (*a*) means there is a period of at least three calendar years from the acquisition of a new domicile during which time liability for inheritance tax remains. For the long-term UK resident who is not domiciled here, there must be an absence of three complete income tax years before he can be free of inheritance tax. Double taxation agreements which cover IHT may affect this provision; see Chapter 7 and Chapter 10.

In the case of *re Clore (deceased) (No 2) Official Solicitor* v *Clore & Others* [1984] STC 609 it was held that an English domicile of origin prevailed as there was insufficient evidence to show a settled intention permanently to reside in Monaco.

Possible changes in the law

Changes to the law on domicile are recommended in a Joint Report of the Law Commission and the Scottish Law Commission entitled Private International Law: The Law of Domicile, CM 200. The report concluded that its recommendations were unlikely to be significant for tax purposes, but that if they were, the use of domicile in taxation law should be reviewed. This has been done in the Inland Revenue Consultative Document of 29 July 1988. The Consultative Document refers in passing to the possibility of relevant legislation being introduced in the Finance Act 1989, but the law has not been changed at the time of writing, and the proposed changes are still no more than recommendations. Not all the changes proposed would or could be retrospective, and an expatriate able to take advantage of present provisions regarding domicile and residence is advised to take any action needed as soon as possible, and to seek professional guidance as soon as the law is changed or impending change is announced.

The concept of fiscal residence

One of the basic principles of UK income tax is to charge to tax any income, no matter where it arises, which belongs to a person who is resident and domiciled in the UK. Furthermore, a person who is not resident in the UK is taxable on any income which arises in the UK.

In determining whether or not a person is resident in the UK, several factors have to be taken into account. There is no single criterion to be satisfied and all the 'rules' of residence have their exceptions, some of which have statutory force, and others which are merely concessionary, ie allowed in practice by the Inland Revenue, although not specified in the Taxes Acts. See Appendix III.

Physical presence

It might be reasonable to assume that in order to be considered resident in the UK a person must be physically present in the country during the tax year. This assumption is given qualified support in what is effectively the Revenue's code of practice contained in the booklet IR20 'Residents and Non-residents Liability to Tax in the United Kingdom' (Appendix I). The qualification that a person '. . . must *normally* be physically present . . .' is, however, important. Under TA 1988, s 334, a British subject or a citizen of the Republic of Ireland whose ordinary residence is in the UK will continue to be taxed as a resident if he is abroad for the purpose only of occasional residence.

In practical terms, it will rarely be necessary to apply s 334. The vast majority of expatriates who do not set foot in the UK throughout a tax year will either be working overseas or permanently settled abroad where other considerations come into play. Where the section will commonly apply is where a person spends a significant length of time outside the UK, but less than a complete tax year. But even there, other considerations must be taken into account.

Residence a question of fact

In *IRC* v *Lysaght* (1928) 13 TC 511 it was indicated that no special or technical meaning was attached to the terms 'resident' and 'ordinarily resident', that it was their normal meanings that should be considered and that a person's residence is a question of fact. It might be assumed from this that to be a resident requires some form of permanent or semi-permanent abode in which to reside. If that is so the question then might revolve around what constitutes an abode. What the case law makes clear is that bricks and mortar are by no means necessary. An American living on board his yacht, anchored in Colchester harbour, was held to be resident; so too was another American who rented a shooting lodge and a Belgian who had the use of a hunting box in Leicestershire *Bayard Brown* v *Burt* (1911) 5 TC 667, *Cooper* v *Cadwalader* (1904) 5 TC 101, and *Loewenstein* v *De Salis* (1926) 10 TC 424 respectively. Then there is that group of individuals who can be described as transients or 'persons of no fixed abode'. The occupier of a cardboard box in a Soho back street or a park bench in Manchester will be no less resident for that. On the other hand, there are cases, eg, *IRC* v *Zorab* (1926) 11 TC 289 and *IRC* v *Brown* (1926) 11 TC 292, where living in hotels or with friends in the UK was not sufficient to render the persons resident for tax purposes.

Dual residence

A person who is resident for tax purposes in the UK is not precluded from also being resident elsewhere, and a claim to non-residence cannot be sustained simply on the grounds of being resident in another state. A person may be resident in two or more states in the same tax year or, indeed, resident in none. Where dual residence gives rise to a double charge to tax then special provisions may exist in a tax treaty between the states which can overrule the purely domestic regulations on residence. See Chapter 7.

Finally, before going on to a discussion of the current practice, it should also be pointed out that *force majeure* will be ignored in any decision as to whether or not a person is resident in the UK. Illness, military service, or even, in borderline cases, the cancellation of a

Domicile and residence 7

flight, can sufficiently extend a stay so as to render the otherwise non-resident person, resident for a particular tax year.

The 'rules' of residence

The booklet IR20 reproduced in Appendix I sets out the Inland Revenue's views on what constitutes residence and ordinary residence. As with most explanatory booklets from government departments, IR20 has no statutory force and it may be that certain views printed therein could be challenged in an appeal. For the most part, however, the guidelines in IR20 are sufficient for all but the most complex circumstances. It is from these guidelines that the following 'rules' have been drawn.

The six-month rule

'If a person is to be regarded as resident in the UK for a given tax year he must normally be physically present in the country for at least part of that year. He will always be resident if he is here for six months or more in the year. **There are no exceptions to this rule.**' (The Revenue's use of bold.)

However, a person who leaves the UK permanently, or who leaves to take up full time employment abroad for a period which includes one complete tax year, may be treated as non-resident and not ordinarily resident from the day following his departure. This treatment can be applied regardless of when during the tax year the person leaves. If, for example, he leaves on 5 January he will have been resident for nine months but will be treated as non-resident for the three remaining months. This treatment is purely concessionary but is a practice of some long standing. (Incidentally, it also provides the exception to another rule that residence and non-residence have to be considered for complete tax years only.)

Analogous treatment is given to people who come to this country to live. If they have not been ordinarily resident in the UK and they intend to stay permanently (or for a period of years, see later) then they may be treated as non-resident for that part of the tax year prior to the day of arrival, and resident thereafter.

The converse of the six-month rule does not generally apply. That is, a person who is not physically present in the UK for six months is not necessarily to be treated as non-resident. Such a person, if a British subject or Irish citizen, may be caught by TA 1988, s 334 or, regardless of nationality, by the rules concerning habitual visits or available accommodation.

Another six-month rule is contained in TA 1988, s 336. This applies to visitors to the UK who are here for purely temporary purposes without any intention of establishing residence. So long as the visit or visits last in aggregate for less than six months in any one tax year the visitor will not be liable to tax under Schedule D, Cases IV or V or under Schedule E except for remuneration for duties in the UK. See Chapter 8—Overseas visitors to the UK.

Under current Inland Revenue practice, six months is regarded as equivalent to 183 days, regardless of whether or not the year is a leap year, and days of arrival and departure are normally ignored.

The six-month/183-day rule can permit a person to stay in the UK for almost a calendar year without becoming resident so long as his arrival falls at the beginning of October. In the extreme case, arrival on 5 October (or 6 October in a year preceding a leap year) followed by departure on the next 5 October would be within the limit so long as the days of arrival and departure were, in fact, left out of account. Such a lengthy visit would, however, preclude any further visits to the UK for at least one and possibly for two years under the rule discussed below.

The three-month rule

Under this rule a person may become resident if he makes regular lengthy visits to the UK. Where the visits are made every year for four consecutive years, and the average length of stay over those four years is three months or more a year, then the visitor will be considered as resident in the UK. Where the pattern of visits is irregular or cannot be foreseen then the residence status will apply after the fourth year. If, on the other hand, the pattern is known and admitted then residence will start from the original date of arrival.

The period of three months, unlike the six months mentioned earlier, is not translated into an equivalent number of days although it can be made up of several visits. Neither is any mention made of ignoring days of arrival or departure. It would therefore seem

Domicile and residence 9

prudent if this rule jeopardises non-resident status to keep visits to no more than 90 days per annum on average.

The accommodation rule

'If a person goes abroad permanently but has accommodation (eg, a house or apartment) available for his use in the UK, he is regarded as resident here for any tax year in which he visits the UK, however short the visit may be.' 'A visitor who has accommodation here will be regarded as resident for any year in which he comes to the UK, however short his visit might be.'

Exception for full-time employees abroad

These two statements from IR20 are all-embracing but must be qualified by TA 1988, s 335. This section states that where a person works full-time in a trade, profession or vocation or is in full-time employment abroad and no part of his work is carried on in the UK, then his residence status will be determined without regard to any accommodation available to him in the UK. In the case of the employee, duties carried on in the UK may be ignored if they are merely incidental to the overseas duties.

The natural follow-on from s 335 is to ask what constitutes 'incidental duties'. The amount of time devoted to the incidental duties is not in itself material unless it exceeds three months (in which case they would no longer be regarded as incidental). What is important is the nature of the duties performed here and their relationship with the employment overseas, *Robson v Dixon* (1972) 48 TC 527. Thus, returning to the UK to report to an employer or to receive fresh instructions will usually be regarded as incidental but a director returning for board meetings would not be so treated. Other visits which are unlikely to come under the incidental duties exemption are those made by couriers or ship and aircraft crew members.

Another case which is not uncommon concerns an employee who, during an otherwise 'incidental' visit, is asked to carry out a specific task, perhaps because of some special skill he has. If he does this he is very likely to lose the protection of s 335 and be treated as resident for the year.

Availability, not ownership, is significant

Returning to the accommodation rule itself, it should be noted that it is the availability, not the ownership, of the accommodation which is significant. Thus rented property, property owned by a company or trust, or any other property which is, *in fact* available will be caught. Conversely, ownership of accommodation does not automatically mean it is available. Where the accommodation has been let on a long lease under which the owner has no right to stay there, then it is not available accommodation and will therefore be ignored. Any accommodation available to one spouse will generally be treated as available to the other.

Where accommodation is rented for temporary visits to the UK, it will be ignored if the renting is for less than two years (in the case of furnished accommodation) or for unfurnished accommodation, less than one year.

The rule does not state that the available accommodation must actually be occupied by the visitor in order that he be caught by the rule. Given also that the rule applies no matter how short the visit, it could be argued that someone with accommodation available could be classed as resident merely by changing planes at Heathrow. While for all practical purposes this possibility is remote, what is much more likely is that the person owning a property in Scotland, say, might spend a week's holiday in London and become resident notwithstanding that he never even crossed the border.

For most working British expatriates the accommodation rule does not present a problem because of s 335. However, where the expatriate is accompanied overseas by his wife he will have to take into account her residence position. If, as is usually the case, the wife is not in full time employment, then in all likelihood, she will remain classed as resident in the UK. The question of residence, unlike many other aspects of UK tax, is determined separately for husbands and wives. There are both advantages and disadvantages for the resident/non-resident couple, and these are discussed in Chapter 2.

TA 1988, s 282(2) provides that a husband and wife are to be treated for tax purposes as if they were not married where one is resident in the UK and the other is not except that this treatment must not result in an increase in the UK tax liability over what it would have been had the normal rules applied. See *Gubay* v *Kingston* [1984] STC 499. This separate treatment can result in significant savings, particularly in the taxation of investment income.

Among the suggestions made in the Inland Revenue Consultative Document of July 1988 is one to scrap entirely the 'available accommodation' rule.

Domicile and residence 11

Residence summary

A person who is resident in the UK will usually have a liability for UK income tax on his worldwide income and would also be liable for capital gains tax on any chargeable gains.

In essence, a person will be considered resident in the UK if:

(a) he makes any visit to the UK, no matter how short, at a time when he has accommodation here available for his use unless he works full-time in a trade, etc, which is carried on entirely abroad or he is in full-time employment, all the duties of which, barring mere incidentals, are carried out overseas; or
(b) he is physically present in the UK for six months or more in the tax year, given that six months are equivalent to 183 days and days of arrival and departure are ignored; or
(c) he makes substantial and habitual visits to the UK; 'substantial' is taken to mean an average of three months or more each year and visits are considered 'habitual' after four consecutive years; or
(d) being a British subject (or citizen of the Republic of Ireland) he has left the UK for the purpose only of occasional residence abroad (TA 1988, s 334).

The concept of ordinary residence

This chapter so far has been concerned with residence, a concept which in the main is concerned with individual tax years, although, in the application of the three-month rule a four year period has to be considered. Ordinary residence, however, involves a generally greater degree of continuity.

In the *Lysaght* case mentioned earlier, ordinary residence was held to be the converse of occasional or casual residence. This can be taken as meaning that where, in the general ordering of his life, a person regularly spends substantial periods of time in the UK he will be considered as ordinarily resident here. Booklet IR20 states that 'ordinarily resident is broadly equivalent to habitually resident; if a person is resident in the UK year after year, he is ordinarily resident here.'

A person who becomes resident under the three-month rule will also be considered as ordinarily resident, as will the visitor with available accommodation, unless exempted by s 335, if he visits the UK in four consecutive tax years, regardless of how long he stays during any one visit. If a person who has been ordinarily resident in the UK goes abroad permanently but retains accommodation available for his use here, he will be treated as remaining ordinarily resident if he visits this country in most years. Again, the exemption conferred by s 335 applies.

Ordinary residence, like residence, is normally applied to complete tax years but the exception mentioned earlier applies. A person may be resident, perhaps under the six-month rule, but not ordinarily resident in a particular tax year. Similarly, a person may be ordinarily resident but not resident in a tax year. If, for example, a person normally lives in the UK but takes an extended holiday covering a complete tax year, he may be treated as ordinarily resident but not resident for that year unless caught by s 334. However, if he is in full-time employment abroad for a complete tax year, the Revenue have confirmed that he would normally be treated as both non-resident and not ordinarily resident for that year.

Whether or not a UK resident is also ordinarily resident here can have a marked effect on how certain types of income are taxed. So far as capital gains tax is concerned, liability may arise if a person is either resident *or* ordinarily resident.

Residence and ordinary residence in the year of departure

A person who leaves the UK to work full time under a contract of employment, all the duties of which are performed abroad, and which will last for a period including at least one complete tax year, will normally be treated as not resident and not ordinarily resident from the day following his departure. This treatment remains provisional until the person has actually remained abroad for a full tax year and, in that year, he has not offended any of the other residence rules. Although the treatment is provisional it does not normally prevent the Inland Revenue from making a tax repayment on departure if, for example, only part of the person's personal allowances had been granted under PAYE. Where the year is split in this way into a resident part and a non-resident part, full allowances are due; there is no apportionment. The intending

Domicile and residence 13

expatriate should obtain the tax repayment claim form P85 and submit it shortly before departure.

For the self-employed expatriate or others who leave with no employment arranged overseas, the tax treatment may not be so straightforward. In these cases the Inland Revenue take the view that they will 'wait and see' for up to three years. During that time a provisional status of ordinarily resident is maintained and at the end of the period, again assuming no breaking of the residence rules in the meantime, the status of not resident and not ordinarily resident may be granted and backdated to the day following departure. Any tax collected in the interim which would not have been payable by a non resident can be repaid.

If it is fairly obvious that a person is emigrating, then provisional non-resident status may be granted. Similarly, the three-year period may be curtailed if events subsequent to departure merit this, for example, the obtaining of employment.

The treatment as non-resident from the days following the day of departure is concessionary, ESCA 11 and D 2, and as such the Revenue reserve the right not to apply it in certain cases, such as where a large capital gain is made immediately following departure (see Chapter 9). Where a concession gives rise to a significant loss of tax to the Revenue its application must be in doubt.

Residence in the year of return

The returning expatriate will normally by concession (see p 14) be considered as resident and ordinarily resident from the day of his arrival in the UK. For the subsequent part of the tax year he will be entitled to the full year's personal allowances. One effect of this is that if he returns to employment here then he may enjoy a period of tax holiday under PAYE until his accumulated allowances are exhausted.

One of the less pleasant aspects, however, is that where the returned expatriate has other sources of income, such as investment income, from abroad taxed on the previous year basis, he may be faced with an assessment on an income which arose while he thought he was beyond the Inland Revenue's reach. Extra-statutory Concession A11 (1985), however, acts to reduce this liability. Under this concession, only that part of the income which is the same portion of the whole as the actual period of residence is of a full year will be charged. That is, if a person returns to the UK on 5 July, say, he will be resident for three-quarters of the tax year, and tax will be charged only on three-quarters of his overseas investment income. This concession does not apply to interest from UK bank deposit accounts. See also Chapters 4 and 5.

2 The expatriate who remains UK resident

The previous chapter explained the terms 'resident' and 'non-resident' and it was pointed out that most working expatriates would achieve non-resident status if their overseas work was for a period that included at least one complete tax year. There are, however, many people who, although abroad for more than 12 months, are not in fact overseas from 6 April to the following 5 April and who do not, therefore, qualify for non-resident treatment.

Although the expression is, literally, a contradiction in terms, we refer here to persons in this category as 'resident' (ie not non-resident) expatriates. A person in this category might, for example, have an 18-month contract commencing in June 1987; his return in December 1988 means that he has spent part of two tax years abroad but not one complete year. Then there is the case of the person whose UK job entails much foreign travel, perhaps for months on end, but whose duties in the UK cannot be described as merely incidental to his duties abroad. This category might include seamen whose voyages start or finish in the UK but who travel the world in between times. Finally among the group of people who are abroad often but either not often enough, or not for long enough to qualify as non-resident for UK tax purposes, are the travelling salesmen, consultants, airline pilots and the like.

What all of these 'semi-expatriates' have in common is that they cannot obtain the tax benefits of the non-resident expatriate proper. They remain liable for UK income tax on their worldwide income. In the 'export or die' atmosphere of the 1970s, the importance of the semi-expatriate to the country's economic well-being was recognised and new legislation was introduced to counter the disincentive effect of domestic taxation for these people. The legislation, mainly contained in TA 1988, s 193, Sch 12, is complex and not without ambiguity. In essence, this schedule provides for total exemption from UK income tax for earnings from work done overseas provided certain conditions are satisfied.

16 *Allied Dunbar Expatriate Tax and Investment Guide*

Long absences

Relief under this category may be obtained against earnings from an employment the duties of which are performed wholly or partly outside the UK. Any duties performed abroad which are merely incidental to those performed at home will be treated as being performed in the UK and will not be taken into account for the purposes of this relief. In order to qualify for relief as a long absentee, a person must perform the duties of his employment in the course of a qualifying period of at least 365 qualifying days. A qualifying period is not restricted by tax years and may span two or more years. For example, a qualifying period may run from September 1987 to December 1988. In that case the Schedule E assessments for 1987/88 and 1988/89 would take account of the emoluments for that part of the qualifying period in each year of assessment and grant the relief accordingly.

A qualifying period consists either of days of absence from the UK or partly of such days and partly of days in the UK. In the former case, the situation is quite straightforward. The person performing the duties of his employment wholly abroad for at least 365 days will obtain the relief. Given that the legislation refers to 'in the course of a qualifying period' there does not seem to be a requirement that the employment must subsist for the whole period. Therefore an absence of 365 days made up of six months work and six months overseas holiday would still be a qualifying period. A day will be considered as a day of absence if the person is outside the UK at the end of the day, ie, at midnight (*Hoye* v *Forsdyke* [1981] STC 711).

The alternative definition of a qualifying period, ie, where there are some days spent in the UK, contains stringent restrictions on the length of time which can be spent in the UK. Between any two periods of absence, the time spent in the UK must not exceed 62 consecutive days. Thus a person abroad for two periods of 155 days with a 60 day break between them will achieve a qualifying period of 370 days and qualify for the relief. In addition, the number of intervening days in the UK must not exceed one-sixth of the total number of days in the period under consideration. In the marginal case of a person abroad for 365 days apart from a 62 day return to the UK, although he does not break the 62 day rule, the period fails to achieve qualifying status because of the one-sixth rule. For seafarers, from 6 April 1988 the limits are relaxed to 90 consecutive days and a total of one-quarter.

The expatriate who remains UK resident 17

Qualifying periods—illustrative example

Going on from the simple case of the single return visit, qualifying periods may be built up from a series of overseas spells interspersed by returns to the UK. But what is vital with this regime is to keep a close check on the length of each stay both at home and overseas. This build-up of qualifying periods to a length sufficient to entitle the employee to obtain the tax relief is best illustrated by an example.

What the example illustrates is that the qualifying period tests have to be applied after every overseas period. An expatriate in this situation must keep a very close watch on his visits to the UK. If Mr

Example: Qualifying periods

Mr Smith is a consulting engineer who has always worked in the UK. In May 1984 he is recruited by A Ltd, an international consultancy, and is appointed to one of their projects in Nigeria for a period of 18 months. His movements over that time are given below.

Period	In Nigeria	In UK	Total		
A	20	—	20		
B	—	12	32		
C	38	—	70 (38)	$\frac{1}{6}$th =	11.7
D	—	5	43		
E	95	—	138	$\frac{1}{6}$th =	23
F	—	15	153		
G	65	—	218	$\frac{1}{6}$th =	36.3
H	—	40	258		
I	120	—	378	$\frac{1}{6}$th =	63
J	—	10	388		
K	60	—	448	$\frac{1}{6}$th =	74.7
L	—	25	473		
M	70	—	543	$\frac{1}{6}$th =	90.5
N	—	90			

In this example, periods A, C, E, G, I, K, M, O are all qualifying periods as they are periods of absence from the UK. None of them individually gives rise to the 100% tax relief because they are each less than 365 days. Period A–C might be a qualifying period if the intervening days do not break either the 62 days or $\frac{1}{6}$th rules. Period B, the intervening days in the UK does, however, break the $\frac{1}{6}$th rule so A–C is not a qualifying period. As a result, periods A and B fall out of the reckoning. A new accumulation process begins with period C. C–E is a qualifying period, so too are C–G and C–I but C–I also exceeds 365 days so the 100% tax relief is due. The qualifying period ceases after period M since period N is more than 62 days. A new progression can commence with period O.

Smith had left the UK one day earlier in period B then period A–C would have qualified.

Holidays taken abroad during a spell of overseas duty or at the end of such a spell will be included in the qualifying period. Holiday or terminal payments at the end of a qualifying period will generally also qualify for tax exemption notwithstanding that the employee might spend his terminal leave in the UK provided the period of absence from the UK amounted to 365 days or more.

Apportionment of emoluments

The earnings or emoluments which qualify for relief are those which are attributable to the period of overseas work. Thus someone who works solely abroad may obtain exemption for all his emoluments. Where a person works partly abroad and partly in the UK (where the UK duties are not merely incidental to the overseas duties) then there is provision for the emoluments to be apportioned between the respective duties (TA 1988, Sch 12, para 2). Inland Revenue practice, however, permits relief against the whole of the emoluments unless there is some question of artificiality about the employee's arrangements with the employer (Inland Revenue letter dated 12 February 1980, reproduced in *Moores & Rowland's Yellow Tax Guide*).

The occasion on which apportionment is more likely to be a consideration is where the individual has two or more associated employments, one in the UK and others overseas. If, for instance, Mr Jones, a colleague of Mr Smith, was employed both by A Ltd and A (Nigeria) Ltd, a subsidiary of the British company, and unlike Mr Smith, Mr Jones spent one year in the UK and one year in Nigeria, then if Mr Jones received a UK salary of £5,000 pa and a Nigerian salary of £50,000 pa he would have some difficulty in persuading the Inland Revenue that this was not an artificial tax avoidance ploy.

In any negotiations over apportionment, the amount which can be relieved is that which can be shown to be reasonable having regard to the nature of, and the time devoted to, the overseas duties in relation to the duties performed in the UK, and to all other circumstances. Returning to Mr Jones' position, he might be able to claim that his overseas duties were substantially more onerous, involved longer hours and greater responsibility, than his UK duties, that local taxes and the cost of living were far higher than in the UK and that, all things considered, £50,000 pa was a fair rate for the job.

The expatriate who remains UK resident 19

Such a claim might well succeed. But if Mr Jones, as is not unlikely, were provided with company accommodation, car, servants and the general panoply of expatriate benefits, and received only £10,000 pa in Nigeria with the balance paid into his UK or tax haven bank account, then his claim would be resisted with a degree of righteous cynicism.

Apportionment apart, relievable emoluments include salaries, bonuses and allowances, benefits in kind and so on. When one considers the nature of the average expatriate remuneration package with its medical cover, possible school fee payments, and other benefits as well as those mentioned earlier, the value of the tax relief becomes apparent. This, perhaps more than anything else, should ensure that the employee keeps a careful eye on his return visits.

One final point to consider about this relief is the timing of the absence itself.

For employees of companies based in the UK which operate PAYE, the relief is normally obtained by the issue of a 'No Tax' code if it is clear that the 100% relief will be due.

Foreign emoluments

This term is used to describe the emoluments of a person **not domiciled in the UK** from an employment with a person or concern which is resident outside the UK. Thus, for example, an American working for an American corporation would be in receipt of foreign emoluments. Whether, and to what extent, foreign emoluments are taxable in the UK depends both on the residence position of the individual and the place in which he carries out the duties of his employment.

Duties performed in the UK are chargeable on the arising basis regardless of the residence status of the individual concerned. Where the duties are performed abroad the individual's residence is crucial. If he is non-resident then there is no liability for emoluments earned outside the UK. If he is resident but not ordinarily resident in the UK, then foreign emoluments for duties performed abroad will be chargeable on the remittance basis. If he is both resident and ordinarily resident in the UK, then the emoluments will be charged on the arising basis unless the duties of the employment are carried out wholly abroad. In this latter case the remittance basis is applied.

In taxing foreign emoluments not related to duties performed outside the UK a measure of relief is available, of 25% of the emoluments (after expenses, etc) provided that the employee held an employment giving rise to foreign emoluments on 13 March 1984 or took up such an employment by 1 August 1984 under an arrangement entered into by that date, provided that he has not resided in the UK in nine out of the previous ten years of assessment. The relief applies for 1987/88 and 1988/89 and ceases thereafter. Further discussion of foreign emoluments is contained in Chapter 8—Overseas visitors to the UK.

Other reliefs for resident expatriates

The normal rules which apply to relief for expenses, ie, that they are incurred wholly, exclusively and necessarily in the performance of the duties of the employment, apply to duties which extend overseas and to the emoluments therefrom. In the usual way the expenses would be deductible from the gross emoluments and the special relief of 100% would be calculated on the net amount. However, for employments which involve working overseas, certain expenses are allowable which would not be so in purely domestic circumstances. In addition, certain benefits which would be taxable in the UK employment are available with no tax penalty for overseas work.

It has already been mentioned that emoluments cover all benefits in kind and that these often form a significant part of an expatriate remuneration package. It follows, therefore, that the 100% relief can cover the benefits so provided. In addition to the generality of this, there are special rules relating to travel costs, board and lodging of the overseas worker and to travel costs of the employee or his family during his spell abroad.

These rules are contained in TA 1988, ss 193, 194 and cover the following situations. In each case the employee is resident and ordinarily resident in the UK and his emoluments are not foreign emoluments (where they are foreign emoluments, see Chapter 8).

(1) If the duties of the employment are performed wholly outside the UK then travelling expenses incurred by the employee to

The expatriate who remains UK resident

Foreign emoluments deduction flowchart for individuals

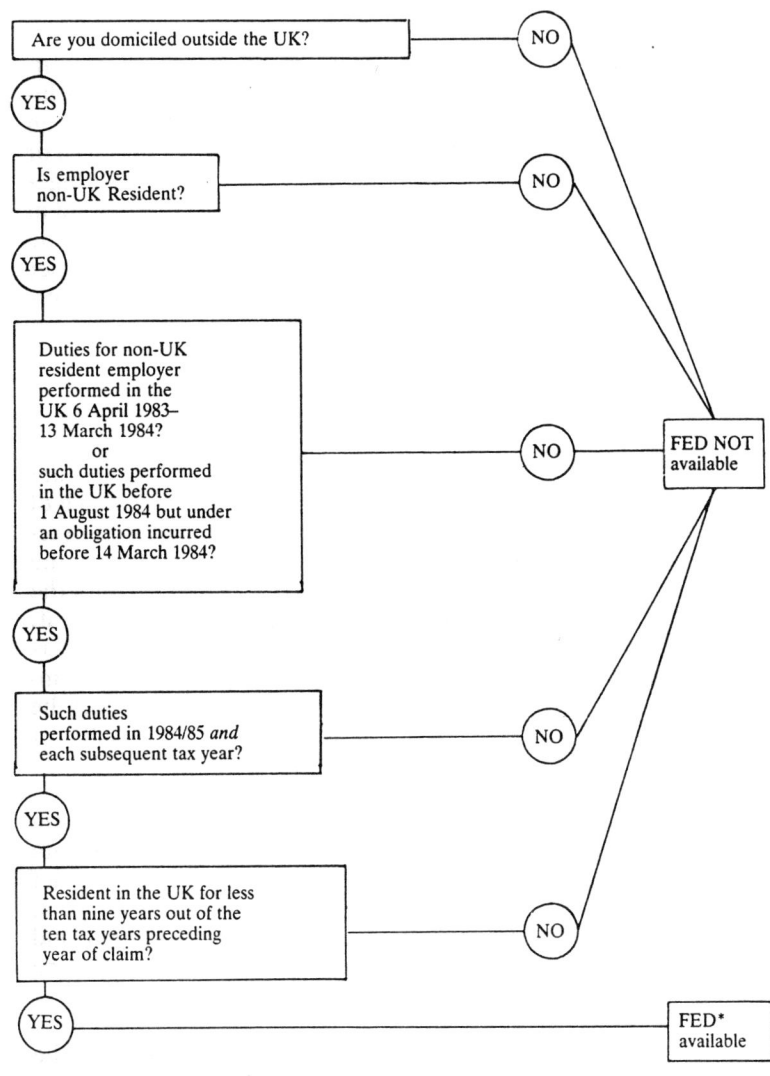

* 50% for tax years 1985/86 and 1986/87 :
  25% for tax years 1987/88 and 1988/89 :
  No relief thereafter

NB—UK resident employee with *EIRE* resident employer : No FED available

Employees Not in Receipt of Foreign Emoluments

UK Residence Status	Employment Performed Wholly or Partly in UK		Employment Performed Wholly Abroad
	UK Duties	Overseas Duties	
Resident and Ordinarily Resident	*Case I* Earnings arising	*Case I* Earnings arising (less 100% deduction where appropriate)	*Case I* Earnings arising (less 100% deduction where appropriate)
Resident but Not Ordinarily Resident	*Case II* Earnings arising	*Case III* Earnings remitted	*Case III* Earnings remitted
Not Resident	*Case II* Earnings arising	Exempt	Exempt

Foreign-domiciled Employees Working for Foreign Employers

UK Residence Status	Employment Performed Wholly or Partly in UK		Employment Performed Wholly Abroad
	UK Duties	Overseas Duties	
Resident and Ordinarily Resident	*Case I* Earnings*	*Case I* Earnings*	*Case III* Amounts remitted to or received in UK
Resident but Not Ordinarily Resident	*Case II* Earnings*	*Case III* Amounts remitted to or received in UK	*Case III* Amounts remitted to or received in UK
Not Resident	*Case II* Earnings*	Exempt	Exempt

* less the 25% deduction in 1987/88 and 1988/89

take up the employment and to return at the end of that employment are allowable as a deduction.

(2) If the cost of board and lodging is provided or reimbursed by the employer this will not be assessable in the case of wholly overseas employment.

(3) Where there are two or more employments and at least one of them is performed wholly or partly outside the UK, then

travelling expenses incurred by the employee getting from one place of employment to another, where either or both places are outside the UK, are deductible against the emoluments of the second employment. Where the expenses described above are not incurred wholly in the performance of the duties of the employment(s), they may be apportioned with relief restricted to that part related to the employment.

(4) Travel expenses for an unlimited number of outward and return journeys to the UK by the employee are to be allowed tax free in the hands of the employee if paid for by the employer.

(5) Where an employee is absent from the UK for a continuous period of 60 days or more certain travel facilities will not attract any UK tax liability. These facilities are for travel by the employee's spouse and/or children under the age of 18 between the UK and the place where the duties are performed and include any accompanying journey at the beginning of the period, or an interim visit; and any return journey. These travel facilities will be tax-exempt for up to two outward and return journeys by any person in any one tax year if provided by the employer or reimbursed by him.

Several points must be noted about the reliefs described above. First, in the case of board and lodgings and the family travel facilities, the relief extends only to cases where the cost is met directly or by reimbursement by the employer. There is no relief available for the employee against his emoluments if he bears these costs himself. Secondly, the relief for travel facilities is restricted to travel to and from the place where the duties are actually performed. There is no allowance, for example, for a family reunion at any halfway house. Thus Mr Green who is working in Australia for three months could not obtain relief for a trip for himself and his family to meet up in Singapore, say. Neither his travel nor that of his family would qualify.

The resident self-employed expatriate

Where a UK resident carries on a trade or profession wholly overseas his profits from that trade or profession are taxable under Case V of Schedule D.

A point to bear in mind when considering profits assessed in these circumstances is that the assessment will be on the profits arising in the previous tax year, not on the profits of the accounting period ending in that year, as would be the case under Schedule D, Case I or II. Unless the overseas profits are already computed on a UK fiscal year basis—an unlikely eventuality—an apportionment of the profits will be necessary.

The profits of a trade or profession carried out partly in the UK and partly overseas by a UK resident are assessable under Case I or Case II in the same way as those of a purely domestic business.

A period of non-residence can be useful for an individual exercising a profession or carrying on a trade which requires his personal involvement, as the preceding year basis of assessment would be preserved on his temporary departure from the UK. Provided an agent is not left in the UK to run the business, a person such as an author, barrister or musician who has had a very profitable year in the UK immediately before a year of non-residence will find that that income would be assessed in the year in which there is no tax charge due to his non-residence. If during the period of non-residence he is employed, the assessment would be under Schedule E on a current year basis and if he is non-resident and the duties are carried on outside the UK there will be no UK tax liability.

Self-employed expatriates also receive travel and subsistence reliefs comparable to those for UK-resident employees working abroad.

Claims for relief

The reliefs available under Schedule E may be claimed within the normal six-year time limit although in most cases involving substantial overseas working, the relief may be initiated by the company's PAYE office with reference to its PAYE tax office.

Relief under Schedule D must be claimed within two years of the end of the year of assessment to which the claim relates.

Overseas earnings of the non-resident

The first part of this chapter has dealt exclusively with the resident and domiciled expatriate or semi-expatriate and the relationship between his overseas earnings and his UK tax liability. Subject to the various reliefs described, such a person remains liable to UK income tax on his worldwide income and to capital gains tax on any gains made, no matter where the assets are located. The expatriate proper, that is the person who is working wholly overseas for a period of years and who has non-resident status, is in a totally different and generally much more favourable situation, at least so far as British taxes are concerned.

The non-resident whose earnings arise from a trade or employment carried on wholly overseas (barring mere incidentals) will have no UK liability on those earnings. There are, however, certain classes of expatriates who, although actually working overseas, may be deemed to be performing their duties in the UK. These include Crown servants and the armed forces, seafarers and airmen, and persons employed in exploration or exploitation activities in a designated area under the Continental Shelf Act 1964, s 1(7). The special circumstances of these individuals are described below.

Crown servants

The duties of an office or employment under the Crown are deemed to be duties performed in the UK irrespective of where they are, in fact, performed. The effect of this is to render the emoluments from such an employment liable to UK income tax under Case II of Schedule E if the employee is not resident and under Case I, but without any of the special reliefs, if the employee is resident. It must be stressed that this deeming provision (TA 1988, s 132(4)(a)) does not, of itself, affect the individual's residence position. If the Crown servant can otherwise satisfy the conditions for non-residence then the other advantages, such as no liability on overseas investment income or to capital gains tax, will still accrue. In addition, certain allowances which are certified as representing compensation for the extra costs involved in living overseas are payable tax free. Under TA 1988, s 278 certain classes of non-resident, including Crown servants, are entitled to some or all of the normal UK personal allowances (for full details see Chapter 5—UK income of British expatriates). In practice, the Crown servant will be taxed under PAYE with an appropriate code for the personal allowances.

One exception to the UK tax liability of Crown servants concerns locally-recruited staff overseas. If they are unestablished staff who are not UK resident and the maximum pay for their grade is less than that of an executive officer in the UK on the Inner London rate, then no tax will be payable (Extra-statutory Concession A25 (1985)).

Armed forces

In general terms, members of the armed forces on overseas duty are treated in the same way as other Crown servants. There is, however, one special relief available to members of the armed forces or their spouses or to a woman serving in any of the women's services. Such individuals will be treated as resident in the UK for the purpose of obtaining relief on qualifying life assurance premiums or policies issued before 13 March 1984.

Seafarers and airmen

Duties by seafarers and members of aircraft crews are deemed to be performed in the UK if the voyage does not extend to a port outside the UK or if the person concerned is a resident of the UK and part of the voyage or flight begins or ends here (TA 1988, s 132(4)(*b*)). This provision is now subject to TA 1988, Sch 12, para 5. This latter provision provides that seamen and aircrew engaged on voyages outside the UK are entitled to the special 100% deduction for long absences (see p 16) in respect of the proportion of voyages or flights spent outside the UK. From 6 April 1988 the conditions for seafarers are more favourable: the limits on intervening days are 90 consecutive days and one-quarter in total instead of 62 consecutive days and one-sixth. The legislation covers two types of voyage or flight: one which begins or ends outside the UK, and any part beginning or ending outside the UK of a journey which begins and ends in the UK.

In a letter dated 22 July 1980, reproduced in *Moores & Rowland's Yellow Tax Guide*, the Inland Revenue expanded on the meaning of this provision, by quoting an example concerning the following voyages. A voyage from Tilbury to Antwerp would qualify as being carried out overseas; a voyage from Newcastle to Tilbury to Antwerp would qualify for the Tilbury–Antwerp portion; a round trip Tilbury–Antwerp–Tilbury would also qualify and that portion of a Newcastle–Tilbury–Antwerp–Tilbury–Newcastle trip would likewise be considered as overseas working. The Inland Revenue practice is that a voyage containing a scheduled call at an overseas port will have an overseas portion, but if there is no such scheduled call, then the voyage will not qualify as constituting overseas working. For the purposes of calculating the number of qualifying days for the 100% relief, a person will be considered as leaving the UK when a ship leaves its berth for a foreign port or when an aircraft takes off.

Also of importance to aircrew and seamen is the question of incidental duties. It has been held that a pilot employed abroad but occasionally landing in the UK performed duties in the UK which were more than incidental (*Robson* v *Dixon* (1972) 48 TC 527) and in this case the pilot was treated as resident in the UK because he maintained his family home here. On *de minimis* grounds, the Inland Revenue will normally ignore a single landing and take-off during the year.

Oil rig workers

For tax purposes, the territorial sea of the UK is deemed to be part of the UK. This area is further extended in the case of employments in designated areas concerned with exploration or exploitation activities. Generally this means that persons employed in the British sectors of the North and Celtic Seas will be treated as working in the UK. 'Designated areas' are those designated by Order in Council under the Continental Shelf Act 1964, s 1(7). Apart from the rig workers themselves, this extension of the UK is also of interest to the crews of ships and aircraft servicing the offshore installations. Flights or voyages to the installations will not constitute overseas working.

The expatriate family

Many aspects of UK tax law treat the family effectively as a single unit. The income of a wife is generally treated as that of her husband, and children's income in as much as it derives from a parental gift or settlement is treated as the income of the parent. This unified treatment ceases in the questions of residence and domicile. The residence or domicile of one spouse does not affect the residence or domicile of the other (TA 1988, s 282(2) and CGTA 1979, s 155(2)). Children will have a domicile of dependence during their minority but are capable of having a residence status quite independent of their parents.

Because each member of a family is considered individually there is some scope for intra-family tax planning. There can also be some pitfalls if this is not done properly.

One of the commonest situations for the family of a working expatriate is that the husband (in the majority of cases) is treated as not resident in the UK from the day following departure on account of his full-time overseas employment, but his accompanying wife remains classified as a UK resident. Now it may be that the wife will acquire non-resident status in her own right but if the family home or any second home remains available for her or her husband's use in the UK, she will be resident in any year during which she visits there. Accommodation available to one spouse is generally assumed to be available to the other unless it can be shown that it is not, in fact, so available.

It is not uncommon for an expatriate wife to have part-time employment abroad and whether or not this is taxable, given that she remains resident for tax purposes, will depend on whether or not she satisfies the qualifying period rules for the 100% relief. If she does not satisfy those conditions then her earnings overseas will be chargeable to UK income tax. Since she is UK resident she will be entitled to a single person's personal allowance.

The expatriate wife with no income of her own, either earnings or investment, is unaffected by her residence status. But if her husband has investment income arising in the UK which is liable to tax, for example, income from letting the family home, there is scope for transferring that income to the wife. It should be noted that the resident wife of a non-resident husband is entitled, not to the wife's earned income allowance but to the single personal allowance. That is, she is treated as a *feme sole*. This means that her allowance can be used to offset investment income, resulting perhaps in a repayment of tax credit or of income tax deducted at source. It is important, however, that income-producing assets should be held in one name only if the income would be exempt in the husband's case. A joint bank deposit account where one of the parties is resident will produce interest all of which is liable to UK tax, whereas a sole account held by the non-resident party would result in the liability not being pursued in view of Extra-statutory Concession B13 (1985) (see also Chapter 5).

The general rule is that UK assets producing taxable income should be held by the wife and UK assets producing an income exempt in the hands of a non-resident should be held by the husband. Non-UK assets should be held by the non-resident spouse.

This separation of spouses can also be useful for avoiding capital gains tax, although there is now less scope for this than there was a few years ago. For details of the potential CGT savings, see Chapter 9.

Children who remain resident in the UK, perhaps staying at a boarding school, are also entitled to a personal allowance. Where the parents are resident in the UK this personal allowance of the children is rarely of significant benefit unless the child has a substantial income from a non-parental source. Gifts from parents to children are treated as settlements and any income arising therefrom is treated as if it were the parent's income. This does not apply, however, where the parent is not resident in the UK (TA 1988, s 663(5)). Because of this, a parent might usefully make a gift of certain income-producing assets to his children who would then be able to claim relief against that income. The tax repayment might, for example, go some way towards paying for school fees, etc. Provided this were an outright gift to the child there should be no charge to inheritance tax.

On the parent's return to UK-resident status, any continuing income from the gift would revert to being taxed as that of the parent until the child reached age 18, or, if earlier, until he or she married.

Non-UK investment income

One of the commonest reasons given for taking up employment overseas is the desire to acquire more capital in a shorter period than is normally possible in the UK. Apart from the often higher overseas salary, a major contribution toward achieving the aim comes from the favourable tax regime under which the expatriate may operate. How favourable that tax regime is obviously depends on where in the world the expatriate is working but in many cases his investment income, if it arises outside his country of residence, will attract little tax.

Chapter 4 of this book considers the various investment media which the expatriate might consider and describes the taxation consequences of using them. For UK tax purposes the overseas investment income of the non-resident is beyond the scope of the legislation. A possible danger point arises, however, when the non-resident returns permanently to the UK. Because of the 'previous year' basis of assessment for certain types of income from investments, income arising while the investor was non-resident may fall into charge to tax after his return. This, and ways in which it might be avoided, are described in Chapter 4.

National insurance contributions

National insurance contributions are payable in respect of employees as Class 1 primary contributions payable by the employee and Class 1 secondary contributions payable by the employer. These contributions are, within limits, earnings related. If the employee is working abroad but the employer has a place of business in the UK, and the employee is ordinarily resident in the UK, and was so resident immediately prior to the employment abroad, the full Class 1 contributions remain payable for the first 52 weeks of working overseas. For national insurance purposes, the DSS normally regards a person as ordinarily resident in the UK if he normally resides in the UK and is likely to return to the UK within a three-year period. In some cases, particularly within the European Community, reciprocal arrangements apply which mean that local social security contributions would be paid and UK national insurance contributions would not be due.

Where Class 1 contributions are not due, it may nonetheless be desirable for the working expatriate, whether resident or not resident for UK tax purposes, to continue voluntary Class 3 contributions (or Class 2, if he or she is self-employed) at a flat rate in order to preserve pension and other benefits. The DSS regards a normal working life for a man to be 49 years, and to qualify for the standard pension, a man needs to contribute for at least 44 years. Since the NI pension, is indexed for inflation, it is in the expatriate's interest as a rule to continue contributing to the scheme. If the employee returns to the UK for a period of 26 weeks or more, unless on unpaid leave, the contribution liability will recommence both for the period of stay and for a further 52-week period of non-residence.

An employee working in the European Community for less than 12 months will not normally be liable to local social security contributions but will remain liable to UK Class 1 contributions.

Similarly a self-employed working expatriate is entitled to continue to preserve his pension and national health service benefits by paying Class 2 flat rate self-employed contributions provided that before his departure he was resident in the UK for a continuous period of at least three years and had paid contributions equivalent to at least 52 times the weekly Class 1 lower earnings limit for each of those years. He would be liable to Class 4 earnings related self-employed contributions only if he remained liable to UK income tax.

A non-employed expatriate may be able to preserve his pension and other benefits by continuing voluntarily to pay Class 3 contributions while abroad.

Information on the national insurance position of an expatriate may be obtained from the DSS Overseas Branch, Newcastle upon Tyne, NE98 1YX.

Occupational pension schemes

The expatriate who has been seconded overseas for a UK company may remain within the UK pension scheme, but if he works for an overseas subsidiary or associated company he may remain within the UK scheme for a three-year period of secondment, provided that he remains contracted to the UK company. This period can sometimes be increased by agreement with the Superannuation Funds Office of the Inland Revenue.

If the expatriate becomes an employee of the overseas company but also retains a UK employment he could only join the overseas scheme with Revenue approval. If he ceases to be employed by the UK and transfers to a foreign employer, he would normally have to withdraw from the UK pension scheme where his pension would be frozen, but may be able to transfer to an overseas scheme.

3 Retiring abroad and the permanent emigrant

The taxation aspects of retiring abroad or otherwise permanently leaving the UK are in some respects simpler than merely going abroad temporarily. The emigrant will most probably be cutting most of his ties with the old country and once away will expect only to return for relatively short visits. Nevertheless he still needs to take some care in his year of departure; he must always bear in mind the rules of residence and non-residence; and he may not totally escape the influence of the Inland Revenue if he has a source of income in the UK.

Immediate considerations

The intending emigrant who has given up his UK employment, sold his house, and has a job and home to go to abroad can usually fill in his Form P85, pack his suitcase and go, reasonably sure in the knowledge that he will be considered not resident and not ordinarily resident from the day after he leaves. The last communication he might ever receive from the Inland Revenue could be an income tax repayment cheque resulting from his P85 claim.

This Inland Revenue treatment is very much the same as that given to a temporary expatriate taking up overseas employment and the non-resident status remains conditional until a complete tax year has been spent abroad and any visits have been kept within the limits described in Chapter 1. Confirmation of the non-resident status is rarely, in fact, given, unless the emigrant has cause to continue to complete UK tax returns because of continuing UK income sources. Although an enquiry might be made of the emigrant to determine whether or not he remains non-resident after the first tax year, as often as not this is a futile enquiry and his tax office file will eventually become a dead file. The Inland Revenue do, however, have remarkable powers of resurrection. The dead file will normally be traced should the emigrant decide to return to the UK again. (This does not, of course, apply to visitors unless their visits are particularly lengthy and involve a period of local employment.)

In the example given, the intending emigrant had sold his UK home. This would be normal for most people leaving permanently and is considered as quite firm evidence of intent by the Inland Revenue. It is by no means crucial for the emigrant who has employment arranged in his new country, because he will in any case be treated as any other overseas employed expatriate.

The retired expatriate

But in the case of a retired emigrant or one who is self-employed, failure to divest himself of his property in this country will mean that he will continue to be regarded provisionally as resident and ordinarily resident for up to three years after departure. A decision on his residence status will be made retrospectively in the light of what has actually happened in the meantime. During the three intervening years, his tax liability will be provisionally computed on the basis that he remains resident in the UK. Such a person will also have a provisional entitlement to personal allowances (since he is provisionally resident) and these will be reflected in any PAYE code operated, for example, against a company pension, or may form the basis of a tax repayment claim if tax is deducted, or effectively deducted in the form of tax credits, from interest, dividends, or other sources of income.

If the emigrant is not working full-time in an employment, trade, or profession abroad, then retaining his UK property can be particularly dangerous. If it is available for his use, then he need only set foot in the UK in a tax year to become resident for that year. Unless, that is, there is a double taxation agreement between his new country and the UK which overrides this provision.

If after three years the emigrant has not broken the rules, then his non-resident, non-ordinarily resident status will normally be backdated to the day following his departure. Any tax paid in the meantime because of his provisionally resident treatment which would not have been payable in the case of a non-resident will then be repaid.

Investment income in the UK

The emigrant who obtains his non-resident status may, of course,

Retiring abroad and the permanent emigrant 35

still have an income tax liability in the UK because of investments there. Certain British investments can generate tax-free income for non-residents, others produce income where tax is deducted at the basic rate and for emigrants in certain countries a double taxation agreement may permit deduction of a withholding tax (generally lower than the basic rate). Because of this continuing liability many emigrants remove all of their investments from the UK when they leave. Although this action is, in the majority of cases, correct from a taxation point of view, the decision to do so should always be taken in the light of the larger considerations of investment performance and flexibility.

Chapter 5 describes the tax regimes applying to most investment vehicles in the UK so far as they affect expatriates. Chapter 14 takes a more detailed look at those investments most suitable for non-residents generally. However, space does not permit an examination of the taxability or tax-efficiency of these vehicles in all the countries which host British expatriates. For that information the reader must consult the tax authorities in the country in question or an international taxation specialist.

Capital gains tax

Capital gains tax is discussed more fully in Chapter 9 but the general rule for expatriates may be summed up here: realise losses before departure but retain gains until afterwards, unless there is a more penal CGT code in the destination country. If capital gains are taxable in the destination country the emigrant will need to calculate his liability both there and in the UK, and adjust his transactions accordingly, bearing in mind that the first £5,000 (1988/89) of gains in this country attracts no tax.

It is not uncommon, particularly with retiring emigrants, for a business to be disposed of, which may give rise to a potential capital gains tax charge. This aspect is considered in Chapter 9.

Inheritance tax

Inheritance tax (formerly capital transfer tax) is fully discussed in Chapter 10 and has already been touched upon in Chapter 1. The criteria for this tax are the location of the assets transferred and the domicile of the transferor. The transfer of assets located in the UK or transferred by a UK-domiciled individual may give rise to an IHT charge.

The emigrant UK domiciliary cannot avoid IHT regardless of the location of his assets for at least three years after changing his domicile. It is important, therefore, to convince the Inland Revenue as soon as possible that a new domicile has been acquired. The evidence required to back such a claim is given in Chapter 1.

For those who do acquire a new domicile but who also retain assets in the UK there is a fairly simple device whereby IHT may be avoided. If the emigrant establishes a company outside the UK and that company owns the assets, then the fact that through his ownership of the company the individual retains control of the assets, is immaterial; what he actually owns is the shares in the company and that asset is located beyond the reach of the tax. There are many organisations in the Isle of Man, Channel Islands and elsewhere which provide companies for this purpose.

It is sometimes felt by non-residents that because they themselves may be beyond the reach of the powers of the Inland Revenue to collect any tax due, they may act with impunity and make what transfers they wish. Perhaps they may; but if the transferee is resident in the UK then the Inland Revenue have power to obtain payment of the tax from that person.

The UK has entered into several double taxation agreements dealing with IHT and its counterpart overseas. These are mentioned in Chapter 7.

Coming home again

If the emigration has not worked out as planned and the emigrant returns to the UK, this can have a profound effect on his tax and investment planning and it may involve a certain amount of unscrambling of complex arrangements. Much of what needs to be done is described in the following chapter.

Where there may be a major difference between the returning temporary expatriate and the erstwhile emigrant is in the field of IHT. If the 'emigrant' had claimed a change of domicile then that would become invalid on his return home. The reversion to the earlier domicile would commence at the time of his decision to return. However, his return could prejudice his intervening domicile of choice if the Revenue can show that his actions indicate that he never actually intended to leave the UK permanently, with the result that the original domicile would be considered as never having been lost. This would have the effect of bringing back into charge any transfers made in the interim which were, at the time they were made, considered to be outside the scope of the tax. This is a point worth making particularly to an elderly couple who retire abroad. It is a common occurrence that after the death of one spouse the survivor decides to come home rather than stay abroad alone. Some contingent IHT planning may therefore be advisable at the outset.

4 The returning expatriate

The successful handling of an expatriate's financial affairs requires careful planning before he leaves the UK, continuous awareness of the taxation consequences of his actions while overseas, and, perhaps most important of all, careful planning and sound advice before his return home. It would, after all, be rather unfortunate to have spent many years building up a substantial amount of capital only to have a large slice of it taken by the Inland Revenue through a lack of foresight on return. Fortunately, much can be done to mitigate potential tax charges, but it is essential for these mitigating devices to be put in train before the expatriate comes back to the UK. Effective tax planning the day after return will, more often than not, prove to be impossible or, at least, illegal or ineffective.

This chapter, in common with the rest of the book, is concerned primarily with taxation and investment, but the returning expatriate has more to consider than this, and an indication of some of the other areas of concern is also provided.

Tax liabilities on return

As already mentioned, the main determinant of a person's liability to UK income tax or capital gains tax, apart, that is, from having an income or a capital gain, is his tax residence position. The mere ending of an overseas employment or a visit to the UK need not result in a change of residence. The change from non-resident to resident will only come about if any of the following circumstances apply:

(a) the person returns to the UK intending to remain permanently or for a number of years; or
(b) he spends 183 days or more in the UK in any particular tax year; or

(c) he visits the UK regularly for periods which average 90 or more days each year over a period of four consecutive tax years; or
(d) he pays any visit to the UK, no matter how brief, while not in full-time employment or self-employment overseas and when he has accommodation available for his use in the UK.

For the majority of returning expatriates, the first condition above will apply. But before going on to review the consequences of this, it is worth considering the not uncommon situation of the expatriate who returns home for a period, perhaps at the end of a contract, but with the intention of finding another overseas job at the earliest opportunity. A person in these circumstances need not become resident in the UK, but most do under the second or fourth condition above. Unlike the majority, this temporary resident will not become resident and ordinarily resident from the date of arrival: rather, he will become resident but not ordinarily resident for that year. The tax consequences here are quite different from those pertaining to the new permanent resident.

Taxation on remittance basis

An individual who is resident but not ordinarily resident will be taxed on the remittance basis, that is, on the income he actually brings into the UK. In some respects this can be a more onerous burden than that of the permanent resident. Income which arises in the UK will be wholly taxable; overseas investment income will be assessed on the remittances made during the preceding tax year (or the current year if the income source is new) as will any remittances from an overseas trade or profession. The remittance of earnings arising in the year of return from overseas employment will also be taxable in the year of return as will earnings arising in previous years from a trade within Schedule D. This latter liability is one of the major differences between the treatment of those who become ordinarily resident and those who do not. Taxable remittances can be in cash or kind or they can be constructive remittances arising through various debt arrangements and similar devices. An expatriate who is likely to find himself in this position would be well advised to seek professional assistance at an early date, before his return, because the degree of tax liability will be determined by many individual factors which are beyond the scope of a general treatment here. So far as CGT is concerned, an individual resident but not ordinarily resident will be fully liable on any gains made worldwide unless he is not domiciled in the UK. In the case of the non-domiciled individual he will be liable in full for gains made in the UK and on any gain remitted to the UK which arose abroad.

Tax on worldwide income

Returning to the majority case, the erstwhile expatriate will become resident and ordinarily resident from the day of his return. From then on, he will be fully liable to UK taxes on his worldwide income and capital gains. There are, however, one or two important exceptions and adjustments to this general rule. The first of these concerns any earnings from the overseas employment. Because, by concession, the tax year is split in the year of return into a resident and non-resident part, the overseas earnings before return escape tax. But, in addition, any subsequent payments including terminal leave pay, bonuses, gratuities, or lump sums from provident funds or in commutation of pension rights, are also allowed tax free where they relate to the overseas employment. Any pension which arises overseas and which is payable by reason of overseas employment is taxable in the UK (whether remitted or not) but 10% of the amount received is exempted from tax.

Where the returned expatriate has a continuing source of overseas investment income this, too, will become taxable on his return. This type of income is taxed under Schedule D, Case IV or V, and the basis of assessment is the income arising in the previous year (with special treatment in the early and closing years—see below). Because of this previous year basis, the new arrival could find himself with an immediate tax bill on income which arose while he thought he was safely beyond the reach of the Inland Revenue. By a further concession the Revenue do not seek to obtain the full amount of tax chargeable. The assessment for the year of return is restricted to that part of the overseas investment income which corresponds to the fraction of the year during which the taxpayer is actually resident. For example, if an expatriate returns to the UK on 5 August 1988 he will be resident in the UK for eight months of tax year 1988/89. If his overseas investment income for 1987/88 was £9,000, the amount assessed for 1988/89 on his return would be:

$$£9,000 \times 8 \div 12 = £6,000.$$

Had he delayed his return until 5 March 1989, the assessment then would be on one-twelfth of £9,000, ie, £750.

Much as the reduction in these assessments may be welcome the net result is still a tax liability on income which arose during the non-resident period. In certain circumstances the whole liability can be avoided.

Current year basis

The normal basis of assessment, as stated above, is the income arising in the previous year. But where there is a new source of income, the assessment for the year in which the income first arises is based on the actual income for that year. This is known as the current year basis. One way, therefore, that the returning expatriate can avoid taxation on the previous year basis, is to ensure that when he returns his investments are all recently purchased. This does not mean that the expatriate should make no investments until just before his return. He should, however, sell his securities and repurchase them the next day for a new account or preferably purchase other securities. Similarly, bank deposit accounts should be closed, the money transferred to a current account for a short period and a new deposit account should then be opened.

One point to bear in mind when contemplating the return home and what to do with bank deposits, is the period of notice required for withdrawals or closure of the account. Many investors use fixed term deposits for three, six, or 12 months and if the interest rate remains attractive at the end of the term, they simply roll the money over for a subsequent term. Breaking a fixed term account, if it is permitted at all, will always involve a stiff penalty in interest forfeited. It is essential, therefore, to ensure that all accounts can be terminated before the return date.

The taxation advantage of using this capitalisation or closure procedure can be best illustrated by an example:

Example: Capitalisation of investments

Mr Swan has been abroad for ten years; he opened a deposit account in a Channel Islands bank five years ago and for the last two years the deposit has been standing at £100,000. Interest has been, and for the purpose of illustration, will continue to be, paid at the rate of 10% a year. The interest earned and paid in June and December has always been withdrawn by Mr Swan and invested elsewhere. Mr Swan's contract ended on 31 December 1987 and he intends to return to the UK on 5 January 1989. If Mr Swan did nothing about his account before coming home he would be assessed for 1988/89 on his interest as follows: interest arising in 1987/88 $\times$ $^1/_4$ (the portion of the tax year during which he is resident), ie, £10,000 $\times$ $^1/_4$ = £2,500.

If he is taxable only at the basic rate this will mean a bill of £625 payable within 30 days of the issue of the assessment.

The returning expatriate 43

If, on the other hand, Mr Swan had closed his account on 31 December 1988 he would have no liability for interest in 1988/89 at all because the first interest payment due from the new source would not be made until June 1989. His first liability would be in 1989/90 and would be calculated on the interest arising in that same year. See Chapter 7 of the *Allied Dunbar Tax Guide*.

The advantage is magnified if, as is often the case, the returned expatriate withdraws a substantial amount of his accrued capital to purchase a house or a business, perhaps. This can be illustrated by considering Mr Swan's actions following his return.

On 1 May 1988 Mr Swan withdraws £50,000 to put towards the purchase of a new house. Assuming in the first instance that he had taken no action over his account before returning, his income tax assessments would be as follows:

1988/89: on previous year basis (reduced), £2,500 = tax of £625
1989/90: ,,   ,,   ,,   ,, (full),   £10,000 = ,,   ,, £2,500
1990/91: ,,   ,,   ,,   ,, ,,   £7,083 = ,,   ,, £1,771
1991/92: ,,   ,,   ,,   ,, ,,   £5,000 = ,,   ,, £1,250

Thus over the four years he would have paid tax of some £6,146 (assuming that the basic rate of tax continues to be 25%).

If, however, the account had been closed, a totally different picture would emerge. The assessments then would be as follows:

1988/89: no liability
1989/90: on current year basis, interest = £7,083 = tax of £1,771
1990/91: ,,   ,,   ,,   ,,   ,, = £5,000 = ,,   ,, £1,250
1991/92: ,,   ,,   ,,   ,,   ,, = £5,000 = ,,   ,, £1,250*

In this case the total tax payable over the period is only £4,271, a tax saving of £1,875. (* If a further withdrawal was made in 1991/92, reducing the interest payable in that year, Mr Swan has the option of having that year's income also assessed on the current year basis, reducing his tax charge still further.)

Although this is one of the simplest pieces of tax planning for the returning expatriate, it is often missed. As the example above shows, it can be an expensive omission. But it only works for overseas bank accounts. If the expatriate has held his money on deposit in the UK he would have had no liability during his period of non-residence but in the year of return this concessionary exemption is lost completely. If nothing is done about a UK account, the full amount of interest paid will be assessed on the previous year basis. There is no apportionment related to the part of the year during which the investor is resident. If the account is closed before return this will make little, if any, difference. The assessment would then be on the current year basis from the beginning of the tax year to the date of closure and on the same basis from the date of reopening until the following 5 April, ie, a full year's interest. The only way around this is to close the UK account in the tax year preceding the tax year of return, transfer the money offshore then use the capitalisation procedure on that offshore account. Because of the hassle involved in this, as well as the need to know the expected return date well in advance, it is better if the expatriate stays clear of UK deposits altogether. The same interest rates, with the same banks, can be obtained outside the UK.

Capital gains tax

Turning to the question of CGT, there is now less scope than there used to be for some tax planning tactics. The basic rule is that where a person is not resident and not ordinarily resident throughout the tax year, he will have no liability to UK CGT. By concession, where the tax year is split into a non-resident and resident part in the year of return, no CGT will be charged on gains made during the period of non-residence. But to qualify for this treatment, the person must have been non-resident for a continuous period of 36 months. If this condition is not met then any gains made in the tax year in which the return falls, will be taxable whether made before or after the return. For short-term expatriates, therefore, any imminent or potential gains should be realised in the tax year before the year of return. For the longer-term expatriate, gains may be taken without penalty up to the day before returning to the UK.

The returning expatriate's aim should be to realise his gains before he returns and hold his losses until he rejoins the UK tax system. The converse, of course, will apply if there is a local CGT regime which is more burdensome than that in the UK. In most cases, however, the investor will not necessarily want to dispose of his holdings. In the case of a married couple where one spouse was resident and the other (the investor) was not resident, the non-resident spouse could transfer the gainful assets to the resident spouse. CGTA 1979, s 44, which normally exempts transfers between husband and wife does not apply if one of them is non-resident; CGTA 1979, s 155(2) and TA 1988, s 282 *Gubay* v *Kingston* [1984] STC 99). This transfer would be deemed to be carried out at market value and the recipient spouse would have this market value as the acquisition cost. When both spouses were resident in the UK once more the asset could be transferred back exempt from tax. Assuming both spouses to be UK domiciled, there would be no IHT complications. On eventual sale, the base cost would be that

The returning expatriate 45

market value crystallised on the first transfer, the overall effect being to wipe out gains which arose during the period of non-residence.

Another simple step is the 'bed and breakfast' operation under which investments are sold and repurchased the following day. The repurchase following the previous day's sale (theoretically, and usually in practice too, at the same price or thereabouts) crystallises any underlying gain and gives an enhanced acquisition cost against which to compute the gain on the eventual disposal. It appears from the exchange of correspondence between the Institute of Chartered Accountants and the Revenue, published on 25 September 1985 as TR 588, in para 16 that the *Furniss* v *Dawson* doctrine would not normally be applied to a properly executed bed and breakfast transaction.

Where the intention is to dispose of certain assets in the near future, perhaps to purchase a house or business, the simplest course might be to sell before return and hold the proceeds on deposit until required. If the assets are showing losses, they should be retained until after return.

So far, this chapter has illustrated ways of reducing the returning expatriate's immediate tax bills. That may be sufficient planning for some expatriates who intend to spend their capital soon after return but for many others it does not go far enough. In particular, where the returning expatriate intends to use his capital to provide an income either to supplement a lower UK salary or to provide a pension in retirement, what is required is longer term planning and the use of a 'tax shelter' and, in this context, good advice is essential.

Dangers of evasion

Many expatriates believe when they return home that so long as their money is left outside the UK they will have no UK tax liability on any income arising from that money or any capital gains made. Others believe that they will only have a liability when they remit the income to the UK. For the British expatriate returning home this is, of course, untrue. Then there are those expatriates who know this to be the case but still take the view that if they leave their money offshore and 'forget' to declare it, the Inland Revenue will never find out. That view, to say the least, is extremely foolish. Just one or two points might help to dissuade some expatriates from this concept. Assuming that the unlawful evasion goes undetected for a year or two, our criminally-minded individual may decide to spend some of his cash on a new house: the Revenue will receive details of the transaction and any half-awake tax inspector will ask where the balance of the purchase price came from. The excuse that it was a legacy from Aunt Freda will not be accepted without sight of the probate documents. Another myth which should be exploded concerns bank secrecy. More and more countries are co-operating with each other in the transfer of information about taxpayers of mutual interest there is often provision for this in double taxation agreements. Even the Swiss banks, those bastions of security where it is a criminal offence to divulge any information about a bank customer, have not proved impregnable to attacks by both the French and American tax authorities. Finally, an incautious word in the golf club may find its way back to the taxman and the subsequent investigation will not be a pleasant experience, quite apart from the substantial costs which will inevitably be incurred.

Miscellaneous investments

The steps to be taken and the points to be considered with a portfolio of conventional investments have largely been covered, but many expatriates also acquire a range of other investments, be they Persian carpets, Chinese ceramics, precious metals such as bullion, coin or jewellery, and so on. Where these are wanted at home for aesthetic as well as investment reasons, the investor should be prepared to pay any necessary duty, including VAT, incurred on importing them. If it is only their investment potential that is of interest, these charges can be avoided by importing them to the Channel Islands and depositing them there. The cost of safe storage and the high cost of insurance, however, must be taken into account.

Unremittable overseas income

Income from and expenditure on woodlands in the UK have been taken out of the tax system with effect from 15 March 1988, subject to transitional provisions, but woodlands remain a tax efficient investment. They still attract inheritance tax privileges.

Where a person has overseas investment income which cannot be remitted to the UK or otherwise released from the overseas country, any tax chargeable in the UK on the income will be held over until such time as the income is released. The unremittability of the income must be by reason of the laws of the overseas country, or executive action of that country's government, or the impossibility of obtaining foreign currency there. In addition the investor must not have realised the income outside that territory for a consideration in sterling or any other freely remittable currency. Where this relief is due it must be claimed before any assessment on the income becomes final. When the income is finally released it will become taxable at that time and relief will be given for any overseas taxes paid. If the investor dies before the income is released then any later release will be charged to his personal representatives.

National Insurance

Some of the benefits available under the British social security system will be accessible to the returning expatriate immediately, regardless of his National Insurance record while overseas, but the major benefits such as unemployment benefit, sickness and invalidity benefit and maternity grants and allowances will only be given where there is an acceptable level of contributions.

Where the returning expatriate has been receiving a National Insurance Retirement Pension at a lower level than that currently prevailing in the UK he will be entitled to have it uprated to the full rate on his resumption of UK residence.

Other matters

The returning expatriate must also consider various legal matters. First, he must make sure to give his tenants sufficient notice if he has let his house and wishes to resume living there. It might be considered wise to seek to terminate the tenancy a month or so before the expected date of return to give time for eviction proceedings to be pursued, should the tenants resist moving. The lost rent is unlikely to be as much as the cost of staying in hotels while the law takes its course.

Another point worth watching is the expatriate's will. It may be that he has made a will under his local legal framework while abroad—this is generally no bad thing. The will should be reviewed on return. It may be worth retaining the overseas will, suitably amended, insofar as it relates to property in the overseas country and to have a new will in the UK. This may assist in releasing overseas assets to the executors in order to pay any IHT required before a grant of probate on the UK will (see also Chapter 10).

Finally, in some countries a tax clearance certificate is required before an exit visa is granted. Where such a certificate is necessary, it is usually essential to apply in good time. There is not a lot of point in turning up at the airport only to be told that you first have to satisfy the local taxman that you have paid all his taxes.

5 UK income of British expatriates

For most expatriates the source of their earnings will be outside the UK. Nevertheless, many who were previously resident will already have investments in the UK and many more will wish to invest there. It may also be the case that an expatriate will also receive earnings from a UK business or a pension from an earlier employment there. In any of these circumstances, a UK source of income will have a tax consequence, but the nature of the British tax system is such that the tax consequence may be different for every type of income. Earnings from employments are treated differently from pensions, which in turn are treated differently from business profits. Earned income is treated in a different manner from investment income and different types of investment give rise to different methods of taxation.

This chapter looks in some detail at the taxation consequences attaching to the major types of income originating in the UK, so far as UK tax is concerned. Income from letting UK property is considered separately in Chapter 6. To obtain a complete picture, the expatriate must also consider any local taxation which will apply in his country of residence and the provisions of any double taxation agreement between that country and the UK.

In considering this topic, reference should also be made to Chapter 7—Double taxation agreements, and to Chapter 9—Capital gains tax.

Interest from bank and building society deposits

Income accruing to a UK deposit account is strictly taxable in the UK under Schedule D, Case III.

Although these provisions take the non-UK resident out of the composite rate scheme they do not exempt the interest from tax.

However, where the beneficial owner of the account is not resident in the UK and certain other conditions are fulfilled, then under Extra-statutory Concession B13 (1985) no action will be taken to pursue that tax charge. Income tax on bank deposit or building society interest is normally paid direct by the bank at a composite rate (23.25% for 1988/89) as a result of which the recipient is treated as having received income which has suffered tax at the basic rate and on which he is only liable to any higher rate charge on the grossed up equivalent of the interest received. This means that a person whose income is below the tax threshold is unable to recover tax paid at the composite rate and as a result he may be better advised to consider investing in a National Savings Investment Account or an offshore bank where the interest is paid gross.

The composite rate tax provisions on bank or building society interest do not apply to a non-resident, provided that he has declared in writing to the deposit taker liable to pay interest that at the time of the declaration he is beneficially entitled to the interest and is not ordinarily resident in the UK. The declaration contains an undertaking that if the depositor becomes ordinarily resident in the UK he will notify the deposit taker accordingly and must be in the form prescribed by the Board of Inland Revenue and contain such information as they may reasonably require (TA 1988, s 481(5)(*k*) and SI 1986/482 reg 8).

The composite rate scheme for bank and building society interest applies to other deposit takers, including local authorities.

Where, exceptionally, a declaration does not incorporate the address of the person making it, it needs to be supported by a certificate from the deposit taker. In such a case, the deposit taker needs to certify that, to the best of his knowledge and belief, the individuals to whom the declaration relates are not ordinarily resident in the UK; that the person making the declaration has undertaken to notify him of a relevant change in residence status; and that if he receives information indicating that any of the individuals concerned are ordinarily resident in the UK, he will bring the deposit into the composite rate scheme. In addition the Revenue are empowered to prescribe or authorise the form of the declarations and certificates.

Extra-statutory concessions

The first condition attached to Concession B13 is that the individual concerned should be regarded as not resident in the UK for the whole of the year of assessment. This means that the concession is not available in either the year of departure or the year of return. Since the basis of assessment for established sources of income under Case III is the previous year basis, this means that the person leaving the UK in May 1988, for example, will be liable for tax on the accrued interest in 1989/90. In the normal course of events this tax would be payable in January 1990, but where a repayment claim (for tax deducted under PAYE prior to departure, perhaps) has been made, this tax will be set off against any repayment otherwise due. The situation on returning to the UK is generally more serious, particularly if the deposit account has been inflated by extra savings during the period abroad. A person returning in July 1988 would be assessed on the interest arising in 1987/88, that is for a year during which he was non-resident. Another Extra-statutory Concession (A11) which can be applied to some other sources of income briefly states that where liability is affected by the person's residence then it will be computed with reference to the period of residence during the year of assessment. For example, someone becoming resident in the UK half way through the tax year will be taxed on only half the assessable income of the previous year if the preceding year basis is applicable (see also Chapter 4—The returning expatriate). This concession is not granted in the case of UK bank interest.

The second condition in Concession B13 is that the non-resident should not be chargeable in the name of any agent or branch with the management and control of the interest.

Finally, if the interest is to be tax free the person must not make any claim to relief in respect of taxed income from UK sources (for example, a claim to personal allowances under TA 1988, s 278).

Joint accounts, where one party is resident and the other is non-resident, as is often the case with married expatriates, are wholly taxable (regardless of whether the account is with a UK bank or offshore) because the interest is generally not apportioned between the two individuals but accrues to them jointly and can be drawn by either of them. This is a point missed by many expatriates.

In general, UK bank and building society deposit accounts are to be avoided. If it is desired to maintain a deposit account with a British bank, it should be made with an offshore branch or subsidiary of the bank, for example, in the Isle of Man. In that way it will be beyond the reach of the UK legislation and attract no UK tax.

Interest from Government, local authority and corporate stocks

Government stocks

In the main British Government stocks are subject to UK income tax and the majority have tax deducted at source. But interest from certain stocks is exempt from tax if they are beneficially owned by a person not ordinarily resident in the UK. The stocks which are currently exempt are listed below.

8¼%	Treasury Loan 1987/90	6¾%	Treasury Loan 1995/98
5¾%	Funding Loan 1987/91	13¼%	Exchequer Loan 1996
11%	Exchequer Loan 1990	15¼%	Treasury Loan 1996
13%	Treasury Loan 1990	8¾%	Treasury Loan 1997
10½%	Conversion Stock 1992	13¼%	Treasury Loan 1997
12¾%	Treasury Loan 1992	15½%	Treasury Loan 1998
9%	Treasury Loan 1992/96	9½%	Treasury Loan 1999
6%	Funding Loan 1993	9%	Conversion Stock 2000
12½%	Treasury Loan 1993	8%	Treasury Loan 2002/06
13¾%	Treasury Loan 1993	9¾%	Conversion Stock 2003
9%	Treasury Loan 1994	5½%	Treasury Loan 2008/12
14½%	Treasury Loan 1994	7¾%	Treasury Loan 2012/15
12¾%	Treasury Loan 1995	3½%	War Loan 1952 or after

Since the majority of stocks suffer tax at source, the non-resident stockholder must apply for the gross payment of exempt stocks. Application should be made to The Inspector of Foreign Dividends, Lynwood Road, Thames Ditton, Surrey KT7 0DP.

Stocks normally paid without deduction of tax include 3½% War Loan, British Savings Bonds and registered stocks and bonds on the National Savings Register.

Exempt stocks have long been a mainstay for the appropriate portion of the British expatriate investor's portfolio because of their competitive yield and high security. They also form the basis of a large offshore gilt fund industry and both direct and fund investment can form part of a sound investment portfolio.

Local authority stocks

Interest from local authority stocks is generally paid after deduction of tax. The only exception to this is where the stock was issued for borrowing in a foreign currency. In that case, and subject to Treasury direction, the interest may be paid gross and be exempt from income tax if the stockholder is not resident in the UK.

Corporate stocks—debentures, etc

These, too, are generally paid effectively net of income tax at the basic rate, although arrangements can be made for interest to be paid gross under a double taxation agreement (see Chapter 7).

Any other interest

Subject to the exceptions described above and to the specific provisions of double taxation treaties (see below) all interest payments made to non-residents should be paid net of UK income tax at the basic rate.

Double taxation agreements

Where there is a double taxation treaty in force between the UK and the country of residence of the recipient, then the treatment of interest may be covered therein. It is normal in these cases for interest to be payable gross and tax to be payable in the country of residence. Many agreements, however, have provision for a withholding tax in the country of origin. The appropriate agreement must be checked.

Dividends

Dividends paid by UK companies are technically paid gross, ie, there is no income tax deducted at source. However, alongside the dividend there is an associated tax credit currently equal to 1/3rd of the net dividend. So far as the payer is concerned, this tax credit is accounted for and paid to the Inland Revenue as advance corporation tax (ACT). This ACT can be used to offset the payer's final or mainstream corporation tax liability in due course. So far as the payee is concerned the tax credit can be treated as analogous to income tax deducted at source. For the UK-resident non-taxpayer, the credit can be repaid, and for the higher rate taxpayer, the quantum of dividend income on which these rates will be calculated is the sum of the dividend plus tax credit.

Thus, where a person receives a dividend of £375, there will be a tax credit associated with the dividend of some £125. For the non-taxpayer, this £125 can be repaid. If the recipient of the dividend had a marginal tax rate of 40%, however, then there would be additional tax of £75 due on his dividend income:

Dividend	£375
Tax Credit	125
	£500
Tax @ 40%	200
Less: tax credit	125
Additional tax due	£75

This tax treatment applies to dividends and other distributions from UK companies, investment trusts, and unit trusts.

In general terms, the non-resident is not able to reclaim the tax credit. However, under certain double taxation agreements payment of the tax credit can be made subject to a UK withholding tax. This withholding tax is 15% of the sum of the dividend plus tax credit, therefore allowing 40% of the tax credit to be paid.

Where an expatriate is entitled to a portion of personal allowances under TA 1988, s 278 then the tax credit can be repaid up to the amount of allowances due but unless the UK dividend income is significant relative to the expatriate's total income, an allowance claim is rarely worthwhile.

Life assurance policies

The benefits payable under UK Life Assurance Policies are liable to UK tax for non-residents and residents alike. However, for a qualifying policy normally there will be no tax liability where the proceeds are payable to the original policyholder or to somebody to whom the policy has been given. In the case of a non-qualifying policy, tax may be payable on the proceeds. (For a single premium bond, for example, the permitted annual withdrawal is a cumulative 5% per annum, which, if taken, could be for a maximum period of up to 20 years.) Tax is only payable by higher rate taxpayers—which includes those who are moved into the higher rate when any gain on

UK income of British expatriates 55

total surrender or excess withdrawal is added to their annual taxable income—and is charged at the difference between the basic and the higher rate of tax (15% for the 1988/89 tax year). For non-UK residents without other significant amounts of UK income, this will generally mean that there is no tax due.

It is important to bear in mind though, that this seemingly beneficial tax treatment is granted to take into account the tax that is paid by UK Life Assurance Companies on the profits and gains within policy funds. Currently, franked income (that from UK equities and gilt edged securities) is taxed at 25%, all other income (from foreign equities and Eurobonds, for example) is taxed at 35%. Capital gains are taxed at 30% but of course the allowance available to individuals to offset the first of £5,000 of gain, is not applicable. For non-UK residents 'offshore policies' may prove to be a better investment. An 'offshore policy' is one issued by a life assurance company resident in a tax-haven where policy funds pay little or no tax on income and gains and the policy proceeds are similarly free of tax.

Expatriates returning to the UK should note that the proceeds of policies effected after 17 November 1983 may be fully liable to tax on the accrued profits ie without the benefit of the basic rate tax credit, although the profit will be apportioned in direct relation to the periods of residence and non-residence during the policy term and only that portion relating to the period of UK residence will be subject to tax. (The proceeds of offshore policies affected before 18 November 1983 continue to be free of liability to UK taxation.)

These comments refer only to UK taxation and non-UK residents must also take account of any local tax liability that may be due on policy proceeds.

Where life assurance premium relief is available (for a qualifying policy issued on or before 13 March 1984) the premiums may be paid net of the relief—currently 15% of the premium reducing to $12^1/_2$% in the tax year 1989/90. The policyholder is eligible for relief if the policy is written on his life or that of his spouse, if either of them pays the premiums, and if the person paying is resident in the UK for tax purposes. Where the policyholder and his spouse will both be non-resident for the whole of a tax year the premiums must be paid gross, but net payments may be resumed when they again take up UK residence.

National Savings

Most of the investments offered by the Department for National Savings are tax-free both for residents and non-residents. However, the yield from these investments largely reflects this in that greater yields can often be obtained elsewhere. As with other 'tax-free' investments there is no guarantee that the proceeds will remain so overseas.

The main taxable National Savings investment is the National Savings Bank account which usually offers a very competitive interest return. This is treated in the same way as other bank interest described earlier in this chapter, except that the composite rate arrangements will not apply to every UK resident.

Pensions

Many expatriates will, whether now or later, receive pension income from the UK and for tax purposes this income may be divided into three separate groups:

(a) State Pensions—these include Old Age Pension and the State Earnings Related Pension Scheme.
(b) Private Pensions—such as an occupational pension payable by a UK employer or self-employed and personal pensions (including the new Personal Pension Plans which became available from 1 July 1988).
(c) Government Pensions—pensions arising from UK Government service: eg an Armed Services Pensions, an NHS Pension, a Teacher's Pension etc.

State Pensions are always paid gross and can be paid in any country. The pensioner is liable for tax in the country where he is resident but where he receives any other pension taxable in the UK (see below), the State Retirement Pension will usually be taxed alongside that other pension. This is carried out either by a reduction of allowances or by the use of the higher rate of taxation in addition to the basic rate.

Private Pensions continue to be liable to tax in the UK—they are likely also to be liable for tax in the country in which the expatriate is resident. Fortunately the UK has Double Taxation Treaties with more than 90 countries including those where expatriate Britons are most commonly to be found. Most of these Treaties include an article covering Private Pensions and provide for the pension to be paid gross in the UK and taxable only in the country of residence.

Government Pensions are always taxable in the UK and, like Private Pensions, they are likely also to be liable for tax in the country of residence. Once again, relief is available where there is a Double Taxation Treaty in force—this will normally provide for Government Pensions to be taxable only in the UK. (More information on Double Taxation Treaties may be found in Chapter 7.)

Non-residents in receipt of a UK pension will usually qualify for at least a proportion of UK personal allowances (see later) and if the pension is substantial these allowances should be claimed. It is proposed that with effect from the tax year 1990/91 the allowance will be available in full for those eligible and this will mean a substantial reduction in liabilities for many expatriates.

Employments

The taxation treatment of employments which are carried on partly within and partly outside the UK is fully described in Chapter 2—The expatriate who remains UK resident. Some non-residents do, however, have employments which are carried on wholly in the UK. Commonly, these are directorships where the non-resident does not work full-time in the employment but attends board meetings, etc, in the UK. The whole of the remuneration from an entirely domestic employment is liable to UK income tax. Taxable too are benefits in kind and travelling expenses from the overseas home to the UK received or incurred in the performance of such employments, unless they are wholly, exclusively and necessarily incurred in the performance of the duties; TA 1988, s 198, *Taylor* v *Provan* [1974] STC 168.

Where a non-UK domiciled individual comes to work in the UK and was not resident in the UK during either of the two preceding tax years or was not present in the UK at any time during the two years up to the date of his arrival, he is entitled to relief for travel between the UK and his normal place of abode abroad for a period of five years, so long as the cost is borne or reimbursed by the employer. The journey includes travel from the home in the UK to the home overseas. Where the employee is in the UK for a continuous period of 60 days or more he is entitled to relief for two visits a year by his spouse and minor children so long as the expenses are paid for or reimbursed by the employer. Apportionment is possible in cases of duality of purpose. There are provisions to prevent double allowances.

Where the employer is not UK resident, the two year period of absence from the UK before claiming relief for the five-year period was not required for 1984/85 or 1985/86, and if relief was available to an employee for either of those years it continues unconditionally until 5 April 1991 (TA 1988, s 195).

Where it can be shown that some part of the duties of the employment are carried out overseas then part of the remuneration should be exempt from tax.

Trades and professions

Where a non-resident has trading income arising in the UK this will normally be liable to UK income tax. It is important, however, to consider the nature of the trade, where it is actually carried on, and whether or not an agent is involved.

A trade *with* the UK should not be confused with a trade *within* the UK. The latter is certainly taxable but the former may not be. A non-resident trader may have a representative office or an advertising department within the UK, he may even have a sales agent in the UK, without incurring any income tax liability (*Grainger* v *Gough* (1896) 3 TC 311; *Smith & Co* v *Greenwood* (1922) 8 TC 193). But care must be taken with agents, as discussed below. An advertising or representative office will not be trading in the UK if, for example, the contracts for the sale of goods, or for services, are in fact made overseas directly with the trader. This would constitute trading *with* the UK. But if the overseas trade was represented by a UK sales office, for example, where orders were taken and paid for locally, then this would constitute trading *within* the UK. In the simple cases of sale of goods and services, the position is fairly clear cut, but if the trade involves both manufacturing and selling in different countries then the situation becomes more complex. Where only selling takes place in the UK, the profit assessed may be limited to the merchanting profit under TMA 1970, s 81. Where UK branch profits do not appear to show the true profit, a proportion of the total worldwide profit may be charged in the UK based on the turnover in the UK, under TMA 1970, s 80. Such a situation

UK income of British expatriates 59

allows for tax avoidance by arranging for profits to be realised in the least onerous fiscal regime. Needless to say, this is counteracted by anti-avoidance legislation such as the transfer pricing rules contained in TA 1988, ss 770–773. See also Chapter 12—Companies.

Where a non-resident trades within the UK he will be liable to tax, but collecting that tax is another matter, given that courts will not normally enforce foreign tax debts. TMA 1970, ss 78 and 79 attempt to get around this by providing that a non-resident trading in the UK will be chargeable in the name of any branch or agent in the UK. Thus the UK sales office mentioned above would be a taxable or chargeable entity in that case. The only exception to this is where the agent is an independent broker or general commission agent carrying on a bona fide brokerage or commission agency.

Royalties and patents

Copyright and UK patent royalties paid to non-residents normally have income tax deducted at source by the payer (see, however, Chapter 7). The payer is assessable even if he fails to deduct the tax. The sale of a patent in the UK by a non-resident vendor involves the deduction of basic rate tax by the purchaser from the consideration paid, under TA 1988, s 524(3).

Where copyright royalties are paid through a third party that party may be liable on the net sum, ie, the royalty less commission, TA 1988, s 536(3), (4).

Maintenance payments

Maintenance payments under a pre-15 March 1988 UK court order are, until 5 April 1989, paid subject to deduction of tax at source unless within the small payment limits of TA 1988, s 351, currently £208 a month for a former spouse, and to a child for his benefit, maintenance or education; and £108 per month to a spouse or other person for a child. Maintenance payments received by an expatriate living abroad would be UK taxable income treated in the same way as any other taxed income. If the UK expatriate is actually paying maintenance to a spouse still living in the UK, tax still has to be deducted from the payments and is payable to the UK Revenue under TA 1988, s 349, although there is obviously no means of enforcement where the payer is outside the jurisdiction of the UK courts. The net amount is grossed up by the recipient and treated as income which has suffered tax at the basic rate notwithstanding the payer's failure to account for the tax (*Stokes* v *Bennett* [1953] 34 TC 337).

The existing rules continue to apply for 1988/89 to payments made under—

— court orders made before 15 March 1988;
— court orders applied for on or before 15 March 1988 and made by 30 June 1988;
— maintenance agreements made before 15 March 1988 (provided that a copy of the agreement has been received by the Inspector of Taxes by 30 June 1988);
— court orders or agreements made on or after 15 March 1988 which vary or replace such Orders or agreements.

Between 6 April 1988 and April 1989, however, the first £1,490 of payments by one divorced or separated spouse to the other is exempt from tax in the recipient's hands.

For payments after 5 April 1989 under pre-15 March 1988 arrangements:

— the payer gets tax relief on payments up to the level for which he got relief for 1988/89; and
— an amount equal to that received in 1988/89 will be treated as part of the recipient's total income.
— however, the difference between the married person's allowance and the single person's allowance (for the relevant year of assessment) will be exempt from tax in the recipient's hands.

All payments of maintenance due after 5 April 1989 will be paid gross—without tax deducted by the payer.

Payers under the existing rules may, if they prefer, switch to the new rules mentioned below. The new rules will then apply to the recipient as well. An election, which will apply for a whole tax year can be made at any time during the year and up to 12 months after. Generally there is no benefit to the payer in making an election for 1988/89. An election may be beneficial in later years if payments increase, and the limit for relief 'pegged' at the 1988/89 level is below the maximum amount of relief available under the new rules.

For court orders and maintenance agreements made on or after 15 March 1988:

— the recipient is not liable to tax on any payments received;
— where one divorced or separated spouse is required to make payments to the other, the payer qualifies for tax relief (at basic and higher rates) for payments up to a limit equal to the difference between the single and married person's allowances (£1,490 for 1988/89) until the recipient remarries;
— there is no tax relief for other new maintenance or alimony payments;
— payments are made gross (ie without deduction of tax).

Trust and estate income

Tax on income received by a non-resident from an estate in the course of administration in the UK is initially charged on income distributed in the year of receipt and ultimately the total income is reallocated over the administration period on a day to day basis unless he has an absolute interest in the residue, or a share of it (TA 1988, s 695). The personal representatives will deduct tax at the basic rate and issue a tax certificate on form R185-E for the tax deducted. The income is then treated in the same way as any other UK-taxed income and a repayment claim may be made or a higher rate liability may arise.

Where the non-resident has an absolute interest in residue the income is again subject to basic rate tax being withheld by the personal representatives but in this case the income under TA 1988, s 696 is allocated on an arising basis and not on a day to day apportionment over the whole administration period. Relief from higher rate tax is available where IHT has been paid on accrued income at the date of death (TA 1988, s 699).

In the case of trust income a life tenant of a UK trust would receive income subject to tax at the basic rate, whereas the beneficiary of a discretionary UK trust would receive his share of income less UK tax at both the basic rate and an additional 10% surcharge, ie currently 35%, under TA 1988, s 687. Again, any overpayment of UK tax may be recovered and any underpayment of higher rate liability remains payable.

Avoidance of higher rate liability

Where UK investment income is sufficient, the non-resident may find that he has an individual liability to higher rate taxation in addition to any basic rate tax that may have been withheld at source. In many cases the tax charge can be limited to the basic rate by transferring investments to an overseas holding company in an appropriate tax haven. For example, if investments were held by an investment company in the Isle of Man with directors in say, Hong Kong, it would be a non-resident company subject, in the Isle of Man, to a flat rate of tax of only £450. As a non-resident company, the liability to tax on its UK investment income would be limited under TA 1988, s 1 to basic rate only.

Despite the obvious attractions, expatriates considering this route should first indulge in some careful consideration. The costs involved in establishing and running an offshore company can be sizeable and in the tax year 1988/89 the savings to be made are much less than in previous years. In the 1988 Budget the Chancellor reduced the basic rate from 27% to 25% and replaced the graded higher rate bands (top rate 60%)—with a flat higher rate of 40%. The maximum saving is thus now 15% instead of 33% as hitherto. Transferring the ownership of assets into an offshore company can also be a costly business especially where there is stamp duty to be taken into account: share transfers are charged at $\frac{1}{2}$% and conveyances of land and buildings are charged at 1%.

Where it is calculated that the tax saving is likely to outweigh the costs involved, there are still a couple of factors to be borne in mind before proceeding. Firstly, in view of the anti-avoidance provisions of TA 1988, s 739 the offshore investment company route should only be considered by individuals not ordinarily resident in the UK and the company should be wound up before UK residence is resumed.

This means that the procedure is only suitable as a means of tax limitation for the long term non-resident.

Care is required, however, because, as in all tax matters, if there is first, a pre-ordained series of transactions and second, steps inserted which have no business purpose apart from avoidance of tax, the inserted steps will be ignored for tax purposes: see *Craven* v *White*, [1988] STC 476.

Lloyd's Underwriters

The taxation of Lloyd's Underwriters is a specialist subject and the

UK income of British expatriates 63

comments here are confined to areas of particular interest to non-resident names.

Lloyd's income arises in the UK and is classified as a trade carried on in the UK subject to UK tax. It is normally desirable for Lloyd's deposits to be arranged by way of letter of credit or bank guarantee as, for example, exempt gilts held as part of Lloyd's deposits or reserves remain UK taxable as connected with a business carried on in the UK (*Owen* v *Sassoon* [1950] 32 TC 101) (apart from $3\frac{1}{2}$% War Loan). The CGT and IHT exemptions however continue to apply.

The basis of assessment for Lloyd's investment income may not be followed by the overseas Revenue which might, for example, assess the investment income as it arises even though it is not distributed until the account is closed. US tax paid which would be refunded to a UK resident is treated as an expense so far as a non-resident is concerned and merely reduces the gross income. Transfers to a special reserve fund would not normally have any effect for foreign tax purposes, although they would affect the UK tax payable and therefore the amount available for credit. Where the UK tax is fully relieved overseas there is no advantage in a transfer to the special reserve fund, although care has to be taken to ensure that foreign tax credits are not inadvertently lost.

There are special rules in certain countries for Lloyd's Names, in particular the US and Canada.

Non-resident's entitlement to UK personal allowances

Certain classes of non-residents may obtain relief against UK assessable income through entitlement to a proportion of the normal personal allowances. The relief operates by restricting the tax applicable to an individual's personal allowances in the proportion that his UK taxable income bears to his total world income (TA 1988, ss 278, 811), which excludes a non-resident wife's non-UK income (*IRC* v *Addison* [1984] STC 540) see SP7/85, Appendix III.

In the first instance the full personal reliefs are given against the UK taxable income but there is a minimum UK tax liability (assuming that there is no double taxation relief (DTR)) which is:

$$\text{UK tax on world income as if income of UK resident} \times \frac{\text{UK taxable income}}{\text{Total world income}}$$

Where the income taxable in the UK is taxable at a nil or reduced rate under a double tax treaty it is left out of the computation in the first instance and the tax calculated separately at the treaty rate. The formula is therefore:

$$\text{UK taxable income subject to DTR as if UK income of UK resident} \times \frac{\text{UK taxable income not subject to DTR}}{\text{Total world income including that subject to DTR}}$$

However there is a further provision that if the world income rate would be lower if there were no double taxation relief (ie applying the first formula) the lower charge prevails.

The classes of individuals to which the relief applies include the following:

(a) all British subjects (including subjects of any part of the Commonwealth, but not mandated states) and citizens of the Republic of Ireland;
(b) persons who are or who have been in the service of the Crown;
(c) missionaries;
(d) servants of British Protectorates;
(e) residents of the Isle of Man or Channel Islands;
(f) persons abroad for health reasons after residence in the UK;
(g) widows of Crown servants;
(h) residents of countries where relief is given under the double taxation treaty.

In addition, double taxation agreements with many countries provide that the relief applies to residents of that country.

This tax relief, while useful in some cases, particularly where the non-resident has a large portion of his income taxable in the UK, is rarely significant for the working expatriate. It may not be worth the trouble of claiming on an annual basis but possibly every few years (the time limit for the claim is six years).

UK income of British expatriates 65

It was frequently the practice of various United Nations Organisations to re-imburse their British subject etc employees for the notional UK tax that they could have reclaimed under this section on the assumption that UNO remuneration was ignored. Actual claims would not generally have been favourable due to the quantum of UNO income. Early in 1978 it was agreed with the Inland Revenue that remuneration of non-resident employees of UNO and its specialised agencies should be ignored for the purposes of computing liability under s 278 thus enabling those persons to submit actual claims. The agencies concerned are:

United Nations Organisation	(UNO)
Food and Agriculture Organisation	(FAO)
International Civil Aviation Organisation	(ICAO)
International Labour Organisation	(ILO)
International Telecommunications Union	(ITU)
United Nations Educational, Scientific and Cultural Organisation	(UNESCO)
Universal Postal Union	(UPU)
World Health Organisation	(WHO)
World Meteorological Organisation	(WMO)

From 1990/91 the restriction to a proportion of world income has been removed and non-residents become entitled to full personal allowances.

6 Tax aspects of UK property
by P A Goodman, *Wilkins Kennedy*

Expatriates often retain property in the UK which is let during the period of absence overseas. The retention of such property ensures that the expatriate has a place to live in the UK on the completion of his overseas work, and may be a protection against significant rises in house prices during the period of absence.

Before entering into letting arrangements, the expatriate needs to give careful consideration to the proposed tenancy arrangements, with particular attention being given to rights of possession. Standard tenancy arrangements may create difficulties at a future date, and consequently advice should be sought from experienced professional advisors in relation to UK Landlord and Tenant Law.

Rental income

Taxation matters in connection with lettings also need careful review. Income from UK property, being income arising from a source in the UK, is chargeable to UK tax at basic and, where applicable, higher rates. Assessment to tax is under either Schedule A (Unfurnished Lettings) or Schedule D Case VI (Furnished Lettings). Expatriates resident in a country which has a double tax treaty with the UK will find that it is normally the case that the treaty provides for rental income to be taxed by the country in which the property is situated.

In preparing the statement of letting income for Inland Revenue purposes, it is necessary to show gross income receivable less allowable expenses paid in respect of the letting incurred during the period covered by the statement. Expenses associated with the letting may include:

- Rates and water rates
- Agents' commission
- Building and contents insurance, and valuation fees for insurance purposes
- Service charges for equipment
- Repairs and maintenance (but not capital expenditure, eg central heating/double glazing installation)
- Ground rent
- Professional charges for preparing the letting statement
- Advertising
- Wear and Tear Allowance (For furnished lettings only – being 10% of gross rent receivable less rates paid by the landlord: Inland Revenue Press Release 13 October 1977)
- Cleaning
- Garden upkeep

Mortgage loan interest is not an allowable expense in arriving at net rental income, but may be allowed as a deduction in arriving at assessable letting income. Overdraft interest is not an allowable expense or deduction for tax purposes. In order to obtain tax relief on interest, a number of conditions need to be met. The loan interest must be payable in the UK on an advance from a bank carrying on a *bona fide* banking business in the UK, or it must be annual interest chargeable to tax under Schedule D Case III. It is prudent for the loan to be taken in the UK from a UK bank or other lender, but it is understood that a loan arranged through the UK branch of a recognised overseas bank will be acceptable. Additionally, the property in the UK must be let at a commercial rent for at least 26 weeks in a 52-week period, and when not so let must be either available for letting at such a rent or undergoing works of construction or repair. Lettings at below the market rate, taking into account maintenance and repairing liabilities, result in loan interest relief being disallowed.

Qualifying interest in excess of net rental income from a property may be set off against other UK rental income. Any unrelieved balance may be carried forward to be deducted against rental income arising in the next year, provided that the property continues to be let at a full commercial rent.

Administration and collection of tax

This is a complex area which can create a great deal of confusion for

Tax aspects of UK property 69

the expatriate. Where rents are paid direct by the tenant to the expatriate whose usual place of abode is outside the UK, then basic rate tax must be deducted from gross rents and paid to the Inland Revenue by the tenant (TA 1988, s 43). Payment of rent into a UK bank account held by the expatriate does not avoid the obligation of the tenant to deduct tax at source. It is important to note that, even if basic rate tax has been deducted by the tenant in these circumstances, it is still necessary to provide the Inland Revenue with a statement of rental income for each tax year in order that the correct income tax liability can be calculated.

Where the property is let through an agent, the provisions of TMA 1970, s 78 apply. This provides that the non-resident owner is assessed and charged to income tax in the name of the agent in the same manner as the non-resident person would have been assessed and charged had he been resident in the UK. The practical effect of this is that the Inland Revenue assess the agent on the net rental income of the expatriate and the agent then discharges the income tax liability. There is no legal obligation on the agent therefore to deduct basic rate tax at source from rents remitted to the expatriate but, given the agent's responsibilities laid down in TMA 1970, s 78, the agent will ensure that sufficient tax is withheld from rents to satisfy the expected tax liability. A statutory right of indemnity from the tenant in respect of tax charged (not interest or penalties which may arise from late payment of tax or failure to make the necessary returns) is contained within TMA 1970, s 83(2). In the event that the agent has made an excessive retention in relation to the tax liability arising, such retention should be repaid to the expatriate once the lettings statement and liability to tax have been agreed with the Inland Revenue.

The agent may, in the interim, place the tax reserve in a gross interest yielding account. Gross bank deposit interest is normally not taxable on the expatriate by virtue of Extra-statutory Concession B13, provided the appropriate certificate of non-residence is signed and the expatriate is not assessable in the name of an agent in the UK. The presence of a letting agent will not generally prevent the application of the concession, provided that the interest arising is beneficially owned by the expatriate, the deposit is not excessive in relation to rent arising, and the agent's authority is restricted to the withdrawal of funds solely for the purpose of discharging the income tax liability arising on the rents.

Tax on lettings income is normally payable on 1 January in the year of assessment.

Furnished holiday lettings

Letting furnished property as holiday accommodation within the terms of the legislation may secure a beneficial tax treatment of expatriates with other UK source income. Furnished holiday lettings are treated as a trade if the following conditions are met:

- the accommodation must be in the UK and let furnished on a commercial basis with a reasonable expectation of making a profit;
- it must be available for letting to the public at large for at least 140 days in any tax year;
- actual lettings must be at least 70 days in the tax year (although in the first and last years in which the trade is carried on the rules are modified);
- in a seven-month period, including the months that the property is let, no single let should normally be longer than 31 days.

The main income tax benefits to derive from the treatment of the activity as a trade relate to the ability to relieve losses against other UK income and the payment of tax in two instalments. There is no change to the administration and collection of income tax as described above. For capital gains tax purposes the expatriate may, in certain circumstances, and especially if a spouse remains resident and has an interest in the property, derive a benefit from the availability of roll over relief and retirement relief relating to business assets.

Mortgage interest relief at source (MIRAS)

MIRAS was introduced in April 1983, enabling UK interest payments to be made net of the basic rate of income tax to qualifying lenders. The loan on which interest payments arise must have been taken out for the purchase (or improvement, before 6 April 1988) of a property in the UK which is used wholly or to a substantial extent as the only or main residence of the borrower, his spouse (or before April 1988 a dependent relative or a former or separated spouse). MIRAS applies only to the first £30,000 of a loan which satisfies these conditions, and expatriates are not, as a class, excluded from MIRAS relief. Qualifying lenders include most UK building societies, banks, insurance companies and specialised mortgage funding schemes.

Tax aspects of UK property 71

An expatriate working full-time overseas may be unable to satisfy the condition that any UK property retained is used 'wholly or to a substantial extent' as his only or main residence. 'Substantial' is not defined in the tax legislation but it is understood that the Inland Revenue regard this as six months or more in the year. If the expatriate's spouse and family continue to live in the UK property then the condition may be satisfied. Additionally, Extra-statutory Concession A27 allows temporary absences of up to a year to be ignored in determining whether a property is used as an only or main residence.

Relief is also granted in Extra-statutory Concession A27 when a person is required by reason of his employment to move from his home to another place overseas for a period not expected to exceed four years. MIRAS will continue to apply to mortgage interest payments in respect of a loan for the purchase of a property used as an only or main residence before working overseas, provided this property can reasonably be expected to be used again as such on his return. Relief is not given beyond a period of four years, but if there is a further temporary absence after the property has been reoccupied for a minimum period of three months, the four-year test will apply to the new absence without regard to the previous absence. It should be noted that if arrangements are entered into to take advantage of the concession for tax avoidance purposes, it is likely that the Inland Revenue will deny the application of the concession (*R* v *IRC, ex parte Fulford Dobson* (1987)).

If an expatriate on an overseas tour of duty purchases a property in the UK in the course of a leave period, and uses that property as an only or main residence for a period of not less than three months before his return to the place of his overseas employment, he will be regarded as satisfying the condition that the property was being used as his only or main residence before he went away, and MIRAS will be applied.

If an expatriate lets his property while he is away at a commercial rent, the benefit of the concession may be claimed, where appropriate, if this is more favourable than a claim for relief against letting income. However, the MIRAS office should be notified of the letting.

Mortgage interest relief is administered by the Central Unit (MIRAS) 1st Floor, St Johns House, Merton Road, Bootle, L69 4EJ.

Capital gains tax: principal private residence

The disposal of UK property by an expatriate during a tax year throughout which he is not resident and not ordinarily resident for UK tax purposes does not give rise to a charge to capital gains tax.

For the tax year of return to the UK, Extra-statutory Concession D2 provides that 'a person who is treated as resident in the UK for any year of assessment from the date of his arrival here but who has not been regarded at any time during the period of 36 months immediately preceding the date of his arrival as resident or ordinarily resident here, is charged to capital gains tax only in respect of the chargeable gains accruing to him from disposals made after his arrival in the UK'. However, extra-statutory concessions will not be given in any case where an attempt is made to use them for tax avoidance and after the judgment in *R v IRC ex parte Fulford Dobson* (1987) care should be taken in respect of any transaction involving a chargeable gain undertaken in the period 5 April to the date of arrival in the UK.

Expatriates who retain their home in the UK during their period of absence overseas should carefully consider the conditions to be satisfied after returning to the UK for exemption from capital gains tax on a subsequent sale. These conditions are as follows:

(1) The property must be the individual's only or main residence throughout the period of ownership except for all or any part of the last 24 months of ownership. If the property has been an only or main residence for part of the period of ownership the gain is apportioned between the exempt and non-exempt periods.

(2) The exemption applies to dwelling houses and land comprising garden and grounds which are for the occupation and enjoyment of the main residence up to the permitted area. The permitted area is defined as one acre (inclusive of the site of the dwelling house), although in any particular case the permitted area may be such area larger than one acre as the 'Commissioners may determine, if satisfied that regard being had to the size and the character of the dwelling house, that larger area is required for the reasonable enjoyment of it as a residence'.

(3) Certain periods of absence from the dwelling are treated as periods of residence provided the dwelling house was the only property eligible for relief and was occupied as such both

Tax aspects of UK property 73

before and after the periods of absence. These periods which can be used on a cumulative basis are—
(a) Any period or periods of absence which do not in total exceed three years; and
(b) Any period of absence throughout which the individual worked in an employment or office all the duties of which were performed outside the UK; and
(c) Any period or periods of absence not exceeding four years in total throughout which the individual was prevented from residing in the dwelling house in consequence of the situation of his place of work or because his employer required him to live elsewhere so that his duties of employment could be effectively carried out.

Expatriates need to pay close attention to condition (b). It is clear that all duties of employment must be performed outside the UK. This is in contrast to income tax rules where incidental duties performed in the UK may be disregarded under the provisions of TA 1988, s 335. The performance of such incidental UK duties could inadvertently jeopardise the capital gains tax relief. The condition is also framed in terms of employment or office and does not cover self-employment.

The requirements as to occupation of the property both before and after the period of absence are of considerable significance. If the expatriate returns to the UK and does not occupy his former main residence because he owns another property, then a chargeable gain may arise on disposal. Extra-statutory Concession D4 provides assistance to the expatriate where he is unable to resume residence in his previous home because the terms of his employment require him to work elsewhere. The concession deems the condition of re-occupation after the period of absence to be satisfied.

Where an expatriate has sold his UK home during his overseas absence and purchased another property which is to be occupied on his return to the UK, the gain attributable to the period of time from purchase to actual occupation may be chargeable to capital gains tax on disposal. This arises if the property has not been occupied as the main or only property on purchase, even though it replaces a former main residence occupied as such, before leaving the UK. Such transactions can present an unfortunate tax pitfall for the expatriate, although the legislation contains specific relief for expatriates who live in job-related accommodation overseas. This is defined as where it is necessary for the proper performance of the duties of the employment that the employee should reside in that accommodation.

Another point to consider carefully is that for the principal private residence exemption to apply, the expatriate must have no other property eligible for capital gains tax exemption as an only or main residence throughout the period of absence. This creates a difficulty as the expatriate may have an interest in a overseas residence— either by way of ownership or rental—which will be a residence eligible for relief. In these circumstances the expatriate should consider submitting to the Inland Revenue an election under CGTA 1979, s 101(5) that the UK property is the expatriate's only or main residence to satisfy the statutory requirements. There is a two-year time limit from acquisition of the interest in the additional property to make the election.

7 Double taxation agreements

Fiscal residence

The UK taxes the worldwide income of a UK-resident and domiciled individual and it also taxes the income arising in the UK of a non-resident. It will be appreciated that as many other countries do likewise, it is possible to be subject to tax on overseas income both in the country of residence and in the country in which the income arises. In many cases this problem is alleviated by a bilateral double taxation agreement between the two countries involved. The text of the OECD 1977 model double tax agreement is reproduced in Appendix IV. The UK currently has more than 90 double taxation agreements, some of which relate only to particular types of income. This book is aimed largely at the British expatriate and it is therefore necessary to consider in the case of income arising in the UK whether there is a double tax treaty between the UK and the taxpayer's country of residence or not. If there is such a treaty, it is then necessary to consider the taxpayer's fiscal residence under the treaty.

Consider for example the case of the expatriate who has retired to Spain where he spends the majority of the winter but who has retained his house in the UK where he spends the summer months. Article 4 of the Anglo-Spanish Double Tax Treaty provides that it is necessary first of all to consider residence according to the rules of the country concerned. Under UK law, because of maintaining a place of abode in the UK, he is resident in any fiscal year in which he sets foot in the UK, as he does not have a full-time employment in Spain. As he spends some nine months of the year in Spain, he is resident in Spain for Spanish tax purposes.

It is then necessary to consider in which country he has a permanent home available to him. As he has a home in both countries, it is then necessary to consider his centre of vital interests; that is the state with which his personal and economic relations are closer. This is debatable. He spends three-quarters of his time in Spain but has by no means severed his ties with the UK. If the country in which he has his centre of vital interests cannot be determined, it is necessary to look to the country in which he has an habitual abode. However, as he has such an abode in both countries it is then necessary to look to his nationality. If he is a UK national, he will be regarded as resident in the UK and non-resident in Spain and taxed accordingly. If he is a Spanish national, however, on the same facts he would be regarded as resident in Spain and not resident in the UK. If he is a national in neither the UK nor Spain, the Revenue Authorities in each country will agree his place of residence. In the circumstances envisaged this would probably be Spain and he would therefore be regarded as not resident in the UK, notwithstanding the fact that he has a home here would normally make him resident under the UK residence rules.

A number of the older treaties do not have this tiebreaker clause with regard to residence and it is therefore possible to be resident in both countries. This also applies where there is no double tax treaty. In this case, the tax liability must be calculated in accordance with the rules of each country and advantage taken of any remaining relief under the treaties and unilateral relief where available.

Exceptionally, the second protocol to the Anglo-US treaty (SI 1980 No 568) provides that for income tax purposes a woman with US citizenship who married a UK domiciled man before 1 January 1974 and therefore acquired a UK domicile of dependence is deemed to have married on that date and may therefore retain her US domicile of origin unless she acquires a UK domicile by choice.

Dividends

A non-resident in receipt of dividends from the UK is not entitled to the tax credit that is available to a UK resident unless the appropriate treaty so provides. The treaty with Spain for example provides in Article 10, para 3 that a Spanish resident entitled to dividends from a UK company is entitled to the same tax credit as a UK resident and is subject to Spanish tax on the gross equivalent of the dividends. However, the UK authorities subject the dividend to a withholding tax of 15% on the gross equivalent and this tax is allowed as a credit against the Spanish tax payable. If therefore a British company paid a dividend of £75, the resident in Spain would receive £75 from the company and the UK Revenue would repay

Double taxation agreements 77

the difference between the tax credit available to a UK resident of £25 and 15% on the gross equivalent: that is £10. He would therefore receive £85 from the UK and would be regarded in Spain as having received dividends of £100 on which tax of £15 had already been paid.

If he were a resident of a non-treaty country, he would be treated as receiving income of £75 and would pay such local tax on that income as would be levied by the country of residence.

To avoid having to apply to the UK Revenue for the repayment of part of the tax credit, it is possible to arrange for the company paying the dividend to repay the appropriate part of the tax credit at the same time. This requires the consent of the company and of the Inland Revenue under the Double Taxation Relief (Taxes on Income) (General) (Dividend) Regulations, SI 1973 No 317. (Usually known as the G arrangement.)

Interest

Interest arising in the UK to a non-resident is normally taxable in the UK under Schedule D, Case III, under TA 1988, s 18(3). There is an exception in the case of bank interest paid direct to a non-resident which is not subject to UK tax in view of Extra-statutory Concession B13 (1985). Annual interest, that is, on a loan exceeding 12 months, paid to a person whose usual place of abode is outside the UK, is subject to deduction of tax at the basic rate at source under TA 1988, s 349(2)(c) unless it is bank interest. A non-resident can arrange that interest is not taxed under the composite rate provisions which apply to UK residents, see p 50.

Interest paid to a non-resident may suffer a reduced rate of withholding tax or be liable in the UK for a reduced rate of tax under the treaty. Article 11 of the Anglo-Spanish Treaty, for example, reduces the tax in the country where the interest arises to 12% which would be credited against the liability in the country of residence. It is possible to arrange with the Inspector of Foreign Dividends to deduct tax at the reduced treaty rate, if any, on payment of interest to a non-resident under the Double Taxation Relief (Taxes on Income) (General) Regulations, SI 1970 No 488. This applies to both interest and royalties.

Royalties

Royalties paid from the UK to a non-resident are subject to a withholding tax at the basic rate of 25% if they are royalties in respect of a UK patent under TA 1988, s 348(2) or in respect of copyright, and are paid to the owner of copyright whose usual place of abode is not within the UK under TA 1988, s 536. It is interesting to note that s 536 refers to a usual place of abode outside the UK, not residence outside the UK, although for practical purposes this will normally be the same. It should also be noted that copyright royalties paid to an author whose normal place of abode is outside the UK are not subject to withholding tax under TA 1988, s 536 in view of a Parliamentary Reply of 10 November 1969 (Hansard Vol 791, col 31). Other royalties arising in the UK are not subject to withholding tax unless they are pure income profit where the non-resident provides no services whatsoever for the royalty received. If it is pure income profit, the tax would be withheld at source at the basic rate in the same way as for any other annual payment. Under the appropriate double tax treaty, it may be possible to reduce the rate of withholding tax and in the treaty with Spain, for example, the rate of withholding tax on royalties is reduced to 10% by Art 12 of the treaty. As for interest, permission may be obtained from the Inspector of Foreign Dividends to pay the interest subject to this reduced rate of withholding tax.

Income from real property

Income from immovable property is normally taxed in the country in which it is situated, as under Art 6 of the Anglo-Spanish Double Tax Treaty. Income from property in the UK is subject to withholding tax under TA 1988, s 43 at the basic rate of tax where payment is made to a non-resident, although it is possible to arrange with the Inland Revenue for payment to be made subject to a reduced or nil level of withholding tax if it can be shown that the income arising will be reduced for UK tax purposes by, for example, mortgage interest paid.

Businesses

Business profits are normally only taxed in the country of residence unless there is a permanent establishment in the other country, see, for example, Art 7 of the Anglo-Spanish Double Tax Treaty. Permanent establishment is very often defined by the treaty, for example, in Art 5 of the double tax treaty with Spain, and includes a place of management, branch, office, factory, workshop, mine, oil

Double taxation agreements 79

well, etc, and in the case of Spain, a building site which exists for more than 12 months.

If there is a permanent establishment of a non-resident in the UK, it will be subject to UK tax on the profits. The assessment may be made in the name of an agent in the UK who is made responsible for the tax under TMA 1970, s 83, and who may withhold UK tax when accounting to his non-resident principal. A non-resident trading with the UK is not, under general law, subject to UK tax and it is specifically provided that a non-resident trading in the UK through a broker who is a general commission agent is not liable to UK tax in view of TMA 1970, s 82. If he is otherwise trading in the UK but not through a permanent establishment the treaty will normally protect him from UK tax. In the case of a business being carried on by a non-resident it is common for the treaty to reinforce the transfer pricing provisions of TA 1988, s 770 to ensure arm's length pricing between the UK and overseas business and in the case of Spain this is contained in Art 9 of the treaty.

Capital gains

A non-resident is not normally liable to UK CGT except in the case of assets used for a branch or business in the UK under CGTA 1979, s 12. Art 13 of the Anglo-Spanish Double Tax Treaty would allow the UK to tax immovable property in the UK, although in fact it does not do so, except for development gains under TA 1988, s 776.

Independent personal services

The self-employed activities of a non-resident will not normally be subject to tax in the UK unless there is a fixed base in the UK, as under Art 14 of the Anglo-Spanish treaty.

Dependent personal services

Employment income of a non-resident from activities in the UK would normally be taxable under Schedule E, Case II although this liability may be reduced by treaty relief. For example under Art 15 of the Anglo-Spanish treaty, if the employer is not resident in the UK and the non-resident employee is present for a period not exceeding 183 days in the fiscal year, he would not be liable to UK tax under Schedule E, Case II for his work in the UK. On the other hand, directors' fees from a UK company would be subject to tax in the UK, in the case of Spain under Art 16 of the treaty.

Artistes and athletes

There are often special provisions relating to the remuneration of non-resident artistes and athletes whose remuneration may be very large. The treaty will usually provide that they are taxable in the country in which the performance is given even though they would otherwise be protected by the treaty, see, for example, Art 17 of the Anglo-Spanish treaty. From 1987/88 there is a withholding tax at the basic rate from the UK earnings of non UK-resident artistes and athletes.

Pensions

Under most of the Double Taxation Treaties that the UK has with other countries, pensions are normally only taxable in the country of residence. The exception is pensions which result from Government Service; these are normally taxable only in the country from which the pension originates unless paid to a national of the country of residence. For example, under the Anglo-Spanish treaty, a UK pension paid to a resident of Spain would be liable for tax only in Spain, by virtue of Art 18. However, if the pension resulted from service with the UK Government or a local authority, it would be taxable only in the UK under Art 19(3), unless the recipient was a Spanish national in which case it would be taxable only in Spain.

Clearly the operation of the agreement is straightforward where the pension is paid gross—one simply makes the return to the appropriate authority. Where the pension is normally subject to deduction of tax at source, obtaining treaty relief is a little more involved. (Those pensions subject to tax deduction at source were outlined in Chapter 5 but briefly, they are likely to be any pension other than State Pensions—Old Age Pension and State Earnings Related Pension—which are paid gross.) Authority for pension or retirement annuity payments to be made gross is granted by the—

Inspector of Foreign Dividends
Lynwood Road
Thames Ditton, Surrey
England KT7 0DP

The Inspector will grant permission on receipt of confirmation that the individual in question is resident for tax purposes in the other jurisdiction. There is an official confirmation form for each country with which the UK has a Double Taxation Agreement—the form may be obtained from either tax authority and is printed in both languages. For instance, in the case of a resident of Spain Form SPA may be obtained from the Inspector of Foreign Dividends or from the local office of the Delegación de Hacienda del domicilio fiscal del residente de España.

UK State Retirement (Old Age) Pension

This is always paid gross to the recipient wherever resident and would normally be taxable in the country of residence.

Occupational Pensions in respect of Government or local authority service

These pensions, for example of civil servants, members of the armed services, state system school teachers etc would be paid subject to deduction of tax under PAYE at the appropriate code number. If the recipient is living in a treaty country it is unlikely that there would be a local tax liability in the country of residence on this income.

Occupational Pensions (not Government)

Occupational Pensions would normally be subject to deduction of tax under PAYE. A non-resident should be able to arrange for a no tax notice of coding from his local district, if he still submits UK income tax returns, or from the Inspector of Foreign Dividends. Such pensions will normally be taxable in the country of residence.

Self-employed Pensions

Deferred annuities are normally subject to deduction of tax at the basic rate although a non-resident should be able to obtain the appropriate authority from the Inspector of Foreign Dividends for the annuity to be paid gross. Such income would normally be taxable in the country of residence.

Students and teachers

There are often special provisions in double tax treaties relating to students and teachers. For example in the treaty with Spain, Art 20 provides that a previous resident of Spain who comes to the UK for training and who receives money for his maintenance, education or benefit is not taxable in the UK. This is obviously useful where the children of expatriates come back to the UK for the purposes of their education. Teachers, as in Art 21 of the Anglo-Spanish treaty, are often allowed a two-year period in another country without becoming liable to tax therein.

Other income

In some treaties there is an article which provides that any other income arising in the treaty country will only be taxed in the country of residence. This article could, for example, apply to maintenance payments from the UK to a non-resident who would therefore receive the income gross or be able to recover the tax from the UK Revenue. In the treaty with Spain the 'other income' article is number 22.

Non-discrimination

Treaties often contain what is known as a non-discrimination article which says generally that a non-resident shall not be treated worse than a resident for tax purposes. In the Anglo-Spanish treaty this is contained in Art 25. Non-discrimination clauses are very often more useful as a negotiating tool than for actual invocation.

Mutual agreement procedure

Most treaties also contain a mutual agreement procedure whereby a resident may ask his own Revenue Authority to negotiate with the overseas Revenue Authority if he considers that he is being unfairly treated, or the double taxation treaty is being ignored or misinterpreted. The mutual agreement procedure is, for example, often invoked or threatened to be invoked in negotiating with the Internal Revenue Service in the US, who tend to have a somewhat cavalier view of the application of double tax treaties with other countries.

Exchange of information

One of the points to watch in living in a country where there is a double tax treaty with the UK, is that the treaty will usually contain a clause overriding the normal secrecy provisions and allow the appropriate Revenue Authorities to exchange information relating to the taxpayer's financial affairs.

Although most treaties are similar in many respects it is extremely important to refer to the actual treaty currently in force when considering the likely taxation charge as there are significant differences.

Inheritance tax

The UK has only ten Double Taxation Treaties covering inheritance tax (IHT) and consequently they are generally of not so much importance as the income tax treaties. The countries with which agreements have been concluded are:

France
India
Italy
Netherlands
Pakistan
Republic of Ireland
Republic of South Africa
Sweden
Switzerland
United States of America

In some circumstances the treaties can change the fiscal domicile of an individual for IHT purposes which would obviously be of extreme importance in determining his UK IHT liability. For instance, under Art 4 of the IHT Double Taxation Treaty with South Africa, a South African national with a UK domicile who had not been ordinarily resident in the UK for seven years would be regarded as domiciled in South Africa and not in the UK. This seemingly arcane illustration is mirrored in other ways in other treaties and must serve as an example of the need to seek professional advice in situations where an individual is living in one jurisdiction and has assets in another.

Where two countries both have a claim to the same assets (for IHT purposes) the potential exists, despite the treaty, for double taxation to occur. For this reason most treaties contain a double taxation relief clause which will remove or, at the least, mitigate the double liability. Where there is no double taxation treaty between countries, unilateral relief against double taxation may be available whereby a credit for the overseas tax paid will be set against the UK IHT liability. The provisions are somewhat complex and are contained in the Inheritance Tax Act 1984, s 159.

Unilateral relief

Double taxation relief is often given unilaterally where there is no treaty or the treaty does not cover the income in question. A UK resident is given unilateral relief under TA 1988, s 790. Unilateral relief will normally give credit for direct overseas taxes suffered but, for example, would not normally give an individual relief for the underlying taxes on a company's profits out of which a dividend is subsequently declared. As far as possible relief is given as if there had been a double taxation treaty in force.

Treaty shopping

In certain cases, it is possible to use a third country's double taxation agreement to reduce a withholding tax. For example, UK patent royalties paid from the UK to a resident of Hong Kong would normally suffer UK tax at 25%. If, however, a Netherlands company were interposed, the UK royalties would be paid gross to the Netherlands under the UK-Netherlands Double Tax Treaty and 7% or so of the royalties would remain in the Netherlands subject to Netherlands tax at 42%. The remaining 93% would, however, be paid on to Hong Kong free of withholding tax as the Netherlands does not levy a withholding tax on royalties.

This could not however be done for dividends from the UK as there is a specific anti-avoidance provision in the UK-Netherlands treaty to prevent the use of the treaty by a third country resident.

Care is required, however, because, as in all tax matters, if there is first, a pre-ordained series of transactions and second, steps inserted which have not business *purpose* apart from avoidance of tax, the inserted steps will be ignored for tax purposes: see *Craven* v *White*, [1988] STC 476.

8 Overseas visitors to the UK

Short visits

An overseas visitor to the UK must consider carefully the rules as to residence and domicile. As explained in Chapter 1, if his visit is for a purely temporary purpose and is not going to exceed six months in any tax year, he would be regarded as not resident in the UK under TA 1988, s 336. If his visit is going to be marginally in excess of six months in a tax year, it might be possible to rely on the tax residence definition in a double taxation agreement to preserve his nonresidence status. Otherwise it might be possible to re-schedule his stay so that part of the period is spent in one tax year and part in another, so that the six-month limit for any tax year is not broken. If the overseas visitor is not regarded as resident for UK tax purposes he may remit money to the UK without suffering UK tax and as there are currently no exchange control restrictions he may take the funds with him when he departs. He will then be liable for UK tax only on income actually arising in the UK as explained in Chapter 5.

Long stays

If the visitor is likely to be in the UK long enough to be classified as UK resident, notwithstanding any treaty protection, then it is necessary to consider his domicile carefully. It is obviously advantageous to show that any overseas domicile of origin has been retained, although a previous UK domicile is likely to be resurrected on a return to becoming resident in the UK (*Fielden* v *IRC* [1965] 42 TC 501).

Where an individual comes to the UK to take up permanent residence or to stay for at least three years, or comes to the UK to take up employment which is expected to last for a period of at least two years, or ceases to reside in the UK, if he has left for a permanent residence abroad, Extra-statutory Concession A 11 (1985) applies to his liability to UK tax which is computed by reference to his period of residence during the year, so that in practice the proportion of the year's income from the date of arrival is subject to tax but the proportion of income prior to that date is not. He is, however, entitled to the full year's personal allowances. The concession does not apply where an individual who had been ordinarily resident in the UK left for intended permanent residence abroad but returned to reside in the UK before the end of the tax year following the tax year of departure, and it has only limited application to changes of permanent residence between the UK and the Irish Republic.

Non UK-domiciled visitor

If the overseas visitor has a UK domicile and becomes resident in the UK he will be subject to UK tax in the normal way. If, however, he has a non-UK domicile there is considerable scope for tax planning, for example, by receiving foreign emoluments as described in Chapter 2.

If he carries on a trade or business in the UK taxable under Schedule D, Case I or II, the whole of the worldwide profits would be subject to tax in the same way as for a UK-domiciled individual. If the business can be structured in the form of a foreign partnership, that is one controlled and managed from overseas within TA 1988, s 112, he would be liable to tax under Schedule D, Case V only on the profits arising in the UK and on any overseas profits remitted to the UK. So far as investment income is concerned the assessment of a non-domiciled UK resident is under Schedule D, Case IV or V in respect of investment income arising overseas on remittances to the UK and not on the income arising. There is therefore considerable scope for a non-domiciled UK resident to limit his UK tax liability by not remitting to the UK income or realised gains assessable on a remittance basis.

Remittance basis

Under Schedule D, Cases IV and V, overseas income is assessed on the basis of remittances in the preceding tax year except in the year of commencement and the year of cessation in which case the actual basis applies with a Revenue option on cessation to substitute the actual basis for the penultimate year, and the taxpayer's option on commencement to elect for the actual basis for the third tax year which would normally be the first year on the preceding year basis.

Remittances to the UK include indirect or constructive remittances such as the satisfaction of a debt incurred in the UK. For example, a cheque drawn on a US bank account and sold to a UK bank was held to be a constructive remittance in *Thomson v Moyse* (1960) 39 TC 291, as was a loan enjoyed in the UK in *Harmel v Wright* (1973) 49 TC 149. Remittances of the proceeds of foreign securities could be remittances of capital if the securities were acquired before the taxpayer became resident in the UK following *Kneen v Martin* (1934) 19 TC 33 but would be remittances of income if the securities were purchased out of foreign income while the taxpayer was resident in the UK (*Walsh v Randall* (1940) 23 TC 55). A non-domiciled individual could make gifts to his wife and family overseas without fear of incurring liability to IHT and if, for example, the wife bought expensive jewellery and the children paid their own school fees out of their overseas bank accounts these should not be regarded as constructive remittances in the light of *Carter v Sharon* (1936) 20 TC 229. If the overseas visitor however enjoyed the assets purchased by the overseas gift, for example, if his wife bought a car which he used in the UK, it is more likely to be regarded as a constructive remittance.

As the UK Revenue will regard any remittance to the UK as primarily out of income unless it can be shown otherwise, it would be sensible for any overseas visitor likely to become resident in the UK to ensure that he plans to take maximum advantage of the remittance basis. He should therefore remit to the UK before he becomes resident a lump sum to enable him to purchase a house, if that is his desire, and to provide for his reasonable wants during his stay in the UK, bearing in mind any income arising in the UK. In this way it should be possible to avoid remitting any funds to the UK during the stay. It may be, however, that this is impractical for various reasons and it is therefore sensible to have a foreign income account outside the UK into which is paid all overseas income. Funds would not be remitted from this account to the UK unless absolutely necessary as such income would be fully taxable. As capital gains made overseas by a non-domiciled UK resident are also taxable on a remittance basis there should also be a capital account for overseas investments sold at a profit. This fund should again not be remitted to the UK but should be used for reinvestment overseas. A third fund of capital held at the time of becoming resident in the UK would also be held which is freely remittable and may be supplemented by the proceeds of any securities sold at cost or at a loss.

A non-domiciled UK resident who is a beneficiary of an overseas trust is taxable only on remittances to the UK under TA 1988, s 740(5). He could, for example, transfer overseas investments to an overseas company in order to accumulate the income outside the UK, because the anti-avoidance provisions of TA 1988, s 739 are specifically excluded in the case of a non-domiciled UK resident by TA 1988, s 743(3) if he would have been exempt had the income been received by him directly. This would normally be the situation so long as the income was not remitted to the UK.

In the case of a non-domiciled individual taxable on a remittance basis who has a business overseas, it might be possible to employ him for a period by an overseas company, in which case the income for duties performed wholly overseas would be limited to the amounts remitted during the course of the employment. If after a period he became self-employed by, for example, joining an overseas partnership carrying on similar activities, he could wait until the 6 April following the termination of the employment and remit the accumulated savings from the overseas employment. Similarly, after a period as a partner in a non-resident partnership, where again the remittance basis applies, he could save up outside the UK the earnings for a period of, say, three years and at the end of the period he would leave the partnership and recommence employment. Any remittances to the UK on or after 6 April following his leaving the partnership should be tax free as the source of income has ceased so far as he is concerned.

Maintenance

Other income taxable under Schedule D, Case V includes foreign pensions, maintenance payments under a foreign court order applied for before 15 March 1988 and made before 1 July 1988 (*IRC* v *Mrs V Anderstrom* (1927) 13 TC 482) and foreign annuities (*Chamney* v *Lewis* (1932) 17 TC 318).

A payment of maintenance under a foreign court order is not a charge on income for UK tax purposes (*Bingham* v *IRC* (1955) 36 TC 254). However, if the order was applied for before 15 March

1988 and made before 1 July 1988 a deduction is allowed in calculating the foreign emoluments assessable in the UK under TA 1988, s 192(3).

Remuneration

The taxability of remuneration in the UK has been explained in Chapter 2. A particular point to bear in mind for the overseas visitor to the UK who is an employee earning more than £8,500 a year or a director is that remuneration includes benefits in kind such as the provision of a company car where the tax liability is in accordance with a scale benefit.

The detailed figures of the car and car fuel benefit scales for 1988/89 (1987/88 in brackets) are as follows:

Table A: Car benefit
Cars with original market value up to £19,250 having a cylinder capacity

Cylinder capacity of car in cubic centimetres	Age of car at end of relevant year of assessment	
	Under four years	Four years or more
Up to 1400 cc	1,050 (525)	700 (350)
1401 cc–2000 cc	1,400 (700)	940 (470)
More than 2000 cc	2,200 (1,100)	1,450 (725)

Table B: Car benefit
Cars with original market value up to £19,250 and not having a cylinder capacity

Original market value of car	Age of car at end of relevant year of assessment	
	Under four years	Four years or more
Less than £6,000	1,050 (525)	700 (350)
£6,000 or more but less than £8,500	1,400 (700)	940 (470)
£8,500 or more but less than £19,250	2,200 (1,100)	1,450 (725)

Table C: Car benefit
Cars with original market value more than £19,250

Original market value of car	Age of car at end of relevant year of assessment	
	Under four years	Four years or more
More than £19,250 but not more than £29,000	2,900 (1,450)	1,940 (970)
More than £29,000	4,600 (2,300)	3,060 (1,530)

Table D: Car fuel benefit
Cars with a recognised cylinder capacity

Cylinder capacity of car in cc	Cash equivalent
Up to 1400 cc	480 (480)
1401 cc–2000 cc	600 (600)
More than 2000 cc	900 (900)

Table E: Car fuel benefit
Cars not having a recognised cylinder capacity

Original market value of car	Cash equivalent
Less than £6,000	480 (480)
£6,000 or more but less than £8,500	600 (600)
£8,500 or more	900 (900)

Notes
(1) The scales give the amounts of the 'cash equivalents' of the benefits, the amounts by which an individual's taxable income is increased. In terms of tax, the average company motorist driving a 1600 cc car will in 1988/89 pay about £6.75 a week in tax for his car (£9.60 if he gets petrol too) compared with £3.65 in 1987/88.
(2) Both the car and car fuel scales are *halved* for the business motorist who does 18,000 *business* miles or more in the tax year. The car scale (but not the fuel scale) is increased by 50% if the car is a second company car or is driven for fewer than 2,500 business miles in the tax year.
(3) The car scale is reduced pound for pound for contributions which the employee is required to make for his private use. The car fuel scale is reduced to nil if the

employee makes good *all* the fuel he uses for private journeys ('all or nothing'). Journeys between an individual's home and his normal place of work are regarded as private motoring.

(4) Tax on car and car fuel benefits is mainly collected through employees' codes which are adjusted each year to take account of the cash equivalent of the benefits.

Remuneration also includes reimbursed expenses except to the extent that these are wholly, exclusively and necessarily incurred for the purpose of the employment.

If accommodation is provided by the employer, this gives rise to a further benefit in kind of the annual rental value as calculated for rating purposes. However, there is a further taxable benefit where the accommodation has cost or costs the employer more than £75,000. The excess is taxed as an additional benefit at 10.5% in 1988/89 (11.5% in 1987/88) as if it were a notional loan. There is no such benefit where it can be shown that it was necessary for the employee to reside in the accommodation for the purposes of the employment. The running expenses of the house can also be assessed as a benefit, limited to 10% of the remuneration.

Other payments by the employer, such as school fees and medical insurance benefits, would be taxed as a benefit.

Ordinary residence

If the overseas visitor is coming to the UK for a period of less than three years he will be regarded as not ordinarily resident even though resident in the UK, and his Schedule E liability on employment earnings will be limited to those arising from duties performed in the UK and remittances from duties overseas. If he is here for more than three years he will become both resident and ordinarily resident from the day of arrival and in these circumstances it becomes preferable for him to have a separate contract of employment for UK duties and for overseas duties, preferably with different overseas companies. Dual contracts with the same company, have, in a number of cases, been successfully challenged by the Revenue on the grounds that there is in reality one employment with duties both in the UK and overseas and therefore the whole of the income is subject to UK tax.

National Insurance

A non-resident coming to the UK employed by a non-UK employer will be exempt from national insurance contributions for the first 52 weeks of business provided that the employer has his business base outside the UK. Thereafter the employee will be liable for his contributions but the employer's contributions will not be payable unless he has a place of business in the UK.

Unremittable income

If the overseas visitor returning to the UK has a UK domicile, and is assessed on an income arising basis he may still be prevented from remitting income to the UK by, for example, overseas exchange control regulations. In such cases TA 1988, s 584 comes to the rescue and postpones the tax charge until such time as the income may be remitted.

Foreign diplomats and members of the armed forces

Foreign diplomats and consular officials are exempt from UK tax under the Diplomatic Privileges Act 1964 or TA 1988, ss 320–322. Effectively, exemption applies to the overseas income of the non-UK citizen and any employment income in the UK from the overseas state.

Private income originating in the UK and private immovable property held for personal purposes in the UK remain within the UK tax net.

Members of visiting forces based in the UK are exempt from UK tax under TA 1988, s 323 provided that they are not UK citizens. This is achieved by ignoring the time spent in the UK for the purposes of residence or domicile or any change therein.

In most cases, diplomats and members of the armed forces based abroad remain liable to tax in the country whose government they serve and in the UK this is achieved under TA 1988, s 132(4). In some cases the exemptions are slightly widened by the appropriate bilateral double taxation treaty as explained in Chapter 7.

Teaching and other academic exchange programmes

As explained in Chapter 7, a teacher, university professor or lecturer visiting the UK for a period of up to two years is often exempt from UK tax under the appropriate double taxation treaty. In the absence of specific relief under a treaty, however, the visiting teacher would remain within the normal tax rules applicable to overseas visitors in the UK.

In some cases the visitor may be employed in research, for example, at a university, and the exemption may only apply if the research is being carried out on behalf of the university itself and not on behalf of some commercial organisation employing the university for this purpose.

9 Capital gains tax

Residence

CGTA 1979, s 2 provides that a person resident or ordinarily resident in the UK is subject to CGT on his worldwide capital gains and it is therefore essential in order to avoid UK CGT to cease to be ordinarily resident in the UK. This would normally require three complete tax years of non-residence or one complete tax year of non-residence where there is a full-time employment overseas. The CGT exemption normally applies from the date of departure in view of Extra-statutory Concession D2 and for an overseas visitor becoming resident in the UK the residence for CGT purposes applies from the date of arrival provided that he had not been ordinarily resident in the UK during the preceding 36 months.

Husband and wife

The residence statuses of a husband and wife are determined independently, and a husband and wife are taxed as if they were not married, if one is resident in the UK and one is not. Despite this, the CGT exemption for assets transferred between spouses married and living together is nonetheless preserved. In *Gubay* v *Kington* [1984] STC 499, it was held that the transfer of a chargeable asset by a UK resident spouse to a non-resident spouse was not a chargeable event. The scope for transferring an asset from a resident to a non-ordinarily resident spouse before sale to avoid CGT is limited as was illustrated in *R* v *IRC ex parte Fulford Dobson* [1987] STC 344. In this case a wife transferred a farm to her husband who went to work in Germany and the farm was sold four days after his departure. The Revenue's refusal to apply Extra-statutory Concession D2 (1985) because an attempt had been made to use it for tax avoidance was upheld.

Emigration

A person emigrating from the UK would normally leave the disposal of his assets showing capital gains until after his departure (taking due account of his liability in the new jurisdiction). The disposal should be deferred until after the following 5 April because the Revenue are likely to refuse to apply Extra-statutory Concession D2 (1985). Investments showing losses would normally be sold before the date of departure in order to crystallise a loss which might be of use on any future return to the UK.

If the assets in question are used in, or in connection with, a business, there are further important considerations. See later 'business gains'.

Immigration

In the case of an overseas visitor arriving in the UK it would normally be desirable, subject to any overseas CGT considerations, before arriving in the UK to dispose of his investments showing a profit and re-acquire them in order to maximise the base value before arrival. This should be done before 6 April preceding arrival because the Revenue are likely to refuse to apply Extra-statutory Concession D2 (1985). Investments showing losses would not be realised until after arrival as the whole of the loss could then be used in the UK. There is no question of apportioning a gain or loss between a period of residence and non-residence. The disposal date is paramount.

Property

Although non-residents may be exempt from capital gains tax in respect of a disposal of most investments it is necessary to look rather more carefully in the case of land and buildings. TA 1988, s 776 provides that a capital profit from dealing or developing land directly or indirectly is assessed to tax under Schedule D, Case VI as UK income irrespective of the residence of the owner. TA 1988, s 777(9) enables the Board to direct that basic rate income tax may be withheld from the sale proceeds, although in practice this has proved ineffective in many cases as the Revenue have not been aware of the disposal until too late to raise the necessary direction and the non-resident has received the sale proceeds gross. Section

Capital gains tax 97

776 does not apply to private residences exempt from CGT as a main residence.

Business gains

Sale of a business

A not uncommon spur to emigration occurs where a person resident or ordinarily resident in the UK is intending to dispose of his business, consisting either of shares in a company or the goodwill of an unincorporated business. This gives rise to a number of problems. Although under Extra Statutory Concession D2 a person emigrating from the UK is *normally* regarded as neither resident nor ordinarily resident from the day following the day of departure this is a purely concessional treatment as, at law, a person resident for part of the tax year is resident for the entire tax year. The Revenue are likely to refuse to apply the concession so the contract for the disposal of the shares or business should be deferred until after the following 5 April. Even then the problems are not necessarily over as the Revenue or the Courts might infer a prior oral contact, or prior agreement sufficient to constitute a contract, where all the terms and conditions of the sale were finalised before final sale. In this connection there is precedent for holding that correspondence between the parties before the final contract can create a binding contract (*J H & S Timber Ltd* v *Quirk* [1973] STC 111) and that the beneficial ownership can pass before any transfer of legal title (*Ayerst* v *C & K (Construction) Ltd* [1975] STC 345, *Wood Preservation Ltd.* v *Prior* [1968] 45 TC 112).

CGTA 1979, s 27 states that the date of disposal for capital gains tax is the time the contract was made, and if the contract is conditional it is the time when the condition is satisfied. It would, however, be hazardous to enter into arrangements designed specifically to postpone the date of disposal in order to allow time for emigration, as this might give rise to a series of transactions or a single composite transaction, the effect of which can be considered together and might result in a date of disposal before emigration (*Furniss* v *Dawson* [1984] STC 153). In particular Lord Bridge's comments in this case are of interest.

'When one moves however from a single transaction to a series of inter dependent transactions designed to produce a given result it is, in my opinion, perfectly legitimate to draw a distinction between the substance and the form of the composite transaction without in any way suggesting that any of the single transactions which make up the whole are other than genuine. This has been the approach of the United States Federal Courts enabling them to develop a doctrine whereby the tax consequences of the composite transactions are dependent on its substance and not its form. I shall not attempt to review the American authorities nor do I propose a wholesale importation of the American doctrine in all its ramifications into English law. But I do suggest that the distinction between form and substance is one which can usefully be drawn in determining the tax consequences of composite tansactions and one which will help to free the Courts from the shackles which have for so long been thought to be imposed on them by the Westminster case.'

The Westminster case held that the form of a transaction takes precedence over its substance in taxation matters. (*IRC* v *Duke of Westminster* [1936] 19 TC 490); this applies only in the absence of a pre-ordained series of transactions or one single composite transaction.

This warning having been given, it is obviously possible to enter into negotiations before leaving the UK which do not amount to a contract to dispose of the shares or business and to conclude these arrangements by a contract for sale after having become neither resident nor ordinarily resident in the UK. As has been explained earlier, to acquire non-ordinary-residence will normally require a period of absence from the UK of at least three complete tax years. However, the Inland Revenue in a letter dated 10 July 1979, quoted in *Moores & Rowland's Yellow Tax Guide*, stated:

'I can confirm that where an employee left the UK on 4 April 1979 and did not return until 6 April 1980 and was on a full-time service contract throughout that period he would be regarded as not resident and not ordinarily resident in the UK throughout the year 1979/80.

However this practice would not be extended to a taxpayer who was only partly in employment and partly self-employed during a similar period. In such circumstances the normal rules for determining an individual's residence status would apply and on the basis that no visits were made during the intervening period the taxpayer would be regarded as not resident but ordinarily resident for the year 1979/80 in these circumstances.'

'These circumstances' would be that there was not a full-time service contract covering the complete tax year.

Capital gains tax 99

It is obviously dangerous to rely on a full-time service contract overseas unless this can be substantiated by the facts of the case. The Revenue are unlikely to be easily persuaded that a person who has emigrated on selling his business in the UK for several million pounds is likely to take full-time employment; and a lot more is required than a mere service contract with some offshore company ostensibly requiring full-time duties, usually of a somewhat indeterminate nature.

If the emigrant disposing of the shares is not granted provisional non-resident and non-ordinarily resident status the capital gains tax would have to be paid and recovered in due course when the non-resident and non-ordinarily resident status was established, retrospectively to include the date of disposal.

In the case of a disposal of an unincorporated business, as opposed to shares, it is important to remember that a business carried on by a non-resident through a branch or agency in the UK remains subject to UK capital gains tax under CGTA 1979, s 12. It is therefore necessary for the business to cease while the owner is still resident in the UK and for him then to depart and thereafter conclude the disposal of the business assets, including goodwill of the former business. This is not easy to do without having entered into a binding contract before leaving the UK despite what the paperwork may purport to provide. In such circumstances it might even be more practical to transfer the business into a company in exchange for shares and claim the roll-over under the provisions of CGTA 1979, s 123, then to emigrate, and then to sell the shares in the UK company. The transfer to the company should be done before entering into any negotiations with possible purchasers, otherwise this would be regarded as a series of transactions within the *Furniss v Dawson* principle. Alternatively, it might be possible to show that the purchasers required the protection of limited liability so that this was the business purpose for the transfer of the business to a company.

Rather than try and argue that the contract was actually entered into after leaving the UK it might well be preferable to give the intended purchaser an option enabling him to acquire the shares after the vendor has become non-resident (CGTA 1979, s 27(2)). 'Conditional contract' refers in particular to a contract conditional on the exercise of an option and makes it clear that the date of the disposal is the date the option is *exercised*. It is tempting to consider entering into a put and call option, but the Revenue have argued strongly in the case of development land tax transactions that a put and call option is the equivalent of a contract for sale and that they are entitled to treat it as a disposal at the date the option was entered into.

If it is not possible to postpone the date of the contract for disposal until the vendor has become non-resident it might be possible to take a large porportion of the proceeds in the form of loan stock. If it can be shown that there is a good commercial reason for the issue of loan stock a claim for roll-over relief on the disposal of the shares should be available under CGTA 1979, s 85, with clearance under s 88. If clearance is obtained it should be possible for the vendor to become non-resident and then dispose of the loan stock, thus crystallising the gain on the shares rolled into the loan stock. It is probably unwise to arrange before departure from the UK for the loan stock immediately to be redeemed or placed with some financial institution, as the Revenue could then argue that the issue of the loan stock was merely an inserted step in what was in reality a sale for cash, again relying on *Furniss* v *Dawson*.

It should be noted that capital gains on Lloyd's investments as an underwriting name are basically subject to capital gains tax as arising from a business carried on in the UK through an agent (CGTA 1979, s 12). However, syndicate investments which form part of the Lloyd's American Trust Fund and Lloyd's Canadian Trust Fund are regarded as not situated in the UK and non-UK securities in the Lloyd's sterling trust fund are also regarded as situated outside the UK. Exempt gilts held as part of a Lloyd's fund would retain their capital gains tax exemption.

Foreign taxes

It is beyond the scope of this book to consider non-UK tax liabilities, but if a business or shares are sold after having left the UK the taxpayer may well have become resident in some other country which imposes a capital gains tax charge or assesses capital gains as income. The general advice given with regard to UK CGT may be overruled if the effective rate of overseas tax on the chargeable gain would be greater.

Local advice should be taken before concluding the contract for disposal, as to whether there is a potential tax charge in the country of residence, and if so what, if anything, can be done about it.

Non-UK domiciled

The overseas visitor who becomes resident or ordinarily resident in the UK becomes liable to UK CGT. He is however exempt from tax on gains arising outside the UK provided that he has a non-UK domicile and provided that the gains are not remitted to the UK. This relief is given by CGTA 1979, s 14 and the constructive remittance rules apply as mentioned in Chapter 8.

Trusts

The UK resident beneficiary of a non-resident trust is liable to CGT if the settlor was UK-domiciled and resident when he made the settlement and if the beneficiary is resident when the gain is distributed to him. If, however, the beneficiary is not domiciled in the UK, FA 1981, s 80(6) exempts him from a CGT charge. See also Chapter 11.

Offshore funds

Before 1984, it was possible for a UK resident to invest in certain offshore funds known as 'roll-up funds', where income to the funds was not distributed but accumulated tax free—when the investment was realised the accumulated profit, both gain and income, was subject to UK capital gains tax only. Complicated rules were introduced to take effect from 1 January 1984 (FA 1984, ss 92–100, now incorporated into FA 1988, s 757) which means that a UK resident investor is now liable to tax on his entire gain in an offshore 'roll-up' fund as if it were income, under Schedule D, Case VI. If the investor is domiciled outside the UK the tax liability will only apply to any gain actually remitted to the UK.

In the case of a UK expatriate there will be no liability to UK tax on realisations of gain from a 'roll-up' fund, so long as he remains non-resident and non-ordinarily resident in the UK, but realisations of gain after he returns home will attract the full liability to UK income tax. This future heavy exposure to UK taxation can be avoided by investing in offshore funds that have been granted 'distributor status'. FA 1984 provided that where a fund meets certain rules—the most important is that the fund must distribute at least 85% of the income received—the investor will be taxed on his income and gain in the normal way, ie Schedule D, Case IV in respect of the income distribution and capital gains tax in respect of realised growth.

Gifts from non-residents

If an asset given by a non-resident to a UK resident is subsequently disposed of by the donee, the donee is treated as acquiring the asset at market value at the time of the gift, and is liable to CGT only on any excess over the acquisition value.

Non-sterling bank accounts

Under FA 1984, s 69 a non-sterling bank account belonging to a non-UK domiciled individual is treated as located outside the UK and therefore exempt from capital gains tax on currency movements unless the account is held at the UK branch of a bank and the individual is resident in the UK.

10 Inheritance tax

As has already been seen, the non-resident working expatriate can, to a very great extent, avoid any liability to UK income tax and CGT. The main determinant of liability for income tax, apart from the location of the income source, is the individual's residence for tax purposes, and CGT is generally only chargeable on persons resident or ordinarily resident in the UK. This is not the case for inheritance tax (IHT).

A charge to IHT may arise whenever there is a transfer of assets, (other than lifetime gifts to an individual (or certain kinds of trust) made more than seven years before the donor's death), no matter where the assets are located, made by a person who is, or was at death, domiciled or deemed to be domiciled (see Chapter 1) in the UK. In addition, IHT may be charged on a transfer of assets located in the UK by a person not domiciled in the UK.

So far as most British expatriates are concerned, although they may be non-resident for many years, their domicile remains the UK and, in consequence, they remain liable to IHT.

What follows is a necessarily brief outline of IHT with the emphasis placed on those aspects which are likely to be of greatest interest or relevance to expatriates. More detailed information is to be found in this book's companion volumes, the *Allied Dunbar Tax Guide* and the *Allied Dunbar Capital Taxes and Estate Planning Guide*.

Note:

It is important to remember that expatriates who do manage to change their legal domicile from the UK will remain liable for IHT for three years following that change because of the 'deemed domicile' provisions described in Chapter 1.

Chargeable transfers

IHT may be payable whenever there is a chargeable transfer of assets. In general terms, a chargeable transfer is one which reduces the value of the transferor's total assets or his estate: in general parlance, a gift or bequest. Tax is chargeable on the cumulative total of chargeable transfers made during the donor's lifetime and on the value of his estate at death. The period of accumulation is restricted to seven years, ie, in year 8, the cumulative total of transfers made will be those of years 2 to 8, and transfers made in year 1 will drop out of account. Following death, the IHT due will be calculated on the value of the estate at death plus chargeable transfers made in the preceding seven years.

For transfers on or after 15 March 1988 the first £110,000 is charged at a nil rate and the excess is charged on death at 40% and on lifetime transfers at a reducing percentage of the 40% rate, depending upon the number of years between the transfer and the death of the donor. Up to three years the full rate is payable, four years is reduced to 80%, five years 60%, six years 40%, seven years 20% and thereafter no IHT is liable.

Following death, chargeable transfers made within the previous seven years are reassessed and the additional tax then becomes payable, but there is no revaluation of the asset transferred at the date of death.

It is fundamental to an understanding of IHT to appreciate that the amount of tax payable is calculated by reference to the total loss to the donor, ie, the amount by which his estate has been reduced by the transfer. It is not the value of the gift in isolation. In practice, this is of greatest importance in connection with unquoted shares. If a father has 55% of the shares in a family company and transfers 10% to discretionary trust, those shares might be worth, say, £100 per share as a small minority interest. However, the father's shareholding has fallen from a 55% controlling interest (shares worth £500 each) to a 45% large minority holding (shares worth, say, £300 each). If there were 10,000 shares in issue, the chargeable transfer (loss to the father's estate) would be not £10,000 (1,000 × £100) but £1,400,000 (from 5,500× £500 to 4,500 × £300).

Exemptions and reliefs

The IHT legislation contains many provisions exempting certain transfers of value from tax. The most important of these are described below.

Potentially exempt transfers

A lifetime transfer by an individual to another individual is a potentially exempt transfer (PET). This means that if the transferor survives for seven years it is exempt, but if he dies within seven years it is chargeable. This also applies to transfers to an interest in possession trust, an accumulation and maintenance trust or a trust for a disabled person.

Transfers between spouses

Where both spouses are domiciled in the UK any transfer of assets between them is exempt. Where the recipient spouse is not domiciled in the UK at the time of the transfer, the total exemption is restricted to £55,000 (by IHTA 1984, s 18(2))—(see also later). Additional transfers would fall first into the usual zero rate band. The spouse exemption applies to both lifetime transfers and transfers at death. There is no similar restriction in other cases where the transferee is non-UK domiciled and the transferor is domiciled in the UK. This may give rise to opportunities for channelling gifts through a non-UK domiciled individual who subsequently settles a discretionary trust, subject to anti-avoidance provisions in IHTA 1984, s 268 and the extended definition of settlor in IHTA 1984, s 44.

Annual allowances

A person may make as many small gifts to as many people as he wishes in a year without incurring any IHT. In order to qualify for this exemption, the maximum gift to any individual in the year is £250 (IHTA 1984, s 20(1)). If the gift is greater than £250 it will be taxable unless it can be covered by one of the other exemptions described below. In addition to the small gifts allowance, there is an annual allowance of £3,000 (IHTA 1984, s 19). This allowance, to the extent that it is unused in the year, may be carried forward for one year only. However, where an annual allowance or part of that allowance is carried forward it can only be used once the annual allowance for the second year has, itself, been exhausted.

Example: Inheritance tax—annual allowance

A does not expect to live long and gives £2,000 to her daughter in 1987/88; she makes no other transfers in that year and therefore has an annual allowance totalling £4,000 in 1988/89. If, however, she only gives away £2,000 in that year, her surplus to carry forward to 1989/90 is not £2,000, but £1,000 again. She has lost the amount carried forward from 1987/88 because she did not fully utilise her 1988/89 allowance. Had she given £3,000 in 1988/89 she would have nothing to carry forward.

These annual allowances are available separately to husband and wife and the value of the gift is calculated without tax, ie, it is not grossed up. These allowances are available only against lifetime transfers.

Normal expenditure out of income

A gift made during a person's lifetime will be exempt if it is shown:

(a) to be part of that person's habitual expenditure;
(b) that, taking one year with another, it is made out of income; and
(c) that allowing for all such transfers out of income, the transferor is left with sufficient income to maintain his usual standard of living.

On the occasion of the first gift out of income it will be considered as exempt if there is clear evidence of further gifts to be made, such as insurance policy premiums on a policy written in trust (IHTA 1984, s 21).

Gifts in consideration of marriage

Wedding gifts into trust or within seven years of death are exempt so far as they fall within the following limits:

(a) up to £5,000 from a parent of either party to the marriage;
(b) up to £2,500 from one party to the marriage to the other or from grandparents or remoter ancestors of either party;
(c) up to £1,000 in any other case.

As with the two previous exemptions, this one is also only available for gifts made during the donor's lifetime (IHTA 1984, s 22).

Dispositions for maintenance of family

This exemption applies to dispositions from one spouse to another and includes any made on the dissolution of a marriage (IHTA 1984, s 11). It also covers those made for the children of either spouse (including any illegitimate child of the transferor) until the end of the tax year in which the child attains the age of 18 or, if later, until the child finishes full-time education or training. Where any person makes a disposition to a child who has been in that person's care for a substantial period, the exemption also applies, even though the person is not the child's parent. Finally, the exemption applies for the maintenance of a dependent relative and, by concession, to a disposition from a child to his or her unmarried mother who is financially dependent on the child.

Other exempt transfers

The previous exemptions have primarily concerned transfers to individuals which are in any case exempt if made more than seven years before death. There are several other exempt transfers of a more impersonal nature. These include transfers to charities, gifts for national purposes, to political parties and for the public benefit (IHTA 1984, ss 23–26).

Finally no IHT is payable on the estate of anyone who dies from a wound, accident, or disease contracted while on active service (IHTA 1984, s 154). By concession, this exemption is extended to the estates of members of the Royal Ulster Constabulary where death is as a result of terrorist activities in Northern Ireland.

Business property relief

Relief is given for the transfer of certain property which is 'relevant business property' by way of a reduction in the valuation of the property under IHTA 1984, ss 103–114. Before relief can be given, there are certain conditions to be met. As well as being relevant business property, the transfer must be of property from a qualifying business (basically a business carried on for gain other than a business which is primarily concerned with dealing in land or securities or holding investments), and the property must have been owned for a period of at least two years prior to the transfer.

Relevant business property falls into four classes:

(1) unincorporated business—property comprising a business or interest in a business attracts relief of 50%;
(2) shares or securities—if these give the transferor control of a company or if the company was an unquoted company and they give away more than 25% of the voting rights, they also attract relief at 50% immediately before the transfer;
(3) land, buildings, machinery or plant used in a partnership or a controlled company or, by the transferor, which was settled property in which he was entitled to an interest in possession—relief is at 30%;
(4) unquoted minority shareholdings—these attract relief at 30%.

NB: In (2) and (4) above a company is still considered to be 'quoted' if its shares are quoted on the Unlisted Securities Market (USM).

Agricultural property relief

Agricultural property in the UK, the Channel Islands or the Isle of Man attracts relief at 50% under IHTA 1984, ss 115–124 where it has been occupied for the two years before the transfer by the transferor for the purposes of agriculture, or where it was owned for the seven years before the transfer but farmed by persons other than the transferor. A further condition to be satisfied for the 50% relief is that the transferor must enjoy vacant possession or be entitled to it within 12 months. In other cases the relief is restricted to 30%.

Potentially exempt lifetime transfers of agricultural and business property

In circumstances where such transfers become taxable due to the death within seven years of the transferor, the conditions necessary for obtaining the relief must still be met at the date of death, Effectively, therefore, the recipient of such transfers must continue to own the property and continue to use it in the manner which qualifies it for relief for seven years after the transfer, or risk forfeiting the relief.

Persons not domiciled in the UK

Overseas assets owned by persons not domiciled in the UK are generally excluded property for the purposes of IHT (IHTA 1984, s 6(1)). That is, any transfer of such property will not give rise to a liability. However, where such persons own assets in the UK, then any transfer of such assets may give rise to a charge to tax. There are, as usual, several exemptions and reliefs available to offset this general rule, in addition to the general potential exemption for transfers to individuals.

Under a double taxation agreement, property may be deemed to be located abroad, thus making it excluded property (see Chapter 7). The property of members of visiting forces or of staff of allied headquarters is excluded property. Where a person holds certain UK government securities, then these will be excluded property if the holder is not domiciled and not ordinarily resident in the UK (IHTA 1984, s 6(2)). For this latter exclusion, it is legal domicile as opposed to the artificial deemed domicile which applies (IHTA 1984, s 267(2)).

Where overseas property is settled property, it will only be excluded property if at the time the settlement was made the settlor was not domiciled in the UK (IHTA 1984, s 48(3)(*b*)). If that is not the case then the settled property will not be excluded, regardless of any subsequent change of domicile of the settlor and regardless of the domicile of any beneficiaries. A reversionary interest in overseas settled property does not come under these rules but is determined according to the general rule which is that if the person beneficially entitled to the reversionary interest is domiciled in the UK, there is a liability, and if he is not, then it is excluded property (IHTA 1984, s 48(1)).

Location of assets

Where an asset is located has to be determined according to the laws of England and Wales, Scotland or Northern Ireland except where these are superseded by special provisions in a double taxation agreement. The commoner types of assets are normally considered to be situated as follows:

(a) cash—where physically located;
(b) bank accounts—the location of the bank or branch (note: foreign currency accounts owned by a non-UK domiciled person but held in the UK are exempt);
(c) registered securities—the location of the share register;
(d) bearer securities—the location of the title documents;
(e) land and buildings—their actual location;
(f) business assets—the place where the business is conducted;
(g) debts—the residence of the debtor (or for specialty debts, such as a life assurance policy issued under seal, the place where the document evidencing the debt is located and, for judgment debts, the country where the judgment is recorded).

The non-UK domiciled spouse

Before 1 January 1974, a wife assumed her husband's domicile on marriage. When the marriage ended, either by death or divorce, the wife retained her husband's domicile unless and until she acquired a new domicile of choice. The current position of women married before 1 January 1974 is that they retain their husbands' domicile (originally a domicile of dependence) as their deemed domicile of choice until, by their own positive actions, they acquire a new domicile of choice. For marriages contracted after 1 January 1974, a wife has had complete independence of domicile and will retain her domicile of origin or any pre-marriage domicile of dependence until she chooses to acquire a new domicile of choice which may or may not be the same as her husband's domicile.

For IHT purposes, a couple of mixed domicile (where one of them is domiciled in the UK and the other is not) have to take extra care in their tax planning. Their situation does, however, offer some opportunities not available to couples where both are UK domiciled.

Dealing first of all with the restrictions, it has already been mentioned that a transfer from a spouse domiciled in the UK to one who is not so domiciled, is exempt only up to a total transfer of £55,000. The reason behind this is obviously to prevent the avoidance of tax which would arise by simply using the non-domiciled spouse as a conduit for transfers of non-UK sited assets to other parties such as children. Nonetheless, substantial value can still be transferred because the UK domiciled spouse will have, in addition to the £55,000 exemption, an additional amount of £110,000 which on transfer will be within the nil rate band. Further transfers may be made using the annual allowance and any subsequent increases in the exempt allowance or the width of the nil rate band. After seven years, the £110,000 transferred initially within the nil rate band will fall out of account.

Where the spouse who is not domiciled in the UK makes any gifts or transfers, there will be no IHT liability so long as the property concerned is excluded property—generally property located outside the UK. One possible pitfall for the non-UK domiciled spouse arises following the family's assumption or resumption of residence in the UK. The Inland Revenue may seek to claim that the originally non-domiciled spouse has acquired a new domicile of choice in the UK. However, they cannot have it both ways. There is a great reluctance in the absence of very strong evidence to accept that a person has shed his or her UK domicile—it should follow, therefore, that there should be equal reluctance to accept that a person has shed a non-UK domicile of origin and acquired UK domicile by choice. But as with most aspects of British taxation, the onus is on the individual to prove the Revenue wrong. The pointers to a change of domicile given earlier should be considered in this light.

In any event, even the person accepted as not being domiciled in the UK in the legal sense, will be deemed to be so domiciled for IHT purposes after a period of 17 years residence here. Strictly, the requirement is to have been resident in the UK in not less than 17 out of the 20 years of assessment ending with that in which the chargeable transfer occurs.

Settled property

If the IHT rules are generally seen as very complex, this is nowhere more true than when considering the question of settled property. There are several types of trusts or settlements which have a useful application for IHT mitigation and these are discussed in some detail later.

For details of the settled property provisions, reference must be made to more specialist textbooks but the following points illuminate, however briefly, some important aspects.

Generally, settlements are themselves subject to IHT at lifetime rates if, when the settlement was made, the settlor was domiciled in the UK. The settlement of any property after 26 March 1974 is a chargeable transfer by the settlor (assuming he is domiciled in the UK) unless the trust is for transfers into an interest in possession trust, an accumulation or maintenance trust or a trust for a disabled person: these are potentially exempt transfers. A person having an interest in possession in any property, is deemed to possess that property for IHT purposes so that when that interest ends, there is deemed to be a potentially exempt transfer of the value of the property, under IHTA 1984, ss 49–53. There is no chargeable or potentially exempt transfer if a person becomes absolutely entitled to the property in which he previously had an interest in possession. The special rules relating to discretionary trusts and accumulation and maintenance trusts are discussed later.

A reversionary interest in a settlement of UK property is excluded property under IHTA 1984, s 48(1) unless it had been acquired for value, is one in which the settlor or his spouse has a beneficial interest or is a reversionary interest under a lease for life treated as a settlement.

Inheritance tax planning

For every tax, there soon springs up a tax avoidance scheme, or many of them. This continuing game between legislators and tax consultants is as obvious in the area of IHT as anywhere else although the Revenue's success in ignoring purely fiscal moves in a composite transaction in *Furniss* v *Dawson* [1984] STC 153 should be noted.

As stated at the beginning of this chapter, the recast inheritance tax is in some aspects similar to estate duty (the predecessor to CTT), which was considerably easier to avoid than the tax which replaced it. On the other hand, the ease of avoiding IHT—by simply making gifts to individuals more than seven years before death—depends on the donor's ability to make outright gifts and lose the benefit of the associated income, because it is no longer possible, as with CTT, to make gifts with reservation of interest.

Basic IHT planning is very straightforward, such as simply making use of the various exemptions and reliefs particularly the exemption for lifetime gifts to individuals. However, rather than merely disposing of cash, some thought might be given to transferring assets which might be expected to grow in value but which have a relatively low value at the time of transfer. Another frequent suggestion is the equalisation of estates between husband and wife with the first to die leaving a substantial part of his or her estate other than to the spouse. In this way maximum use can be made of each spouse's entitlement to allowances and the nil rate band.

Example: Inheritance tax—estate planning

A husband has an estate worth £220,000 and the wife £40,000; in their wills each leaves his or her estate to the other. On the second death, everything goes to the children. Under these provisions there would be no IHT payable on the first death and, assuming no previous chargeable transfers, an IHT charge of £60,000 on the second death. If, however the husband transferred £90,000 to his wife during his lifetime and they each decided to leave £110,000 to their children with the balance to the spouse, there would still be no IHT to pay on the first death and on the second death, when the estate is £150,000 the IHT payable would be £16,000, a saving of £44,000.

One reason for equalising the estates rather than simply making enough available for the wife to use the nil rate band is to allow maximum flexibility on the first death following which a written variation of the will (see later) could be used in the light of prevailing circumstances.

The transferor should not so reduce his estate that the surviving spouse cannot sustain a required standard of living. In addition, payment of IHT should be postponed from the date of the first death to the second death by leaving the estate on the excess over the nil rate band to the surviving spouse.

Insurance policies

To use these policies, the transferor or the intending transferor effects a policy on his life written in trust for his beneficiaries. The sum assured under such a policy should be the amount of the anticipated IHT which will be due on the estate passing at death. Where there is a relatively short period of liability to the tax as, for example, when a person emigrates permanently but remains deemed domiciled in the UK for three years, a three year term policy would be the cheapest and simplest form of IHT protection. Similarly, if a major transfer of assets is made to take advantage of the lower lifetime rates of tax, it may be worth insuring for the difference between the tax paid and the tax which would become payable if death occurred within three years of that transfer. In most circumstances however, a term policy is unlikely to be the wisest course because as the potential transferor gets older renewing the policy can become very expensive. A better solution is to take out a whole of life policy and write it in trust at a reasonably early stage. Premiums paid by the life assured/settlor in respect of the policy in trust are, of course, transfers of value into the trust and hence can amount to either immediately chargeable transfers or potentially exempt transfers depending on whether the trust is a discretionary trust. However, the exemption for gifts out of income and where necessary, the £3,000 annual exemption can normally be applied to those transfers of premium and, where this is so, the payments will be totally exempt. These exemptions can also be applied to the premiums paid on an investment oriented policy written in trust and this, too, can be a useful way of transferring a growing asset to others.

The family home

One asset which can sometimes prove difficult to plan for effectively is the family home, and for many people this is their main asset. Normally a couple will own their house as joint tenants. On the death of one of them the deceased's share is automatically transferred to the survivor. Assuming the couple are married, and are both either UK or non-UK domiciled, there will be no IHT payable on this occasion but on the second death, the whole value of the house will be counted in calculating the tax. The effect of this is illustrated in the following example.

Example: Inheritance tax—the family home

A couple have joint net assets of £310,000, of which £220,000 represents the value of their house, the remaining £90,000 being invested to provide income. The house is owned under a joint tenancy and each holds about £45,000 of investments. Under their wills each leaves his or her estate to the other. The couple have two children who will inherit everything on the second death. Because the survivor after the first death will still require a similar income, it is not practicable to leave anything to the children on that occasion so the eventual IHT bill will be £80,000.

The bill can, however, be reduced by changing the way the house is owned. If the couple own the house as tenants in common, rather than as joint tenants, their individual shares do not automatically go to the other on death but may be dealt with in the same way as any other asset. Thus, in the previous example, although the income producing assets could not be left to the children, a share of the house could be.

If, on the death of the first spouse his or her half-share in the house was left to the children, this would be a chargeable transfer of £110,000 with no IHT payable. The estate on the second death would be £200,000 on which the IHT would be £36,000, a saving of £44,000.

But tenancies in common are not without their drawbacks. There must be a high degree of trust among all the parties so that the widow or widower can continue to live in the property only half of which she or he will own. There can also be a problem if the co-owner is declared bankrupt. It is very important for anyone contemplating such an arrangement to discuss it fully with his solicitor who will also give an indication of the cost of changing an existing joint tenancy to a tenancy in common, which usually requires only a simple notice of severance served on the co-owner.

Wills

Anyone whose assets are other than negligible should make a will, at least if he has any concern as to the disposition of those assets after his death. Anyone who dies without leaving a valid will dies intestate and his property will be disposed of according to the laws of intestacy. Only rarely will this procedure coincide with the deceased's wishes. For the expatriate who may have assets spread around different parts of the world, a will is more necessary than ever. Or more importantly, several wills are necessary.

The expatriate, or indeed any international investor domiciled in the UK, should have a valid UK will which allocates all his worldwide property according to his wishes. He should also have a will covering assets held outside this country which is valid in the overseas location. Someone with assets in several countries might require several wills. The reasoning behind this is basically twofold. First, there is the simple efficiency in dealing with a local estate under local law with a locally accepted document. Secondly, from the UK viewpoint a grant of probate or Letters of Administration will not be given until any IHT has been paid. Since assets will not normally be released until the grant is made, the only way to pay the tax bill is to borrow the money. If overseas assets can be speedily released through a local probate these can be used to pay the UK tax and thereby hasten the release of the UK assets.

One point to bear in mind about overseas property is that not all countries allow the testator complete freedom to dispose as he pleases. There may be requirements that, for example, children inherit a part with the remainder freely disposable. These restrictions most commonly apply to land and the investor should always check with a local lawyer whether or not any such potential problems exist. In this respect Scottish law is different from that in the rest of the UK.

Even in the very liberal UK a will may be challenged and the dispositions altered by the court if, for instance, no provision has been made for a person who was financially dependent on the deceased. A will may be challenged on several other grounds also, but that is beyond the scope of this book.

Will trusts

A UK will may grant an absolute interest to a beneficiary or may create a will trust under which the assets are left to trustees for the benefit of various beneficiaries. The types of possible trust are discussed in Chapter 11. The most common will trust is to leave the majority of the estate to the surviving spouse for her life with remainder to the children or grandchildren. The advantage of this arrangement is that the life interest to the surviving spouse is treated for IHT purposes as her absolute interest and therefore the IHT exemption on leaving assets to a surviving spouse still applies. However, the ultimate destination of the assets is assured so that should, for example, the wife re-marry and have further children by the second marriage, the deceased former husband's estate passes through to his own children and cannot be diverted to the children of the second marriage. It is possible to leave the reversionary interest to the grandchildren rather than to the children and so avoid a IHT charge on the death of the children. Whether this is desirable of course depends on the children's assets and the respective ages of the parties.

Incidence of IHT

It is also important to bear in mind when drafting the will the

Inheritance tax 117

incidence of IHT. IHTA 1984, s 211 following *Re Dougal* [1981] STC 514 makes it clear that IHT on death in respect of personal property and of real property in the UK is a general testamentary expense payable out of residue in the absence of contrary provisions in the will. If, therefore, the intention is that any legacy should bear its own share of IHT, it is important that the will makes this clear. There are complicated provisions in IHTA 1984, ss 38–42 to deal with the case where part of the residue is left on an exempt legacy such as to the surviving spouse, and part on a chargeable legacy such as to the children.

Overseas assets subject to IHT will normally be subject to their proportionate share of the IHT applicable thereto. For the avoidance of doubt, it is preferable to draft the will so that it is made perfectly clear which, if any, legacies are to bear their share of IHT.

As already noted, the provisions of a will can largely determine the amount of IHT which will fall due. A will can, in fact, be looked upon as a IHT planning tool. However, if family circumstances at the date of death are significantly different from what was envisaged when the will was prepared, or if the will is highly inefficient in a tax-planning sense, the will provisions may be altered by a written variation. If this is done within two years of death, no IHT will be charged on the variations or rearrangements if the parties concerned so elect, and the tax payable will be computed on the basis that the varied provisions were effective at death. Stamp duty is no longer payable on the value transferred under a written variation (FA 1985, s 85).

Written variations

The problem with the written variation is that it requires any beneficiary whose share is being reduced to be legally competent (ie, adult and of sound mind), as any attempts so to modify the interest of a child beneficiary would require the consent of the Court. In practice, it may be preferable to leave that part of the estate which, for example, may or may not be required by the surviving spouse to trustees of a discretionary settlement with the intention that the trustees would, within two years of the date of death, redistribute the assets among the various beneficiaries in accordance with their needs.

Written variations are treated for IHT purposes as a disposition on death under IHTA 1984, ss 17 and 142 and for CGT purposes by

CGTA 1979, s 49(6). However, for income tax purposes, the income in the period from the date of death to the date of the variation (or distribution from any discretionary trust) remains that of the original beneficiaries. It is also likely that a variation in favour of children would be argued by the Revenue to be an indirect settlement by the original beneficiary so that for income tax purposes, any income distributed to the child during his minority would be treated as the income of the parent under TA 1988, s 663. A variation or two-year discretionary trust should therefore be regarded as a useful opportunity to fine tune the dispositions given by will rather than a substitute for a carefully planned will reviewed at frequent intervals.

Example: Inheritance tax—written variation

Mr Bird died in January 1989. His net estate was valued at £400,000 including a house worth £100,000. Apart from £25,000 to his son, the estate was left to Mr Bird's widow. When Mr Bird's will was drawn up many years previously the value of his estate was only about £150,000 with the house worth £50,000. He felt at the time that his widow would require £75,000 to provide her income and that was his rationale for the structuring of his will.

As it happens, in 1989, there will be no IHT to pay following Mr Bird's death (he has made no previous transfers) but there is a potential tax charge on Mrs Bird's death, assuming she leaves her estate to the son (she has personal assets worth £50,000) of £126,000. She and her son therefore effect a written variation whereby the son receives £100,000 instead of £25,000 and his children receive £10,000 in total. There is still IHT payable on the estate. The potential charge on the death of Mrs Bird is reduced from £126,000 (on £425,000) to £92,000 (on £340,000). The written variation has therefore saved IHT of £34,000.

Dying is never a pleasant thing to think about, but perhaps the only thing worse is to die and leave too much money to the Inland Revenue. IHT planning and a regular review of testamentary arrangements are essential to protect the family who remain.

11 Trusts

A trust or settlement is a legal relationship which is established when a person transfers assets into the care of others for the benefit of a third party. The three parties concerned in this relationship, the settlor, trustees, and beneficiaries respectively, may all incur tax liabilities stemming from the trust in different ways. A detailed explanation of trust law is beyond the scope of this book and readers are referred to the *Allied Dunbar Capital Taxes and Estate Planning Guide* for further information. Trusts constitute an extremely complex area of the law and good professional advice is essential.

This chapter can only provide an outline of the major tax planning aspects of trusts as they affect, or might affect, the expatriate. It must be stressed that to establish a trust is not a job for a layman. Perhaps more than in any other field of tax planning, trust work requires the assistance of expert professional advice.

The residence of trusts

For income tax purposes, a trust is resident outside the UK if all the trustees are themselves so resident and the administration and management of the trust are carried out overseas (*Kelly v Rogers* (1935) 19 TC 692, *Reid's Trustees v IRC* (1929) 14 TC 512). For CGT purposes, CGTA 1979, s 52(1) only requires a majority of trustees to be non-UK resident. A trust which is not resident in the UK may enjoy substantial tax advantages over the domestic settlement but there are numerous provisions in the UK legislation which seek to prevent tax avoidance by the use of such vehicles by or for the benefit of persons ordinarily resident in the UK. The three main UK taxes income tax, CGT and IHT can each have an impact on trusts and on each of the parties involved. Tax liabilities are determined not only by the residence of the trust and the individuals concerned but also by the type of trust which is involved. The following section on the taxation of trusts outlines the tax consequences which attach to each of the main types of trust with which the expatriate may be concerned.

Resident trusts

It may be useful to make the first distinction between types of trusts as between those where the settlor is alive and those where he is deceased. The main thrust of the anti-avoidance legislation is concerned with preventing a settlor using a trust mechanism to provide himself with a tax-sheltered 'piggy bank' for his own or his wife's benefit. To that end there are numerous provisions which seek to tax trust income as that of the settlor and these are described below. Where the settlor has died, whether the trust was set up during his lifetime or under his will, the taxation rules are somewhat less complex.

In general terms, a UK trust is liable for basic rate income tax on all its income, wherever arising. Where trust income has already suffered tax at source or is accompanied by a tax credit, this will be accounted for in the trust assessment. Where the trust has overseas income which has been taxed abroad then relief for double taxation may be available either to the trustees or the beneficiaries. The income of discretionary trusts and accumulation trusts, after deducting expenses, is also liable for an additional charge (10%)—TA 1988, s 686. The income tax assessment of trusts is generally made in the name of the trustees and the tax due is payable out of the trust funds. Where trust income is distributed to beneficiaries it is treated as received net of tax at 35% under TA 1988, s 687 (or 25% in the case of a beneficiary absolutely entitled to the income, that is where the trust is not a discretionary trust).

A non-resident trust is liable to UK tax on its UK income at the basic rate and, on accumulations, at the additional rate as well. See *IRC v Regent Trust Co Ltd* [1980] STC 140.

Trusts are also liable for CGT in much the same way as individuals but the annual exemption is restricted to 50% of that available to individuals. For 1988/89, the trust exemption is therefore £2,500. For trusts formed after 6 June 1978, this exemption is split among all trusts with the same settlor, ie, if he made four trusts, each would be entitled to exemption on the first £625. For trusts formed before that date, the full £2,500 is allowed. Certain trusts for the mentally disabled and those in receipt of attendance allowances are entitled to the same exemption as an individual; CGTA 1979, Sched 1, para 5.

Some of the aspects of IHT and trusts were mentioned in the preceding chapter. *What is perhaps of the greatest importance is to note that, for IHT purposes, the residence of the trust is largely immaterial.* A trust may incur a liability to IHT on its worldwide assets if, at the time it was set up, the settlor was domiciled in the UK (IHTA 1984, s 48(3)(*a*)). If the settlor was domiciled elsewhere, the IHT liability will be restricted to transfers of trust assets located in the UK.

Trusts created *inter vivos*

Where a settlement is made during the lifetime of the settlor, the taxation rules are particularly rigorous to prevent the avoidance of tax. An outline of these anti-avoidance provisions is given below.

Income tax

The basic rule a settlor must obey in order to avoid having the trust income assessed on him, is fully to divest himself of the assets he is transferring into the trust. If he retains an interest in either the income or the assets of the trust then any income not distributed to beneficiaries will be treated as the settlor's income (TA 1988, ss 673–674). A retained interest is widely defined but generally means that the settlor or his or her spouse is able to obtain some benefit from the income or assets of the trust at any time. Even where the income is distributed to others any excess of higher rate tax over the basic rate on the distribution will be charged to the settlor.

Akin to retaining an interest is a power to revoke the trust. If the trust can be revoked in whole or in part, and on revocation the trust property reverts to the settlor or his spouse, then the income of the trust (or a part thereof corresponding to the partial revocation) will be treated as the income of the settlor (TA 1988, ss 671, 672). The power of revocation may be immediate or postponed, but in the latter case, if the power cannot be used for at least six years, the income will not be treated as that of the settlor until the power becomes exercisable. Power to revoke includes a power to advance the whole of the capital, or to diminish the assets of the trust or the income receivable by beneficiaries other than the settlor or his spouse. Whether it is the settlor or another person who has the power to revoke is immaterial.

Where there is a settlement of income such as a covenant, it is essential that the payments should be capable of being made for a period of at least six years (TA 1988, s 660). The six-year rule applies to settlements generally but is normally of particular relevance to income settlements. Where a covenant fails on this rule, it will be treated as income of the settlor and not the payee. Nevertheless, the payment will still be deemed to have been made to the covenantee and then returned to the settlor; the settlor is then treated as receiving investment income, even if the payment was made out of earned income or capital. As a result, the settlor may find that he has more tax to pay because of a failed covenant than he would had he not instituted it in the first place (*Ang* v *Parish* [1980] STC 341). However, since 15 March 1988 there have been no tax advantages in covenanting money to an individual.

Where a capital sum (which includes a loan or loan repayment) is paid by trustees to the settlor, his spouse, or a third party directly or indirectly at the settlor's direction, that sum is treated as the income of the settlor and is assessed on him under TA 1988, s 677. The assessment, however, is restricted to the amount of undistributed income in the trust but includes income previously accumulated. The tax charge is based on the amount of undistributed income grossed up at the basic rate plus the additional rate and credit is given for tax already charged on the trust. Where the undistributed income is less than the capital sum, there is provision to carry forward the excess of the capital sum to subsequent years. The settlor will then be charged to the extent of undistributed income in those years until the capital sum is fully extinguished. For capital payments made after 5 April 1981, the period for carry forward is restricted to eleven years (capital payments made before that date are to be treated as made on that date so as to fall within the new rules, so far as they have not been charged).

Under a discretionary trust, that is, one where the trustees may apply the trust property and/or income at their discretion, the settlor and his spouse must be specifically excluded from benefit, otherwise the income will be charged on the settlor whether or not he receives it. This does not apply where the benefit may accrue to the widow or widower of the settlor.

Settlements for the benefit of the settlor's infant children do not generally provide an income tax advantage, in view of the effects of TA 1988, s 663. The exception to this rule is an accumulation settlement; TA 1988, s 664. Any income belonging to a child which is derived from a parental source is deemed to be the income of the parent for tax purposes. This applies not only to settlements made by parents but to any transfer of assets from the parent to his or her child. For example, if a parent gave his child shares in a company any dividends paid to the child until he reached the age of majority would be treated as the parent's income. Similarly taxed too would be the interest in a child's bank account where the capital came from a parent. Where there is a court order directing a father to make payments directly to his child, the Inland Revenue do not regard these payments as creating a settlement. Under these circumstances, the child's income would not be aggregated with that of either parent.

The use of accumulation trusts is one way to create a settlement for the benefit of minor children. Where there is an irrevocable settlement of capital and the trustees are empowered or directed to accumulate the income arising from it for the ultimate benefit of the settlor's children, the settlor will not incur any income tax liability so long as the income is actually accumulated. The trust income is taxed at 35% in the name of the trustees. If any sums are paid to or for the benefit of the child before his or her eighteenth birthday or earlier marriage, such sums will be treated as the settlor's income. When the accumulated income is paid to adult beneficiaries, it is normally treated as capital in their hands. See also Chapter 10 and below, regarding the favourable treatment of these trusts for IHT purposes.

All of the above provisions apply generally but where the settlor is either not domiciled, not resident, or not ordinarily resident in the UK, certain other considerations come into play. Under TA 1988, s 681(1), income arising under a settlement includes any income chargeable to income tax and any income which would have been so chargeable if it had been received in the UK by a person domiciled, resident and ordinarily resident in the UK. But where, in any year of assessment, the settlor is not resident, etc, in the UK then the settlement income in that year will not include any income which would not have been chargeable on the settlor, had he been entitled to it, by reason of his non-residence, etc.

The other consideration concerns settlements for the settlor's children. Where the settlor is not taxable as a UK resident then there is no aggregation. Any income from such a settlement paid to the child will not be treated as the parent's income for any year in which the parent is not resident in the UK. Under these circumstances, the child beneficiary will be able to reclaim the tax deducted on his income from the trust up to the amount of the single person's allowance. Where tax has been deducted at 35% he will also be able to reclaim the 10% additional rate tax on the income beyond his personal allowance.

Capital gains tax

CGT may become payable on the creation of a trust, on gains made in the trust, and on certain deemed disposals of trust assets. On the first of these the liability is likely to fall on the settlor, while on the second and third, the tax will be payable by the trustees out of the trust funds.

Whether a settlement is revocable or otherwise, a transfer into a settlement is considered to be a disposal of the entire property which becomes settled (CGTA 1979, s 53). This implies a deemed disposal by the transferor and the disposal will be treated as being made at market value. If this results in a capital gain then the transferor may elect to have the gain held over, under FA 1980, s 79 and FA 1982, s 82. If the deemed disposal shows a loss then this loss may normally only be utilised by the transferor against subsequent gains arising in his transactions with the trust (CGTA 1979, s 62(3)). Gains may only be held over where the trustees are resident in the UK (FA 1980, s 79(1)).

During the administration of a trust, gains and losses will accrue to the trustees as they would to an individual managing his portfolio. Net gains are chargeable at 25% (or 35% for a discretionary or accumulation settlement) subject to the restricted exemption mentioned earlier. In the case of trusts where the settlor or settlor's spouse could receive any benefit, the gains are aggregated with the settlor's to determine the rate of tax.

When property ceases to be settled property, if, for example, it is distributed or a person becomes absolutely entitled to it, that is a deemed disposal and an occasion of charge on any gain (CGTA 1979, s 54(1)). Where property ceases to be settled on the death of a life tenant, there is also a deemed disposal but there will be no chargeable gain (CGTA 1979, s 55(1)). If the trustees and recipient of the disposed property agree and so elect, the gain accruing may be held over provided the recipient is resident in the UK (FA 1982, s 82). Where a life interest in settled property comes to an end, there is no charge if the property remains within the settlement; there is no deemed disposal.

Inheritance tax

When a person creates a settlement there will be a diminution of the settlor's estate unless he settles the property on himself for life (IHTA 1984, s 3). This transfer of value may give rise to a liability for IHT. The IHT legislation treats differently settlements where there is or are interest(s) in possession, and those where there is no interest in possession.

Where a person is beneficially entitled to the interest in possession of settled property, he is treated as being beneficially entitled to the property in which the interest subsists (IHTA 1984, s 49(1)). Thus if two people had equal interests in possession of a trust worth £200,000, each would be treated as being entitled to £100,000. On the death of one of these persons IHT would be payable on the deemed transfer of £100,000 in addition to any other estate the deceased might have. Other events will also be treated as dispositions of the property by the person beneficially entitled to the interest in possession; if, for example, the interest is terminated during the life of the person or if it is disposed of by way of assignment or surrender. Where the disposal is for a consideration in money or money's worth, IHT will be charged on the value transferred less the consideration received.

There are, however, exceptions to this rule. If a person becomes absolutely entitled to the property or to another interest in possession, that will not be treated as a chargeable transfer (IHTA 1984, s 53(2)). Other exceptions include where the property reverts to the settlor or his spouse (if she, or he, is domiciled in the UK) or to the widow or widower of the settlor within two years of the death of the settlor (IHTA 1984, s 53(3)–(5)).

A reversionary interest is a future interest under a settlement. For IHT purposes, a reversionary interest is normally excluded property unless it was acquired at any time for money or money's worth (IHTA 1984, s 48(1)).

With one major exception, trusts where there is no interest in possession are treated harshly for IHT purposes. The major problem with the normal discretionary trust is the liability for the periodic charge under IHTA 1984, s 64. This charge is levied every tenth anniversary of the settlement date (falling after 31 March 1983) and is charged at 30% of the rate which would be payable on a notional transfer of the value of the property in the trust at the end of the ten-year period. The rate is the lifetime rate of the settlor and is calculated on the settlor's previous chargeable transfers in the ten years preceding the creation of the settlement IHTA 1984, ss 65 and 67. For further details, see the *Allied Dunbar Capital Taxes and Estate Planning Guide.*

IHT is also payable on other occasions when property is distributed from the trust to beneficiaries (including the settlor and his or her spouse) in anticipation of the ten-year charge (IHTA 1984, s 65).

The exception to this highly taxed regime is the accumulation and maintenance settlement. Such settlements are greatly favoured and narrowly defined by IHTA 1984, s 71. They are settlements where one or more beneficiaries will, upon attaining a specified age not exceeding 25, become entitled to an interest in possession in the settled property; no interest in possession subsists in the settled property and the income from the property is to be accumulated insofar as it is not applied for the maintenance, education, or benefit of a beneficiary; and either not more than 25 years have elapsed since the trust was created or became an accumulation and maintenance trust, or all the persons who are or have been beneficiaries are or were grandchildren of a common grandparent.

The commonest use of such trusts is along the following lines: S creates a settlement under which his children obtain an interest in possession at age 21 and at age 35, say, or upon earlier marriage, they receive the capital. Income up to age 21 is to be accumulated apart from any payments made for the beneficiaries' maintenance. No lifetime IHT is payable on transfers into accumulation trusts, on any maintenance payment made, on the beneficiaries' acquisition of the interest in possession, or on the release of capital and accumulated income (IHTA 1984, s 71(3)). Neither is there a periodic charge on these settlements (IHTA 1984, s 58(1)(*b*)). But one point to bear in mind if a payment is made for the benefit of the child under age 18 and unmarried, is that it will be treated as the income of the settlor if the settlor is the parent, under TA 1988, s 663.

Accumulation and maintenance settlements offer one of the most tax-efficient ways of transferring capital to children or grandchildren.

Non-resident trusts

Non-resident trusts may have a particular appeal to the expatriate who is used to having his investments sheltered from the Inland Revenue and who wishes to retain a similar advantage on his return either for himself or for the benefit of his children. There can certainly be advantages in setting up non-resident trusts but the anti-avoidance legislation is a veritable minefield for the unwary. It is essential to consider this legislation most carefully before opting to place substantial sums in what can be an expensive attempt to establish shelter and then finding that it does not achieve its main aim.

As mentioned earlier in this chapter, a trust will be treated as resident in the UK unless the general administration of the trust is carried on outside the UK and the trustees, or, for CGT purposes, a majority of them, are not resident or not ordinarily resident in the UK. For income tax purposes, a single UK resident trustee with two non-resident trustees is not liable to UK tax on trust income from foreign assets held for non-resident beneficiaries, administered abroad and not remitted to the UK.

The UK income of a non-resident trust is liable to UK income tax at the basic rate and, so far as it is to be accumulated or is payable under a discretion, at the 10% additional rate: see *IRC v Regent Trust Co Ltd* [1980] STC 140. It should be noted, however, that where the income has tax deducted at source or has an accompanying tax credit, the additional rate is charged only on the net income. For example, a non-UK-resident trust receiving dividends of £750 (with tax credit of £250) would be liable for additional tax of £750 × 10% = £75 leaving a net income of £675. A UK-resident trust would have suffered total tax of £350 (tax credit of £250 plus £1,000 × 10%) leaving a net £650.

From an income tax point of view, general principles can be applied which indicate that income paid to a beneficiary, where he is entitled to that income, will form part of his income for tax purposes. Where the trust is an accumulation trust, then accumulated income will not be taxable on the beneficiary and this may be paid to the beneficiary as capital in due course. General principles apart, there are several anti-avoidance provisions which also come into play.

The most important of these income tax provisions are contained in TA 1988, s 739–746. Section 739 is seen as one of the most widely drawn anti-avoidance provisions. Where an individual transfers assets so that someone not resident or domiciled in the UK receives any income from these assets, and that income can be used currently or at some future time by the individual who transferred the assets, then that income will be treated as income of the transferor.

What this means in the context of trusts is that if an individual, ordinarily resident in the UK, has established a non-resident trust under which he may benefit, then the income of the trust will be treated as his income whether or not it is distributed. It will be similarly taxed if the settlor's spouse may benefit. Section 739 will not apply while the settlor is not ordinarily resident, but a non-resident trust established during a period of non-residence will be caught when the expatriate returns to the UK. This section relates only to income and does not, therefore, operate to tax capital gains (see later). If income from or accruing to a non-resident trust is to escape UK income tax then the settlor and his or her spouse must be totally precluded from any possible benefit, and the words 'power to enjoy' are widely construed under TA 1988, s 742(2). Alternatively, if it can be shown that the trust was established for *bona fide* commercial reasons, such as the establishment of a pension scheme, and that the avoidance of tax was no part of this reasoning, the section will not operate (TA 1988, s 741). This will be very difficult to prove especially since exchange controls (once a useful commercial reason) no longer operate in the UK.

It should be noted that non UK life assurance policies held in a non-resident trust are subject to UK tax on maturity under TA 1988, s 553(5).

On a more positive note, non-resident trusts can be established for the benefit of, for example, the settlor's children without any UK tax liability on the income as it arises overseas (see earlier for income arising in the UK). This is all well and good so long as the trust funds are accumulated. Unless the settlor and his spouse are excluded from benefit, TA 1988, s 674 can deem the trust income to that of the settlor. Where there is a distribution of income that income becomes chargeable on the beneficiary under TA 1988, s 740 if he or she is ordinarily resident in the UK. Where a benefit is received under the trust, then that benefit will be taxed to the extent that the trust has relevant income. Where the benefit exceeds the relevant income then the excess will be taxed in later years as the trust accrues further relevant income. Relevant income is income of the trust which can be used to provide a benefit but is restricted to income which arose on or after 10 March 1981. If, for example, a non-resident trust established in 1975 accrued income at the rate of £2,000 a year, then in May 1988 the total income is £26,000 of which, say, £14,000 is relevant income. During that year, £30,000 is paid to a beneficiary. The beneficiary's income tax liability in 1988/89 would be on £14,000 and, if income continues to accrue to the trust at the same rate, a further liability on £2,000 a year for the next eight years. If, however, the trust also had realised capital gains accrued since 10 March 1981, then to the extent that there is insufficient relevant income in the year of distribution, the surplus or a part of it will be allocated to the accrued capital gains and taxed accordingly.

In general terms, a non-resident trust is not liable to UK CGT (except where it is carrying on a trade in the UK). However, where the settlor was domiciled and either resident or ordinarily resident in the UK when the trust was established, or in a relevant subsequent year when trust gains are distributed to a UK-domiciled beneficiary (FA 1981, s 80), those gains will be treated as accruing to the beneficiary and taxable on him. Gains of the trust are computed each year and the cumulative total of gains is treated as trust gains for the year. When a capital payment is made to beneficiaries, the trust gains will be attributed to them in proportion to the capital payment received by them up to the amount of that payment. Unattributed gains, ie, where total gains are in excess of the capital payment, will be carried forward as trust gains for subsequent years. Gains are not apportioned to non-UK domiciled beneficiaries.

As far as IHT is concerned, non-resident trusts are treated in very much the same way as resident trusts. The important point for the tax liability of these trusts is the domicile of the settlor at the time the trust is first established. If the settlor is not UK domiciled, then trust assets located outside the UK will be excluded from any IHT liability. The professional adviser has a duty to return details of any non-resident trusts established for a UK-domiciled individual under IHTA 1984, s 218. Reference must be made, however, to any double taxation agreement in force. Where a non-resident trust has a IHT liability, this normally falls on the trustees but if, for whatever reason, the liability is not met by them, the Inland Revenue may obtain the tax from any of the following under IHTA 1984, s 201:

(a) any person entitled to an interest in possession in the settled property;
(b) any person for whose benefit the property or income therefrom may be applied at or after the time of the transfer; or
(c) the settlor, if the transfer is made within his lifetime.

In summary, non-resident trusts can be very useful in tax planning. Where the settlor and his or her spouse are precluded from income, the income payable to beneficiaries is effectively taxed on a remittance basis. Capital gains, whether accruing to the settlor or others, are similarly taxed on an effective remittance basis. Before embarking on any trust scheme, the expatriate must be totally clear on what he hopes to achieve and must be professionally advised in order to achieve it.

12 Companies

In most cases an expatriate is not involved in complicated corporate structures involving overseas companies and this book is not the place to explore the advantages of international financial royalty companies for a multinational group. Reference is, however, made to a number of common cases where expatriates find the use of a company advantageous.

Residence

Companies which are incorporated in the UK after 14 March 1988 are resident in the UK for tax purposes. If they transfer their trade or business to non-resident companies, a capital gains charge arises in the normal way. Companies incorporated in the UK and carrying on business before 15 March 1988 but not resident in the UK under previous rules become resident in the UK on 15 March 1993 with certain exceptions. Even in such cases, if central management and control of the company is transferred to the UK, the company irrevocably becomes UK resident.

Where a company ceases to be resident in the UK on or after 15 March 1988 it is deemed for capital gains purposes to have disposed of its assets and immediately re-acquired them at market value. This does not apply to UK assets of a branch or agency which remain here. Where a 75% subsidiary company migrates but the principal company remains resident in the UK, the charge on the foreign assets of a foreign trade can be deferred.

A company incorporated outside the UK is resident for UK tax purposes at the place of its central management and control following the case of *Calcutta Jute Mills Co Ltd* v *Nicholson* (1876) 1 TC 83. The place where the Head Office or shareholders' general meetings are held is irrelevant (*De Beers Consolidated Mines Ltd* v *Howe* (1906) 5 TC 198). A foreign registered company can have a

UK residence (*Bullock* v *The Unit Construction Co Ltd* (1959) 38 TC 712). If such a company wishes to migrate it must notify the Inland Revenue and make suitable arrangements for payment of tax.

Formerly a UK-registered company could have a foreign residence if its central management and control were overseas (*Todd* v *Egyptian Delta Land & Investment Co Ltd* (1928) 14 TC 119).

A company's domicile is the country of its incorporation (*Gasque* v *IRC* (1940) 23 TC 210) but a company's domicile is of little significance under UK tax law.

The country of incorporation is also important in many countries overseas and, for example, a company incorporated in the Netherlands is resident there and a company incorporated in one of the states of the USA is resident in the USA for US tax purposes. It will be appreciated therefore that even though a company may have only one place of central management and control it may nonetheless be dual resident if, for example, it is controlled from the UK but incorporated in the USA. On 27 July 1983, the Inland Revenue published a long and detailed Statement of Practice 6/83 giving the Revenue view on company residence but this is now generally relevant only to companies incorporated abroad.

A company, like an individual, may be resident for tax purposes in more than one country. Formerly a subsidiary company could be dual resident and obtain relief, say for losses, in two countries: the losses could then be surrendered to related profitable companies. This was stopped in most cases from 1 April 1987 by what is now TA 1988, s 404 and Sched 17.

Trading in the UK

An expatriate trading in the UK may well wish to use a company as his trading vehicle. If such a company is incorporated in the UK it is normally UK resident, whether or not it is managed and controlled in the UK, and is subject to corporation tax on its profits in the normal way.

Alternatively, a company registered overseas, but managed and controlled outside the UK, is liable under TA 1988, s 11 to corporation tax on profits arising through a branch or agency in the UK, but otherwise only to income tax at the basic rate on its UK non-trading income. It should be noted that if the expatriate controls a UK resident but foreign incorporated company before his emigration he must not leave the UK without considering the question of the company's residence. If the directors physically move from the UK, but retain the management and control of the company, the company becomes non-resident. It is deemed to have disposed of and immediately re-acquired its assets, other than UK assets of a branch or agency, giving rise to gains. It must also notify the Revenue of its intention with a statement of its tax liabilities, including PAYE etc, and how it intends to secure their payment. Guidance on the procedure was issued by the Revenue on 4 August 1988. Alternatively it would be possible to appoint directors in the UK that would continue to control the company from the UK following the emigration of the shareholders.

Instead of a company, the expatriate could consider using a Scottish limited partnership of which the partners are two non-resident companies. The partnership is thus not resident for tax purposes, but is a legal entity in the UK, registered in Edinburgh under the Limited Partnerships Act 1907. Its notepaper will give the UK address and registered number but need not disclose the companies who are partners.

Investing in the UK

An expatriate investing in the UK may well do so through an overseas investment company so that the company owns the UK assets and the expatriate owns the shares in the investment company. Such a company can be incorporated in almost any tax haven and non-resident Channel Islands or Isle of Man companies are fairly commonly used for this purpose. The advantage of this course of action is to limit the UK income tax to an effective basic rate liability on UK investment income. The other advantage is that if the expatriate has acquired an overseas domicile and dies, his estate would be left holding shares in a non-UK company which is foreign property and therefore not subject to UK inheritance tax even though the underlying investments are in the UK. A direct holding of investments in the UK would be subject to inheritance tax in these circumstances.

Property development in the UK

Sometimes an expatriate wishes to trade in the UK but is unable to do so without having a permanent establishment in the UK. For example, a property development in the UK could consist of an acquisition of land where the contract was signed outside the UK, a building contract for the property to be built, which again could be signed outside the UK, and the subsequent sale of the complete property. The Revenue might argue that this was an acquisition of land which is developed with the sole or main object of realising a gain from disposing of the land when developed and therefore taxable under Schedule D, Case VI on the expatriate, notwithstanding his non-residence for UK tax purposes. If, however, the development takes place through a Jersey resident company as a trading activity of the Jersey company, it should be protected from UK tax under the UK-Jersey Double Tax Agreement with the result that the profits are subject to Jersey income tax at 20% instead of UK corporation tax. If the Jersey resident development company is in turn owned by a Jersey non-resident investment company, it may be possible to agree with the Jersey Comptroller of Income Tax that 90% of the profits of the resident development company may be paid as a management charge to the non-resident investment company which would suffer corporation tax in Jersey of a flat rate of £500 a year. The effective rate of tax on the development profit is therefore limited to 2%.

Treaty shopping

In the meantime, the Netherlands Antilles continues to be used as a vehicle for routing income from a high tax country to a suitable tax haven. If, for example, the expatriate, receives royalties from France he could well suffer withholding tax of 33.3% of the gross. He might however consider a structure whereby he owns the shares in a Netherlands Antilles company, which in turn owns shares in a Netherlands company. The Netherlands Antilles company, will own the intellectual property giving rise to the royalties and license the Netherlands company which in turn would license the exploiters in France. Royalties would be paid to the Netherlands company free of withholding tax under the France-Netherlands Double Taxation Agreement. By agreement with the Netherlands Revenue, 7% of the royalties would remain in the Netherlands subject to tax at 42%. The remaining 93% of the royalties would be paid down to the Netherlands Antilles intellectual property owning company, where they would suffer tax at between 2.4 and 3% in the Netherlands Antilles as an offshore company. The Antilles company would pay a dividend free of withholding tax to the expatriate.

It is obviously not cheap to set up or run a structure of this type and therefore it should only be contemplated where the sums involved are fairly large.

A non-UK resident non-domiciled expatriate may well hold shares in a Netherlands Antilles company directly in his own name. In other cases, it may be desirable for shares in such a company to be held through an offshore trust arrangement. See Chapter 11.

Anti-avoidance provisions

The main UK anti-avoidance provision against the use of non-resident companies by an individual resident in the UK is TA 1988, s 739. This section enables the Revenue to look through an overseas investment company and tax the UK resident investor on the gross income of the company (*Lord Chetwoode* v *IRC* [1977] STC 64). The provisions of this section are very wide, and include the indirect enjoyment of overseas income. In fact the Revenue considered that the section was sufficiently wide for them to assess each of the beneficiaries of an offshore trust to the whole of the trust income. The section was however interpreted in a distinctly more restricted manner by the House of Lords in *Vestey* v *IRC* [1980] STC 10 which resulted in the introduction of what is now TA 1988, s 740. TA 1988, s 739 applies to individuals resident or ordinarily resident in the UK and therefore has no application to the non-resident expatriate. The overseas visitor who becomes resident in the UK, but who is domiciled outside the UK, is not caught by the section provided that the income is not remitted to the UK in view of TA 1988, s 743(3). The UK resident and domiciled individual potentially caught by s 739 may escape if he can show that the transfers to an overseas company and any associated operations were *bona fide* commercial transactions and were not designed for the purpose of avoiding UK tax, and that such avoidance was not one of the purposes of the transfer.

A period of non-ordinary residence by an expatriate must be a good time to liquidate an overseas company held in an overseas trust, distribute the proceeds to the trust as a capital sum and appoint the non-resident a beneficiary of the trust and distribute to him before his return to the UK. He should then be able to bring back the proceeds to the UK free of UK tax.

Offshore funds

The UK anti-avoidance provisions relating to material interests in offshore funds include an interest in a non-resident company, unless the shareholder has the right to have the company wound up and in such event would be entitled to more than 50% of the net assets of the company. An interest would only be within this provision, however, if it could reasonably be expected that during the seven years beginning with the acquisition of the shares, the shareholder would be able to realise the value of his interest by transfer, surrender or in any other manner. These provisions were primarily aimed against the use of offshore roll-up funds by UK residents and there is an exemption whereby the fund can show that it distributes more than 85% of its income (TA 1988, s 760). A shareholder is only deemed to be able to realise the value of his interest if he can realise an amount which is reasonably approximate to the appropriate proportion of the company's net assets. A minority shareholder in an overseas company would normally not be able to realise the asset value in this way, and would apparently escape the charge. The charge is arrived at by calculating the capital gain in the normal manner, but without indexation, and charging it to income tax under Schedule D, Case VI. A non-UK domiciled resident is restricted to a charge on amounts remitted to the UK by TA 1988, s 761(5). As the charge is based on making a chargeable gain in the first instance, a non-ordinarily resident expatriate would not normally be within the provisions unless the investment were connected with a·business in the UK.

Controlled foreign companies

An expatriate owning shares in a UK company which in turn has non-resident subsidiaries may have to contend with the controlled foreign company legislation in TA 1988, ss 747–756.

A controlled foreign company is one which in any accounting period is resident outside the UK, is controlled by persons resident in the UK and is subject to a lower level of taxation in its country of residence.

The charge to UK tax arises only if there is a direction by the Board of Inland Revenue. Where a direction is made, it is necessary to compute the chargeable profits of the overseas company for its accounting period, and its creditable tax, if any, which are then apportioned to the shareholders in accordance with their respective interests. An amount equal to corporation tax is calculated on the profits apportioned to a UK-resident company. UK individuals could be assessed under TA 1988, s 739. The creditable tax is the overseas tax paid on the profits and is similarly apportioned to the shareholders and may be credited against the corporation tax liability.

A direction cannot be given if the controlled foreign company pursues an acceptable distribution policy by distributing 50% of its profits if it is a trading company and 90% in other cases. There will also be no direction where the company is carrying on exempt activities, which broadly means trading in the country in which it is resident subject to various exceptions. There is a *de minimis* limit whereby there will be no direction if the profits of the controlled foreign company do not exceed £20,000 a year. Finally, a direction may be avoided if the motive test is passed. This is where it appears to the Board that the transactions in the accounting period were carried out for *bona fide* commercial reasons and they did not achieve, or were not designed to achieve, a material reduction in UK tax and that it was not one of the underlying reasons for the company's existence to divert profits from the UK. The provisions of the controlled foreign company legislation are extremely complex and as it is unlikely that an expatriate would hold shares in an overseas company through a UK company, the provisions are not examined in detail.

Pre-return planning

An expatriate thinking of returning to the UK should consider carefully any action required in connection with his overseas companies before his return. It may be sensible to liquidate a company and bring the funds in as capital or, if an overseas domicile of choice has been established, to consider transferring shares into trusts before a return to the UK and the resurrection of a UK domicile of origin. In view of TA 1988, s 739 it is unlikely that it would be advantageous to retain a direct shareholding in an overseas investment company after the return to the UK.

Non-resident Irish companies

A company may be incorporated in Ireland without necessarily being resident there for Irish tax purposes. There will be an Irish tax liability on any income or certain capital gains arising in Ireland, but a number of non-residents have found it useful to use an Irish company for transactions entirely outside Ireland. A registered office address in Ireland can sometimes give an air of respectability to a trading company which may or may not be justified. Such companies are often thought to raise fewer enquiries from foreign tax officials, who possibly assume erroneously that as the company is incorporated in Ireland it must pay Irish tax at high rates and therefore is not being used for tax avoidance purposes. In practice, many overseas tax officials are aware of the benefits of a non-resident company.

It must also be appreciated that an Irish company, whether resident or not, has to file accounts with the Registrar of Companies which become public documents. It is however a relatively straightforward matter to modify the structure slightly so that the non-resident Irish company is acting not for its own account but as trustee of, for example, a Jersey non-resident trust. In this case all the trading transactions, although on the face of it entered into by the company, would in fact be entered into (outside Ireland) by the company acting in its trustee capacity, and the only transactions reflected in the company's accounts would be the trustee fee that it charges and any expenses incurred in the actual running of the company. The trading transactions would be those of the Jersey trust and there is no necessity to file the accounts of such a trust except possibly with the tax authorities of those countries in which the trading is taking place. A non-resident Irish company acting as trustee for a Jersey trust, buying goods from Japan and selling them to Italy, could be managed and controlled from Hong Kong without there being a tax liability anywhere. So long as there was no permanent establishment in Japan or Italy and no contracts entered into in those countries the trust would be trading with and not in those countries and would not be liable to tax therein. There would be no Jersey taxation, as the trust is a non-resident trust so far as Jersey is concerned, with a non-Jersey settlor and beneficiaries. The company is only incorporated in Ireland and is therefore outside the scope of Irish tax, and because the trading does not take place in Hong Kong, which operates a territorial system of taxation, there is no Hong Kong tax either.

Exchange control approval from the Irish Central Bank would be required for the investment by the non-resident in the Irish company. Approval should be forthcoming on the grounds that it was to provide an agency or trustee service for a non-resident trust, but might be withheld if there was any indication of non-commerciality.

13 Other taxes

Value added tax

UK VAT is payable at the standard rate of 15% in respect of goods or services supplied in the UK by a registered business. Registration is compulsory where the taxable turnover exceeds £22,100 a year or £7,500 per quarter. Certain items are exempt from VAT, while others are zero-rated, for example, most food. So far as the expatriate is concerned, the most important VAT relief is that relating to exports of goods or services. If goods are exported from the UK the sale is zero-rated, and therefore VAT should not be charged. Certain supplies of international services are also zero-rated; for example, an expatriate obtaining advice from a UK business, on his personal tax affairs, will receive a zero-rated bill if he is resident outside the EC. However if he is resident inside the EC the charge will be standard-rated. A supply to the expatriate of taxation advice for business purposes is zero-rated whenever he is resident outside the UK.

Importation of goods into the UK, on the other hand, is an occasion for charge to VAT. VAT due on imports of goods is paid at the time and place of entry or, if the importer has approval for deferment, by direct debit covered by banker's guarantee on the fifteenth of the month following the month in which the goods enter the UK.

VAT exemptions and zero-rating

The main VAT exemptions are set out in VATA 1983, Sched 6 the main headings are land (but see 'Property' below) insurance, finance, education, health, burial and cremation. Zero-rating for VAT purposes is given by VATA 1983, Sched 5, the main headings of which are food, books, news services, fuel and power, construction of buildings (however the construction of commercial buildings will cease to be zero-rated from 1 April 1989), international services, including services relating to land outside the UK, letting goods for hire outside the UK, the supply of cultural, artistic, sporting, scientific, educational or entertainment services performed outside the UK, valuation of goods outside the UK, the supply to a person in his business capacity of services listed in VATA 1983, Sched 3 to a member of the European Community and in any capacity to a person belonging elsewhere, and the supply of insurance and allied services and export and transhipment services. Goods sent to the UK for repair and subsequently re-exported are also included in this heading. Schedule 3 refers to services supplied where received such as transfers and assignments of intellectual property, advertising services, professional services of consultants, engineers, lawyers, accountants, etc, banking, financial and insurance services, the supply of staff and certain restrictive covenants. If these services are supplied by a person who belongs outside the UK to a UK business registered for VAT, then the same consequences apply as if the recipient had himself supplied the services in the UK and that supply was a taxable supply ie, he would have to account for VAT on the value of that supply by the overseas person. Therefore if the UK business was partially exempt for UK VAT purposes, and these services received related to exempt supplies, it will suffer a disallowance of VAT input tax on these expenses. A UK business will therefore not obtain an advantage by using services supplied from abroad, which do not have a VAT charge on them, as opposed to services supplied in the UK which will bear VAT. Other zero-rated items include transport, caravans and houseboats designed for permanent habitation, gold, children's clothing and certain supplies by charities.

Property

Expatriates with property in the UK should appeciate that although the purchase price of property is free of VAT, alterations as well as repairs and maintenance are subject to VAT. However it should be noted that following the decision of the European Court of Justice on 21 June 1988 zero-rating will cease to be applied from 1 April 1989 on the construction of buildings for industrial and commercial use and in the community and civil engineering sector. Also from 1 August 1989 the landlord will have the option to charge VAT on rents and to capital sums received on the supply of non-domestic buildings and developed land used for non-domestic purposes. By electing to this, the landlord will be able to recover input tax on repairs and maintenance expenses. Therefore expatriate owners of commercially let property in the UK should consider registering for UK VAT and appointing an agent in the UK to deal with their UK VAT affairs.

Car tax

Cars supplied in the UK other than for export are subject to a car tax in addition to VAT.

An expatriate returning to the UK and importing a car could be liable to both VAT and car tax on the value of the car at the time of importation, plus import duty if the car is not of EC origin (see below).

Excise duties

Many items imported into the UK suffer excise duties in addition to VAT. Examples include the obvious ones of alcohol and tobacco, perfume and gold and other less likely items such as cigarette lighters. Items acquired in the UK for personal export may be acquired in duty-free shops or those operating a personal export scheme under which the VAT, but not excise duty, may be recovered.

Personal belongings

The importation of personal belongings is normally subject to import duty, VAT and car tax (if relevant). The value for import duty is basically the secondhand value (exclusive of VAT) in the UK of identical or similar objects. The value for VAT is the same but inclusive of import duty. The value for car tax is the trade value inclusive of import duty but exclusive of VAT. (See Customs and Excise Notice 252.)

There are relieving provisions and these relate to three categories of belongings;

(1) cars, aircraft and caravans,
(2) boats, and
(3) other effects.

The appropriate customs formalities including the claiming of the reliefs must be complied with.

(1) Motor cars, motor bikes, aircraft and mobile homes can be admitted entirely tax and duty free if belonging to a person coming into the UK for a stay of at least six months which are already his personal property and have been owned and used abroad by him or his spouse for six months excluding time he has spent in the UK. Furthermore, the vehicle must be for personal use and not sold, hired, etc for one year from importation under penalty of forfeiture. Release may be granted, if all duties and tax are paid. There is also a temporary importation relief for a visitor intending to stay less than six months in the UK, but the vehicle must be exported at the end of this period (see Customs and Excise Notice 3, and the Private Vehicle Memo).

(2) Boats are not in any case subject to import duty if more than 12 metres long. All boats designed or adapted for recreation or pleasure are subject to VAT as are other boats of less than 15 tons gross. The relieving provisions are virtually identical to those for motor cars (see Customs and Excise Notice 8A and later Customs and Excise Notice 8).

(3) Other baggage, personal and household effects (including pets) are relieved in the same way as cars, etc, except that these goods need only have been owned and used in the expatriate's normal home for three months if he is returning from the EC: the six month rule applies if he is returning from outside the EC and the goods are not disposed of for 12 months. These rules also apply to someone setting up a secondary home in the UK. Certain prohibited or restricted goods are not within this relief, eg, goods bought under a tax-free scheme. The normal duty-free allowances apply in addition to this relief (see Customs and Excise Notice 3).

(4) In addition to the above reliefs, a person who is resident outside the EC and who intends to become normally resident in the UK on the occasion of his marriage can bring in, duty and VAT free, wedding gifts up to a value of £700 each provided that they are from non-residents. Personal and household effects need not have been used abroad, but the goods should be imported within two months before, or four months after, the wedding.

Stamp duty

Stamp duty on the conveyance of UK shares is chargeable at $\frac{1}{2}\%$.

Other taxes 143

In the case of property the charge is 1% unless the value transferred is £30,000 or less. Stamp duty on gifts was reduced to 50p from 26 March 1985 by FA 1985, s 82.

Of particular interest to expatriates is the stamp duty provision under which a stampable document signed outside the UK and kept outside the UK is only stampable within 30 days of being brought into the UK (Stamp Act 1891, s 15(2)(*a*)).

14 Investment by Richard Sayer, *International Investment Marketing, Allied Dunbar Assurance plc*

Introduction

The expatriate investor very soon discovers that the process of constructing an investment portfolio is far from straightforward. There is a wide and bewildering range of investment media available from which he can choose and there is an equally large number of important criteria that he must take into account when making that choice. The subject is so wide-ranging and so important that it merits a book all on its own, and indeed, the *Allied Dunbar Investment Guide* gives an excellent commentary on the many types of investment available and the criteria for making a selection. This chapter contains a brief outline of those criteria for the major investment media likely to be considered by an expatriate investor. It also contains the most important tax implications of each medium, although reference should also be made to the earlier chapters for a detailed account of the taxation of specific investments.

When choosing an investment the expatriate should always remember that the investment itself is the primary consideration and the taxation treatment the secondary consideration. However, where two contending media are, on investment considerations, of apparently equal merit, if one of them benefits from a favourable tax regime, the balance must tip in its favour.

Finally, it should be borne in mind that this chapter can only discuss the major considerations in detached terms whereas, clearly, the individual circumstances of each expatriate will need to be taken into account when making a decision as to one investment medium or another. It is in this part of the process—matching the needs of the investor to a suitable investment—that the services of a qualified and competent specialist adviser will be invaluable.

Establishing the objective

Pick up any expatriate magazine or turn to the money pages of your daily newspaper and you will find a veritable cornucopia of investment opportunities. The avid but untutored investor can while away his time considering the merits of precious stones versus financial futures say, or traded options compared to limited edition prints and still reach no clear cut conclusions. This is usually because he has given no consideration at all to what he wants to achieve—he has no 'Investment Philosophy'.

When designing an investment strategy for himself the expatriate should begin with the basic precept that any investment proposal must address his specific financial circumstances. It is not possible to make a considered choice of an investment medium until the objective or purpose of the investment has been established with the utmost clarity. In essence the investor must ask himself three broad questions:

- What do I want my investments to achieve for me?
- In what timescale?
- Within what constraints?

Obviously the more general the question, the more difficult it is to give an accurate, satisfactory and qualified answer. The individual factors that need to be taken into account to arrive at a considered investment strategy are many and varied. The following list is not necessarily exhaustive but it does include the major questions that need to be asked:

- What amount is available for investment, and when;
- What proportion of the total investment portfolio this represents;
- What other investments are held;
- What part this investment should play in the overall spread and balance of the total portfolio;
- What is the investor's base currency;
- What known liabilities are to be met;
- Whether there is any expectation of adding to the investment, and when;
- Age of the investor and, where relevant his dependants;
- The investor's attitude to risk, having due regard to the usual relationship between risk and reward;
- The need for access and the likely timescales involved;

- The personal motivations of the investor;
- The rate of inflation in the country in which the investor is, and will be, resident;
- Whether immediate income from the investment is required and if so at what level;
- Where relevant, the required balance between high immediate income and future growth in income;
- Whether capital appreciation alone is the principal present aim;
- Personal tax liabilities of the investor, both current and anticipated. Whether different rates of tax will be applied to income and realised gains;
- Inheritance tax considerations which may affect the choice of investment;
- Any other relevant constraints which may limit or influence the choice of investment; for example, exchange controls, protective securities legislation, investment subject to trust, double tax treaties etc.

Constructing a portfolio

For many investors the most important feature of their investment portfolio will be security. Few investors have so much money that they can afford to invest without first assuring themselves that the risk/return profile of their proposed investment is consistent with their own philosophy. If the investment is pitched too high on the risk/return curve, it becomes little more than speculation, mere gambling if you wish. Pitched too low, the returns will be dull and unexciting, leaving only dissatisfaction and little reward.

Security comes through spread. It is extremely unlikely that a single investment area will meet all of an investor's needs. What is required is a spread of investment sectors, a spread of countries and a spread of currencies. Only then can the investor look forward, with reasonable confidence, to a secure and growing investment return.

Choosing the individual components of an investment portfolio can be confusing. Performance statistics often serve to mislead rather than inform. There is a disturbing tendency these days, among some sectors of the financial press, to measure investment performance over unrealistically short timescales. Apart from causing confusion when attempting to compare the performance of different shares, sectors or investment funds—it makes comparisons between different investment media meaningless. Perhaps the most important difference between the mainstream investment areas is the time-frame within which they can be expected to provide effective performance. The prudent investor will use published investment statistics with caution, taking care to obtain sufficient information to indicate clearly the track record of his chosen investment.

So armed with all this information, what kind of investment does the expatriate need to satisfy his aims? Where should he start looking?

Leaving aside the esoteric sorts of 'investment' opportunities mentioned earlier—emeralds, rare stamps, coffee futures and the like—most private investors will find their needs catered for by the mainstream investment areas—Bank Deposits, Government Bonds and Equities. These three areas account for well over 90% of privately invested monies. Before we go on to examine specific investment vehicles, we will look at the main characteristics of these media.

Monies placed on deposit have a secure capital value in money terms, but the income produced will vary depending on the prevailing interest rate. This means, contrary to popular belief, that the overall return from a deposit type environment is far from guaranteed. If we go further and consider the overall return in real-value terms (as opposed to the meaningless 'money' return), it is clear that in an inflationary climate the longer the investment is held the more vulnerable it becomes.

An investment into Government Bonds is almost the reverse of this situation in that the income is generally guaranteed (in money terms) but now the capital value will fluctuate, depending again on the prevailing interest rate climate. The Bond will usually have a guaranteed capital value at redemption of course, but once again only in money terms, not in real value.

It will be seen that in the case of the two main investment areas where guarantees are common, the main effect of the guarantee is to provide a secure and dependable return in the short term, but to restrict the overall return over the longer term. If one is looking for realistic growth rates over longer timescales, experience has shown that they have only been achieved by investments in real assets such as shares, which produce both income and a capital return.

Investment 149

There can be no guarantees or predictions but in a capitalist society, which is expected to remain so, security will more likely be achieved in the long term by investing in a well balanced carefully managed portfolio of equities—providing the investor's timescales are long enough to iron out the fluctuations caused by the ebbs and flows in world market conditions and the market sentiments generated by political climates. Historically, five years upwards has been the right sort of timescale to consider equity investment to have sufficient security. If equity investment is contemplated over shorter periods than this, it stands the risk of being speculation rather than an investment.

Most investment advisors would, for the majority of their clients, recommend a balance between the highly liquid, short-term, high income bank/money market deposit, and the longer term equity-linked investment, offering capital appreciation, with characteristic fluctuations in value and a lower but secure percentage income yield. The actual income will rise as the capital value appreciates and, therefore, this element of the portfolio is the key to providing the growth in income that is necessary to offset the erosive effects of inflation. The middle ground will be held by Government Bonds (such as Gilt-Edged Stock or Eurobonds).

Quite how the proportion between deposits, Bonds and equity-linked investment will be determined, depends on the answers to the list of questions in the previous section of this chapter, and hence the particular needs of the individual investor. As a rule of thumb (and a potentially hazardous one, since any such rule must make assumptions about average needs) a classically constructed portfolio might have anywhere between £2,000 and £20,000 on deposit. Of the balance, one quarter to one third might be in Bonds, with the rest in equity linked investments (frequently mutual funds such as unit trusts or offshore funds).

To summarise:

- There must be a spread of investment sufficient to contain the volatility and depreciation risks that are incurred with an overly weighted exposure to one investment medium, one market sector, one country or one currency.
- Within individual stockmarket holdings there should be a balanced mix of investment sectors eg manufacturing, engineering, property, finance, leisure etc.
- The resulting portfolio must be under active daily management to ensure that the results obtained continue to meet the investor's needs.

Clearly, this is an ideal situation which the average investor may find difficult or impossible to achieve by direct investment. He may not have the expertise to guide his choice or the time to actively manage a balanced portfolio. Even where the time and expertise are to hand, the required spread may be impossible to achieve in all but the largest private portfolios without striking 'minimum bargains' where the dealing costs are disproportionately high.

For many investors, the answer is to construct their portfolio from large 'building blocks' such as the wide range of collective investment media that are available. The main areas from which the choice may be made are described in the following section.

Principal investment media

Banking and deposits

Whether an individual's financial affairs are very simple or extremely complex, successful financial planning begins with establishing proper and effective banking arrangements. Apart from providing a home for money in its own right, a bank provides the mechanisms which link and give access to whatever other financial arrangements need to be made.

Obviously, the services that any one individual will require will depend on personal circumstances but most expatriates are liable to need some or all of the following:

- Sterling current account—expatriates tend to keep higher balances than their onshore counterparts so this should, preferably, be interest bearing.
- Sterling deposit account—as mentioned earlier this forms an important part in constructing a secure investment portfolio.
- Currency deposit account—many expatriates are paid in foreign currency and, according to their domestic arrangements, may well have this currency as their base currency giving rise to a need for appropriate deposit facilities.
- Currency conversion facilities.
- Loan facilities—expatriates will often have the need for both short and longer term borrowing, perhaps in the latter instance to buy a home in the UK.

Investment 151

- Standing orders.
- Direct debit facilities.
- International money transfers.
- Eurocheque facilities.
- Credit card payment facilities.
- International money orders and drafts.

These facilities can be provided by most banks, whether offshore or onshore. Whilst we have already said that the tax treatment of investments should not be the only consideration, in the matter of banking it is of primary importance. Interest arising on a UK bank account or deposit is a UK source of income for a non-UK resident. The tax treatment of such income is covered elsewhere in this book—the non-resident can avoid the problems of UK taxation by making his banking arrangements offshore. There is the additional consideration for the non-UK domiciliary that a deposit in the UK is treated as a UK sited asset for IHT purposes, unless the deposit is in a currency other than sterling (see Chapter 10).

Apart from the taxation implications, there is a more fundamental reason why the expatriate should conduct his banking affairs offshore. It will be clear that he has particular problems and needs which are not common to UK residents and these are more likely to be understood and catered for by an offshore bank or branch which specialises in the banking needs of expatriates. If that bank or branch operates from either the Channel Islands or the Isle of Man there are two further important advantages:

(a) These offshore centres are outside of the UK tax jurisdiction but have access to the UK banking network which means that the full facilities of a UK clearing bank, such as cheque books and cards, for use in the UK can be made available.
(b) Jersey, Guernsey and the Isle of Man have all recently enacted Financial Services Legislation which mirrors the UK's Financial Services Act so the investor is assured of substantially the same safeguards and protection as if he had made his financial arrangements with an institution on the UK mainland.

Building society deposit

Building societies are in competition with banks for deposits and they tend to offer a range of deposit accounts, viz share accounts, higher interest accounts (the rate of interest paid will normally depend on the minimum withdrawal notice—the longer the notice the higher the interest), term bonds and Save-As-You-Earn contracts.

Where investment and tax considerations are concerned, a UK building society deposit provides broadly similar advantages and disadvantages to a deposit with a UK bank, therefore, many of the comments above will apply equally here.

In recent years the major building societies have extended their range of services to include many of the facilities previously only offered by banks such as, cheque books and cards, automatic telling machines and standing order/direct debit facilities; however, they are still unable and are unlikely to be in the foreseeable future, to provide the full range of facilities, that the expatriate investor will require. It is rare also for the expatriate to benefit from the other claimed advantages for a building society depositor, that is to say, 'High Street' convenience and priority in the queue for mortgage funds.

In general, therefore, an expatriate should think twice about keeping deposits with a building society, despite the comfortable feeling of familiarity it may offer. There is, perhaps, one exception to this piece of advice and that is where the building society in question has an offshore branch. During 1988 a number of building societies have exercised the freedom given them by recent legislation to open offshore branches in such places as Gibraltar, Jersey and the Isle of Man. These offshore branches can offer deposit facilities that compare very favourably with the offshore banks. The overall caveat remains, however, that the deposit part of an investor's portfolio should not be allowed to grow out of proportion to the rest of the portfolio since there is no capital growth on a deposit.

National Savings (UK)

National Savings investments are sponsored and guaranteed by the Government of Great Britain; there are several different schemes designed to appeal to the different classes of investor eg National Savings Bank accounts, National Savings Certificates, National Savings Index-linked Certificates, National Savings Income Bonds, National Savings Deposit Bonds and National Savings Yearly Plan.

Many of these schemes can be compared with bank and building society deposits in that they are an acceptable investment for investors with an income tax liability; indeed, some of the tax exempt investments (National Savings Certificates, National Savings Index-linked Certificates and National Savings Yearly Plan) are particularly useful for higher rate taxpayers. They are unlikely to be attractive to non-tax payers like most expatriates as their yields are generally less than can be obtained elsewhere.

The gross return from National Savings Bank accounts, National Savings Income Bonds and National Savings Deposit Bonds is usually good, but for the expatriate it shares the same problems as interest from accounts with UK banks and building societies.

An investment in National Savings will generally be best left until the expatriate returns to the UK.

British Government Stocks

British Government Stocks (also known as British Funds or Gilt-edged Securities) are the instrument used by the Government and certain nationalised industries to raise capital. The stocks are guaranteed by the Government and consequently are totally secure. Investors can be sure that the stated rate of interest will be paid and the nominal principal returned, in accordance with the provisions of the loan.

Gilt-edged securities normally have a fixed rate of interest, known as the 'coupon', which is expressed as a percentage of the nominal value; so, for example the holder of £100 nominal of Treasury Loan $8^3/_4$% 1997 will receive £8.75 a year until that date (normally subject to deduction of income tax at the basic rate—but see later) regardless of the price at which he purchased the stock or its market value from time to time. In addition to paying interest during the life of the stock, the Government also has a requirement to repay the loan at the nominal or par value of £100, on the date stated—this is known as the redemption date.

The market value at any given time will depend upon the coupon, the amount of time to run to redemption and prevailing interest rate conditions. Clearly the closer a stock is to redemption the nearer the market price will be to the nominal value. Stocks are usually classified according to the length of time to run to redemption, as follows:

- 'Shorts'—five years or less to redemption.
- 'Mediums'—between five and 15 years to redemption.
- 'Longs'—over 15 years to redemption.

In addition there are also undated or irredeemable stocks with no final date specified for redemption.

The key factor, certainly for the mediums and longs, in determining the capital value from time to time is prevailing interest rate conditions compared to the coupon of the stock. If the prevailing interest rate falls, the value of the stock will rise. If the interest rate falls below the stock's coupon then the value of the stock will rise above its par value and can be sold for a (tax free) capital gain. Naturally, a stock bought above par and held to redemption has an inbuilt capital loss. Conversely, if interest rates rise then the capital value will fall and if interest rates rise above the coupon, the stock's price will fall below par and if sold at that time would generate a capital loss. A stock brought below par value and held to redemption has an inbuilt capital gain.

The expatriate should, in general, make his choice from the range of 'approved' or 'exempt' gilts, where the income can be paid without deduction of tax. Normally interest is paid net of basic rate income tax but investors who are resident and ordinarily resident outside the UK can arrange with the Inspector of Foreign Dividends to have the interest paid gross.

Because the investment is guaranteed by the Government and the coupon and redemption value are both fixed, gilt-edged securities are ideal for the investor who places a high premium on security. Also, as mentioned above, gilts have their place within an otherwise equity related portfolio, where they can introduce some stability. It will be seen however, from the bewildering range and different types of stock available, that some professional knowledge is still necessary to invest successfully in this market. For this reason many investors, instead of holding stocks directly, will choose to invest via some kind of collective investment medium—see later.

Overseas Government Securities & Eurobonds

The structure of both these types of stock or bond is fundamentally

Investment 155

the same as that of the gilt. An Overseas Government Security is a stock issued by a foreign government but normally priced in sterling—for this reason they are often known as 'Bulldog Bonds'. The yields available are usually higher than on gilt-edged securities and the interest is paid gross on some issues.

A Eurobond is a stock which circulates outside the country in whose currency the bond is denominated. Eurobonds are normally issued in 'bearer' form with interest coupons attached; the interest is paid without deduction of tax. In addition to the usual investment considerations for Government Stocks there is an additional, and major, consideration for Eurobonds, namely the performance of the currency in which the bond is denominated against the investor's base currency. The Eurobond market is not an easy one for the private direct investor unless he has a great deal of money to invest. He can deal through a stockbroker but small deals, and small is defined as less than £25,000, will be difficult to arrange. There are a number of offshore funds (see later) specialising in collective Eurobond investments and these provide a convenient medium for the private investor who wishes to include the effects of such bonds in his investment portfolio.

Collective investment media

The individual private investor who is looking to construct a well balanced portfolio consisting of, perhaps, a mix of gilt-edged securities, Eurobonds and particularly, equities will find that there are a number of practical difficulties which may conspire to prevent him meeting his aim. The principal problems will be:

- 'Small' investors may have difficulty in achieving a sufficient spread of investment areas, sectors, countries and currencies to iron-out the volatility that can occur with an overly weighted exposure to one area.
- Even 'large' investors may have difficulty in achieving an adequate spread without dealing in such small parcels that they incur lots of minimum charges which will increase the overall costs.
- Few investors have the expertise necessary to choose and then actively manage a properly spread portfolio.
- Those investors who do have the expertise will seldom, unless perhaps they are retired, be able to devote the amount of time necessary for effective management.

- Expertise can be bought, but for smaller investors, the cost involved will very often be out of proportion to the size of the investment.
- There is a great deal of administration and paperwork involved in running a successful portfolio, dealing with such things as dividend warrants, scrip and rights issues, bonus issues, voting rights etc.

It was for investors for whom these considerations weighed too onerously that collective investment media were developed. A collective investment, commonly known as a mutual fund, enables a large number of individual, and probably smaller, investors to pool their resources so as to become collectively a large investor. The common fund thus created can be managed by professional managers at a proportionally lower cost, the paperwork can be dealt with by the fund's administrators and, most importantly, a greater degree of security can be achieved by spreading the risk over a much wider range of investments than could be achieved individually.

Over the years, a number of different kinds of collective investment medium have evolved such as Investment Trusts, Unit Trusts, Insurance Bonds and Offshore Funds. The differences between these different media are lessening as time passes, given the 'level playing field' created by new onshore and offshore financial legislation. Despite this, there are still significant differences between the various investments particularly in the way they are taxed. These differences will lead to one being more suitable for a particular market than another. Unsurprisingly, those investments which are based offshore will usually prove the most suitable for the expatriate but we will look at the main features for each of the investments in turn. First, however, it will help to over-view each medium.

An Investment Trust is not, in fact, a trust at all but an investment company having limited liability. Investors may buy shares in the company and so share indirectly in its assets and income which, of course, will be the investments it makes. An Investment Trust is subject to normal rules for trading in shares which cannot be sold direct to or bought from, shareholders; instead, the shares are bought and sold by investors on the Stock Exchange and the share price is subject not only to the value of the underlying securities, but to normal market sentiments.

A Unit Trust on the other hand *is* a trust fund and the investors have a direct beneficial interest in the underlying assets of the trust. Unit trusts are normally open-ended investment vehicles which means that units—which are a bit like shares—are created or liquidated as necessary, to meet the demand by investors for sales or redemptions. The investor can deal direct with the unit trust company and the value of his units is directly related to the value of the underlying holdings.

Insurance bonds are, in reality, 'single premium non-qualifying life assurance policies' and are an alternative form of lump-sum investment. There are certain tax advantages conferred by their status although these advantages are likely to be of interest chiefly to the higher rate UK taxpayer. Historically, insurance bonds have been permitted a wider range of underlying investments, direct holdings in property for instance, but the Financial Services Act 1986 provided similar wide investment powers for Unit Trusts. Insurance bonds are discussed in more detail under the heading Life assurance policies.

The term 'Offshore Fund' is a generic title which covers both Unit Trusts and Investment Companies based outside the UK. They are usually to be found in jurisdictions where their operations will involve little or no local taxation, such as the Channel Islands, Isle of Man, Luxembourg, Bahamas, Bermuda, Cayman Islands, British Virgin Islands etc. Shareholders who are not resident in the jurisdiction can receive both income and gains without liability to tax of the country in which they have invested.

UK unit trusts and investment trusts

These are the two mainstream collective investment media available in the UK and, of the two, unit trusts are the more popular. This is largely due to the fact that units in a unit trust can be bought and sold in a simple manner—the unit trust managers make a market in their own units—whereas dealing in shares in an investment trust can only be done via the Stock Exchange. For investment and tax purposes it is convenient to consider the two together. Both enable the investor to have an exposure to a wide range of investment sectors: UK equities, foreign equities, government securities, real property, commodities, and cash. Each have a widespread of investment, under expert management with the minimum of red tape and paperwork.

There are many hundreds of trusts available in the UK having different investment aims and objectives—an investor would have to be very pernickety indeed to be unable to find one which matched his own investment philosophy. Some trusts will have as their investment aim the accumulation of capital for the future, in which case the income yield will be low; others will be managed for income, in which case the yield will be higher, but still with the capacity for capital appreciation. In general, the capital appreciation oriented trusts will be more suitable for the expatriate investor owing to the tax treatment of unit trust income and distributions.

Franked income of the trusts (dividends from UK equities and income from UK Government securities) is received net of withholding tax at the basic rate (or UK ACT)—there is no further liability to taxation within the trust and the tax deducted is passed on as a credit to the unit holder.

Unfranked income (which includes deposit interest, income from overseas government securities and non-UK dividends) is subject to corporation tax within the trust. To reflect this the unit holder is granted a basic rate tax credit but, of course, if the trust is liable to corporation tax at the standard rate there will be a differential (10% in the tax year 1988/89). As mentioned, income is distributed net of withholding tax at the basic rate (or UK ACT) and is accompanied by a corresponding tax credit for use by UK residents. The non-resident investor may have little or no opportunity to reclaim the tax deducted and he should therefore restrict his exposure to the various trusts which aim for capital growth, with a very low yield.

The capital appreciation of approved investment trusts and authorised unit trusts is free of capital gains tax within the trust; realised gain on redeemed holdings is taxable in the hands of the investor in the normal way. The investor who is resident and ordinarily resident outside the UK will have no liability to UK capital gains tax.

Units of a UK unit trust and shares in a UK investment trust rank as UK sited assets for inheritance tax purposes and this will be an important factor for the non-UK domiciliary (whether resident in the UK or not) to take into account.

Offshore funds

As stated earlier, offshore funds can be structured in a similar manner to a UK unit trust or, quite commonly, as an open-ended investment company which can make a market in its own shares. Their main purpose is to provide pooled investment opportunities similar to UK unit trusts and investment trusts, but with reduced taxation. The exact taxation effects for the fund will depend on a number of factors, including where it is resident, where it invests and the existence or otherwise of relevant Double Tax Treaties. The general position is that although such funds do not benefit from Double Tax Treaty advantages on equity dividends received, no corporation tax is payable within the fund and no withholding tax is imposed on distributions of income to investors.

The tax treatment of income in the hands of the investor will obviously depend on the tax regime(s) at the time he receives income or redeems his investments. Most countries in the world will tax their residents on a worldwide arising basis for income whether remitted or not and, therefore, it will often be advantageous to invest in low yield, growth orientated funds so that the investment can roll-up with minimal exposure to taxation.

Investors in funds which capitalise income ('roll-up funds') will have their total gain taxed as income, on realisations made when UK-resident. Investors in funds certified as distributing ('distributor-status funds') will avoid this special taxation. The subject is dealt with in more detail in Chapter 9—Capital gains tax.

Holdings in offshore funds operated from a tax haven will not be subject to local inheritance taxes (tax havens don't usually have them!) but, remember, there may well be a liability to inheritance taxes under the laws of the country in which the investor is domiciled.

The expatriate investor is spoilt for choice in the offshore fund market as there are many thousands available. When narrowing down his selection the investor should follow the usual guidelines regarding quality of management, previous track record etc, but will also need to take into account the jurisdiction from which the fund operates. It is regrettable but true that some of the fringe offshore centres have very loose and lax controls so that the investment on offer may not provide the security and safeguards that the investor requires. In general the UK expatriate will find all the choice and variety he could possibly want on offer from offshore investment houses operating out of the Channel Islands, Isle of Man and, perhaps, Luxembourg. The first two areas have the additional advantage that they have both enacted Financial Services Legislation that provide investor safeguards mirroring those available to UK investors via the Financial Services Act 1986. It is expected that before the end of 1988 Jersey, Guernsey and the Isle of Man will all have been granted 'Designated Country Status' under the UK FSA which, apart from being an endorsement of the investor safeguards provided in those countries, will enable locally authorised investment houses to market their funds in the UK.

In general then, and subject to the usual caveats about quality of management, offshore funds are likely to provide the most practical and efficient form of investment vehicle for the expatriate investor.

Life assurance policies

A life assurance policy is a contract between the individual policy holders and the life assurance company. The life company maintains the underlying investment funds in its own right but, depending on the nature of the policy, it undertakes to pay the policy holder either a specified sum, or a sum which is increased periodically out of the profits of the company, or one which varies from time to time with the value of that part of the underlying fund 'earmarked' for that particular investor. One of the most important characteristics of the life assurance policy as an investment is that it does not produce an income (which would, of course, be exposed to taxation) but is essentially a medium to long term accumulator.

Naturally, all life assurance policies provide life cover—a sum assured payable upon death. Most policies, other than temporary assurances, usually also provide investment benefits—sums payable on surrender or maturity of the policy. Life assurance policies may be divided into three categories depending upon the emphasis that is placed on savings or on protection (life cover):

(a) An endowment policy—has a high savings element and is one under which the benefits are payable at the end of the predetermined period (the endowment term) or on death, if earlier.
(b) A whole of life policy—one under which the benefits are in general payable on death, whenever it occurs.
(c) A term policy—a temporary assurance, the sum assured being paid only if death occurs within a specified period.

Term assurances are used entirely for protection against financial hardship on death and will not be considered further here. Within

Investment 161

the endowment and whole of life categories the life policies can be one of three different types, depending on the way in which the sums payable by the company are determined:

(a) With profit contracts are policies under which a minimum sum is guaranteed to be paid by the life company on certain specified events, augmented from time to time by bonuses declared by the company according to its profits. These bonuses may be reversionary (bonuses added to the sum assured, either yearly or triennially) or terminal (bonuses declared at the end of the policy as an increment to the final payment).

(b) Without profit contracts are policies under which the life company guarantees, on certain specified events, to pay an absolute sum and invests the premiums in such a way as to produce that sum, bearing any short-fall in the return or retaining any profit in excess of the guaranteed return.

(c) Under unit-linked policies the life company maintains an underlying fund, which is divided, for accounting purposes, into 'units' and undertakes to pay to the policy holder an amount equal to the greater of any guaranteed sum and the value of the units allocated to the policy. The underlying fund might consist of specific types of investment media (such as property, equities, unit trusts, investment trusts, Government securities, local authority and bank loans or deposits, or building society deposits) or the fund may consist of a combination of some or all of these ('managed' or 'mixed' funds).

A life company generally has full investment freedom as to the type of investments it chooses, subject only to the investment being a suitable 'match' for its liabilities. In the case of unit-linked policies the Insurance Company Regulations only permit linkage to certain types of assets, such as those listed above. If the contract is one which incorporates a guaranteed maturity value, the investor knows that he will get at least that sum. At the same time, in the case of with profit policies, he has the advantage of having the guaranteed sum augmented from time to time by reversionary and terminal bonuses. With unit-linked contracts, the value is augmented by the movement of the value of the underlying fund (capital appreciation plus re-invested income).

Life policies can be sub-divided into two main types depending upon how the premiums are payable:

(a) Regular premium policies are those under which premiums are payable annually, half yearly, quarterly or monthly, either

162 *Allied Dunbar Expatriate Tax and Investment Guide*

throughout the duration of the policy or for a limited premium-paying period. This type of policy is suitable for the regular saver, probably investing out of income, who is looking to amass a capital sum for the future.

(b) Single premium policies—generally known as single premium bonds, are purchased by way of one single premium or lump sum payment. Clearly, they are designed for the capital investor.

The usual logic for making investments through the medium of a life assurance policy is that the proceeds, when taken from the policy, can benefit from advantageous tax treatment in the UK. The tax treatment of both 'qualifying' and 'non-qualifying' policies is dealt with in more detail in Chapter 5—UK income of British expatriates.

It will be seen that, so far as policies issued by a UK company are concerned, the disadvantage to be weighed against the advantage mentioned above, is that the life fund in which the investment is being made is itself taxed. Income received and realised gains made by the fund are both taxable. Policies issued by offshore life offices will, in general, not suffer from the taxation disadvantages but neither can they offer an advantageous treatment of proceeds, following the Finance Act 1984 (now incorporated in FA 1988).

The Act, however, provides (Sched 15, para 6), in the case of a regular-payment policy (such as a 10-year endowment policy—the shortest period for which a qualifying policy can be issued) for a special offshore/onshore hybrid where a UK policy is issued in substitution for an offshore policy when and if the policy holder becomes UK-resident. Providing that this is done within a year of coming to the UK, the tax advantages on the taking of proceeds are preserved. Unfortunately, in January 1988 the UK Inland Revenue announced fundamental changes to their interpretation of contract law as it concerns the exercise of options in life policies, which have effectively removed one of the main advantages of this type of policy. The options specifically attacked by the Revenue are the 'Regular Withdrawal Options' contained in many endowment policies (including the offshore/onshore hybrid type) which enable the policy holder to reduce the premium to a nominal amount (eg £1 a year) and take a tax-free 'income' from the policy after a qualifying period, usually ten years. This option was, obviously, particularly attractive to the higher taxpayer. The Revenue action means that it has not been possible to sell such qualifying policies containing such an option since 25 February 1988. Existing policies and offshore/

onshore hybrids which were issued before 25 February 1988 are not affected.

The offshore investor seeking to hold his investment through a trust should also note than an offshore life policy written in trust or transferred to non-resident trustees after 19 March 1985 is subject to tax on income on the full gain irrespective of the policyholder's period of non-UK residence, FA 1988.

The two kinds of policies normally considered by investors are the ten-year endowment and single premium bonds. The single premium bond can be considered as an alternative investment to unit or investment trusts and/or offshore funds but investors should note the disadvantageous tax treatment of offshore bonds compared to onshore bonds (see Chapter 5). The ten-year endowment policy can play a useful role in an expatriate's portfolio of investments, provided that the role it is to play is a considered one. A wise investor will seek professional advice before making his decision.

In this chapter we have considered life assurance as an investment only. Clearly, many expatriates will have a need to provide life assurance protection for themselves and their family to guard against the problems caused by premature or unexpected death. Life assurance is the most effective way of providing such protection but this aspect is outside the scope of this chapter. Investors needing more information should contact their usual advisor.

Pensions

An expatriate who intends to retire and who also expects to enjoy a reasonable standard of living in that retirement, will generally need to make his own provisions. Many will consider the possibility of effecting a UK Pension Plan but, in all probability, this will be neither possible nor desirable.

A UK Pension Plan does have its attractions but they are often misunderstood. Any Pension Plan is a two stage affair: stage one is producing the retirement fund; stage two is turning that fund into an income.

The perceived attractiveness of a UK Pension Plan arises from the tax treatment of stage one—the ability to fund out of gross income into a gross fund. This benefit is more usually described as 'the ability to obtain tax relief on the premiums and invest in a tax-free fund'. This is undoubtedly an attractive proposition but there is a threefold price to be paid:

- The invested capital is 'locked-up' until at least age 50.
- Only part of the benefit may normally be drawn in cash—the remainder must be in the form of an income.
- The whole of the income, when received, is taxed as if it were earnings.

Despite this, it does hold true that a Pension Plan is usually the best way for a UK domiciled/UK resident to provide for retirement. It is also true that individuals who are non-UK domiciled and/or non-UK resident ie expatriates, may be able to achieve many, if not all, of the advantages of a UK Pension Plan, whilst at the same time avoiding the disadvantages by making private arrangements offshore.

In fact, there may be no choice but to make alternative arrangements as many expatriates will not be eligible to be a member of a UK Plan. To be a member of an approved Occupational Pension Scheme (one set up by an employer) an individual must normally be in receipt of income chargeable to tax under Schedule E. This would, of course, normally exclude expatriates living and working abroad but the Inland Revenue booklet IR12, which sets out the practice notes for occupational schemes, outlines a number of circumstances where an expatriate can be a member of a UK approved scheme:

- Where he works for a UK-resident employer.
- Where he is only on secondment from a UK-resident employer for a limited period (usually not more than three years).
- Where he is serving with a non-resident company in a group where the parent company is resident in the UK and the parent company retains control over his movements.

It is perhaps worth mentioning that an employee not spending sufficient time abroad to become non-resident for tax purposes, may, under the '365 day rule', be entitled to 100% tax relief against his earnings. He could either be a member of his firm's pension scheme or (because, technically at least, he is in receipt of non-pensionable earnings) effect a Personal Pension Plan.

Although, therefore, it is possible under some circumstances for an expatriate to take advantage of UK pension arrangements, there are a number of downsides of which the major ones are:

- The drawbacks mentioned above.
- The employee is unlikely to get tax-relief on personal contributions and, indeed, may be taxed on his employer's contribution.
- The employer may not get tax relief on contributions.
- The pension may be based on a fixed and notional UK salary rather than on the expatriate's actual emoluments.
- The expatriate may intend to remain permanently outside the UK so that a UK based sterling denominated pension might not be appropriate.
- Many expatriates will wish to retire and draw their pension rather earlier than is permitted by Inland Revenue and pension scheme rules.

There is one circumstance in which it seems desirable from both the employer's and expatriate's point of view for him to be a member of a UK Pension Plan. This is where an existing employee who is already a member of the company scheme is sent abroad for a short tour of duty which is unlikely to be repeated. Removing him, albeit temporarily, from the scheme may well have a serious effect on his benefits which cannot be offset, in the limited time available, by alternative funding.

It is clear then, in the majority of cases, that an expatriate will and indeed should make his own arrangements. The expatriate worker enjoys a very different life style from his UK based peers of course and his pattern of employment will often seem fractured and indeterminate when judged by UK norms. His pension needs are often equally unconventional and may only be properly met by an arrangement which incorporates the utmost flexibility. The main areas of concern will be the need for:

- Simple administration when communications may be difficult or delayed.
- Easy variation of contribution levels.
- Flexibility of payment period.
- Open-ended maturity date.
- Choice in the type of benefits available—capital, annuity income, investment income, growth portfolio etc, and on a single or joint life basis.
- Choice of underlying investment areas/currencies.

- Maximum tax efficiency.
- Maximum flexibility on return to the UK.
- The ability to change, at short notice and without penalty.

Surprisingly, there is in fact no such animal as a genuine Offshore Pension Plan. There are a number of pre-packaged arrangements on offer to the expatriate but they are based on one or a combination of the following conventional investment vehicles:

- Offshore Endowment Policy (usually with a minimum ten-year investment period).
- Offshore Insurance Bonds (often in a 'funding' arrangement).
- Non-resident Trusts.

One could, of course, argue, that the actual method used is immaterial providing that it achieves the desired results. This last point is fundamental and the investor should take care to ensure that his chosen solution provides the benefits he requires with adequate flexibility to meet changes in circumstances which can, and often do, occur at short notice.

When the expatriate feels unable or unwilling to commit himself to a longer term arrangement it will still be possible for him to achieve most, if not all, of his desired aims by making regular investments into an offshore investment fund. Some of the advantages of this route are:

- There is no set contribution level—he can pay as much or as little as he wishes according to cash flow.
- The payment period can be as short or as long as desired and contributions may be suspended at any time—whilst between contracts for instance.
- The benefits are accessible, in whole or in part, at any time and at short notice—the money is not 'locked-up' until some distant retirement date.
- The benefits can be enjoyed in any form or in any combination he wishes eg cash, purchased life annuity, investment income, future growth etc and can be held in single or joint names.
- Offshore funds give access to a very wide range of investment areas and currencies.
- If 'distributor status' funds are chosen and especially the low yielding varieties—there will be minimum exposure to income taxes, even after a return to the UK. The main return will be in the form of capital appreciation and most retiring expatriates

Investment 167

should be able to schedule their allowances so as to avoid capital gains tax completely.
- If the expatriate returns to the UK to work in the future, the accumulated funds can be drawn on to subsidise UK pension funding.
- Because there are no arbitrary rules—only those the expatriate sets for himself—he can make whatever changes to the arrangement he wishes whenever he wishes.
- If a 'Death in Service Benefit' is required it can be taken care of by a stand alone assurance policy of a level and type exactly suited to his needs.

In this area of financial planning as in many others there is a wide range of options open to the expatriate investor and, with proper advice, he can be sure of arranging matters to his satisfaction.

Miscellaneous investments

In addition to the mainstream investment media already mentioned there is an enormous range of minor and fringe investments from which the investor can choose, ranging from race horses to Texan oil wells. In general, these appeal either because the investor happens to like race horses or because some startling tax advantage or investment performance is claimed. All startling claims should be examined with care and, perhaps, suspicion. Personal preference may be allowed a place in choosing an investment but the investor should recognise that the desire to be part-owner of a race horse may be obscuring his view of the true investment considerations.

Objects, such as fine art, antiques and precious stones, are sometimes bought as investments and may turn out to be not only pleasurable but also profitable. They are, however, oddities as investments since they produce no income. This means that their total investment performance is in capital appreciation and this is nearly always highly volatile. Such an investment tends to be illiquid, since it is not always possible to find a buyer, let alone a good price. Insurance and safe-keeping costs are high, as are dealing costs. This type of investment is only for those prepared to take a potentially very long term view, who have the expertise necessary to guide their judgment and, ideally, who also derive from owning them a pleasure quite apart from their own investment value.

Exchange controls

Following the abolition of UK exchange controls in 1979, the UK resident is generally free to invest where he chooses. This freedom is not always necessarily available to the expatriate investor, since he may be resident in a jurisdiction which still imposes exchange controls. If this is the case then due account must be taken of such controls and any other local investment restrictions when the expatriate is planning his finances.

For example, the working expatriate who commonly receives the whole of his income in local currency, may be able to arrange that some or all of his salary is paid to his offshore bank account. He will then ensure that he remits to the country where he is resident, only that amount of money he needs for living expenses thus ensuring that his surplus income, that which is available for investment, is not trapped by local legislation. The retired expatriate who is living in a country still subject to exchange controls, will be well advised to keep his capital outside the country so as to avoid that capital becoming locked in by rules preventing or limiting the repatriation of capital.

Making such arrangements for income and/or capital will not usually have any effect on the expatriate's tax position as most countries in the world will tax their residents on a worldwide arising basis, which means that tax is due whether or not the income is remitted to the country in question. Keeping investment capital outside the country of residence will also be important to those who are able to benefit from a remittance basis of taxation in that country; an example is non-UK domiciliaries resident in the UK. There may also be benefits, so far as inheritance taxes are concerned, in keeping assets in a jurisdiction which does not impose such taxes (for example, the Isle of Man), although the UK domiciliary would, of course, not thereby avoid an inheritance tax liability.

Methods of holding an investment

In the main, this chapter addresses itself to investments held directly by the individual investor. It is quite common, however, for investments to be held in a manner or through a medium quite different from this. As an example, an investment may be held jointly by a husband and wife; where this is the case, and the spouses are resident for tax purposes in different jurisdictions, there may be some unexpected results. These may sometimes be desirable and sometimes not; in any event, they need to be taken into consideration.

Investments may be held via a nominee. This will not alter the investor's beneficial title to the investments and hence will not usually affect his liability to tax. The virtues of holding investments via a nominee are, perhaps, largely logistical; the nominee will have instructions to act on the investor's behalf, may be geographically closer to the investment than the investor and thus easier to contact, and would be the registered holder (as distinct from owner) of the investment. It is likely that the nominee will, in the circumstances described, be able to act more swiftly in executing an investment decision than could the investor himself from his more remote location.

A trust or a company—or sometimes a combination of both—can be used as a vehicle for holding an investment. The perceived benefits of such a method can be many but the actual effect is to interpose a third party (the trust or the company) between the investment and the ultimate investor. The trust or company will be a legal and, generally therefore, taxable entity in itself and this can result in a modification of the eventual tax liability. The investor must take account of any anti-avoidance provisions which may seek to look through the company or trust for tax purposes and might therefore negate some of the advantages he may be seeking. Before deciding whether to hold investments through the medium of a trust or company, the investor should take due consideration of not only any potential tax saving, but also the costs of such an exercise. These costs will include the setting up of the arrangement and the continuing running costs. The latter, particularly, should not be ignored since, for example, the trustee fees charged in some tax havens can be quite startling.

Making the choice

Matching investments to needs is rarely simple. A detailed knowledge of the characteristics of each investment type is essential and enables a choice to be made between two apparently similar and competing investments. Advice on which investments to choose is widely available these days. It is worth seeking such advice since, at the very least, it should provide a yard stick against which to gauge one's own conclusions. Advice on the related matters of taxation, exchange control and holding companies and trusts is more difficult to find but nonetheless important to seek out if the intended investment aims and objectives are to come to fruition.

15 Investment and floating exchange rates by Howard Flight, *Guinness Flight Global Asset Management Ltd*

Introduction

In an international financial system, such as that operating in most of the world at present, in which currencies (broadly speaking) find their own level on the foreign exchange markets through the interplay of supply and demand, they play a dual role. They still act as tokens of value for the purposes of international trade in goods and services, but they also behave as and are viewed as financial assets in their own right, like shares or bonds, with a similar potential for gain or loss. Expatriates who live in one country and receive current income from another are vulnerable to day-to-day fluctuations in relative currency values. For example, Britons living in retirement in Spain and drawing sterling-denominated pensions found to their cost in 1986/87, when, for a short period, the peseta rose against the pound. Over the longer term, expatriates with assets denominated in more than one currency are obviously exposed to the vagaries of the 'invisible hand' of floating exchange rates.

Factors driving exchange rate movements

There are essentially five major currencies in the world at present: the US dollar, the Japanese yen, the German D-Mark (especially as representing the European Monetary System currencies), sterling (still an important independent currency), and the Swiss franc (although it has been closely tied to the DM for a decade). In addition, the Australian dollar and the Canadian dollar, both representing economies based on commodities, are of growing importance, and likely to become more independent than they are at present; and the currencies of the dynamic Pacific Rim economies are also likely to become more important over the next decade. The five major currencies, and the Australian dollar and Canadian dollar are all freely convertible, and part of the floating exchange rate regime operative since 1973, when it became clear that the system of fixed exchange rates devised at Bretton Woods in 1944 could be maintained no longer.

Comment on foreign exchange markets is published daily in the *Financial Times*, which also publishes several useful indicators every day: for sterling and the dollar against the other main currencies it gives 'spot' (today's) rates and one- and three-month forward rates; exchange cross-rates and 'trade-weighted exchange rates' (providing an 'averaged' parity measurement for a particular currency, useful in a historical perspective of bear or bull phase); and prevailing interest rates for the major Eurocurrencies.

The strength or weakness of any particular currency depends ultimately on the demand for it on the part of traders and investors and, more recently, Central Banks, through intervention. A number of factors interact in the market to determine this demand and, indeed, the supply of the currency needed to meet it. These factors can be divided into two broad categories: macroeconomic, expressed in objective statistics about such matters as economic growth, trends in productivity, inflation rates, money supply trends, interest rates, current and trade deficits and surpluses, international capital flows, and so forth; and intangible and largely subjective factors such as political change or threatened change, market sentiment, and changes in national attitudes to consumption and saving, which in turn affect key statistical factors.

It is unwise to try to forecast exchange rate movements on the basis of two or three historical relationships between any of the factors listed above, let alone any one single relationship. Exchange rates move for a variety of short to medium-term as well as longer-term financial and economic reasons, with the shorter-term factors sometimes predominating until the longer-term factors assert themselves. Another important point is that the various factors themselves change in importance over time. That caveat having been entered, it is still possible to say, for example, that differentials between interest rates in different currencies are usually the main short-term factor affecting capital flows. In the longer-term, the correlation between exchange rates and relative or differential inflation rates has proved extremely reliable. In other words, a country with persistent, higher than average inflation will tend to see its currency depreciate against those of its trading partners to offset this, to a degree that can be mathematically correlated with

Investment and floating exchange rates 173

the gap between its own rate of inflation and that prevalent in the countries with which it trades.

Exchange rates and equity investment

For the international investor, exchange rate movements are at present the single most important factor affecting the value of his holdings in equities, bonds, collective funds and cash, wherever the market place. The effect on cash and bonds, in both the long and short-term, is more direct than that on equities: exchange rates affect not only prevailing capital values as a result of movements in interest rates, but also the international purchasing power on sale or maturity of a particular bond or, obviously, of cash held in a particular currency. Thanks to postwar developments in telecommunications and information technology, the world's main stock markets, like the foreign exchange markets, now operate globally, except in matters of administration. In this environment, exchange rate movements can mean the difference between profit and loss; or, in a stock market crash, the difference between a small loss and a large one. When, for example, stock markets fall worldwide—as they did on 'Black Monday' in October 1987—a major factor affecting relative loss measured in an investor's home base currency is the recent and accompanying strength or weakness of the currencies in which his investments are held.

After Black Monday, US investors found that they had suffered less on their foreign investments measured in dollars than investors in other countries (measuring their investments in other currencies). Because the US dollar fell against the yen, D-Mark, and sterling, shares in these three currencies that had been bought with US dollars fell in value much less *in dollar terms* than in local currency market-value terms, to the extent that the dollar weakened against the currency in question. This example shows that profitable international equity investment cannot be achieved unless the exchange rate factor is taken into account in the investor's calculations. Currency weakness is generally good for profits and share prices in certain sectors (eg export-led sectors), when considered in local currency terms; resulting equity gains, however, will naturally be reduced or may be erased in the currency terms of the foreign investor. The expected depreciation of the currencies in question must be included in calculations of comparative projected total investment returns. For example, an investment in a US company in a sector benefiting from future dollar weakness may be expected to show a 100% return in dollar terms, thus attracting Japanese investors. But if the dollar is expected to depreciate by 25% against the yen, the expected return in yen terms will be, in fact, only 60%.

Exchange rates and bonds

The market value of a bond is tied to the interest rate (and yield curve) of the currency in which it is denominated: when interest rates fall, the value of the bonds normally increases, and vice versa. Under a regime of fixed exchange rates, such as that established at Bretton Woods, the only scope for capital gains in bonds was in local currency terms: the return achieved depended on the investor's ability to assess correctly the future course of interest rates. Nowadays, however, there are opportunities for returns on investing in bonds internationally, to be increased as a result of currency movements, and there is also scope (of course) for these returns to be reduced for the same reason. Exchange rate movements also influence the ultimate value of the proceeds of the bond when repaid at maturity, in terms of its global purchasing power.

Exchange rate movements have a strong direct influence on international investment in national bond markets and, in turn, on bond interest rates of the various currencies. Bond markets with a large volume of foreign funds invested in them will be more influenced than others by the strength or weakness of the local currency. Bond markets funded largely by domestic investors will be less vulnerable to movements in exchange rates. The British bond market has for many years been influenced by the strength or weakness of sterling, mainly because a large volume of foreign funds has been invested in gilts, attracted by Great Britain's political stability and reputation for honest dealing, and reflecting sterling's past role as the major reserve currency. If sterling is strong, foreign investors normally buy more British bonds, and they normally sell their gilts, or at any rate buy less, when sterling is weak. By contrast, the majority of buyers of US bonds have until recently been resident in the USA, so that US bond prices and yields have been less influenced by dollar strength or weakness. But this state of affairs is changing because the huge US foreign trade and current account deficit and federal budget deficit have created the need for greater flows of foreign capital into US government bonds to finance both deficits. This means that increasingly US bond yields will have to be at whatever levels are required to attract and sustain adequate inflows of foreign capital.

Exchange rates and cash

Especially at a time when equity markets have to be approached cautiously, many investors are concerned with managing liquid assets of one kind or another, and again international investors, including expatriates, must take account of the impact of exchange rate movements. But more and more investors are realising that cash investment (in the form of bank deposits or 'financial paper') on an international basis represents a major investment opportunity in its own right. International investment in a managed spread of currencies is the logical approach for cash investment. With a managed currency fund, investors buy shares or units in a fund whose liquid assets are invested in a managed spread of, normally, the five main currencies. The currency constitution of the fund is changed over a period of time in accordance with the fund managers' assessment of expected exchange rate movements. For each particular currency, assets are held in a mixture of deposits, certificates of deposit, floating exchange rate notes and, when interest rates appear likely to fall, in part in fixed-interest securities. In broad terms, the commonsense approach is to invest in a diversified portfolio of undervalued currencies in terms of economic fundamentals entering, or soon to enter bull market cycles, and to avoid any significant exposure to currencies in either mature bull cycles or in long-term declining trend.

There is no doubt that foreign exchange markets can be volatile. To hold cash in a single currency only is, from an international perspective, high risk or speculative. A diversified and managed investment in currencies is the opposite of this, but will inevitably underperform as measured against the strongest currency in the short-term. Most managed currency funds have shown themselves to be highly conservative and bearing a lower risk than either investment in a single specific currency or international investment in equities or bonds. Equities of this nature carry higher risks than bonds; bonds carry higher risks than cash. In an international context, investment in the equities, bonds or cash of one country only is higher in risk than diversified investment across a range of currencies and in those three areas. Just as the performance of a unit trust or offshore fund can never match or outperform the best performing shares within it in the short-term, so the performance of a managed currency fund should not be expected to match or outperform that of the strongest currency in the short-term. Over the longer-term, however, managed currency funds have outperformed and should outperform the returns on holding liquid funds in any one single currency—even the strongest over a five or ten-year period.

16 Checklists of do's and don'ts

Going abroad

One of the most daunting things about going abroad to work is gathering together all the information necessary. Obviously the intending expatriate needs full details of his contract, health, visa and permit requirements and many more. On the financial front, the following are some of the most important things to consider:

- *Do* bring your UK tax affairs up to date;
- *Do* submit a P85 and claim any PAYE rebate if leaving part way through the tax year;
- *Do* inform the Department of Social Security, check if any contributions will be necessary and, if not, obtain an application form for voluntary contributions;
- *Do* make arrangements for offshore banking (including a current account for remaining UK commitments and a small amount in a deposit account);
- *Do* close any building society deposit accounts;
- *Do* inform any mortgagee that the mortgaged property is being left vacant, or if it is to be let, ask his permission;
- *Do* check the continuing validity of all protective insurances, both life and personal effects, property, etc;
- *Do* take legal advice on letting property;
- *Do* make or revise a will;
- *Do* review existing investments not already mentioned;
- *Do* consider comprehensive insurance protection while overseas;
- *Do* make use of duty-free facilities in purchasing a car or household appliances if appropriate;
- *Do* inform bankers, solicitors, accountants and other advisers of the new address;
- *Do not* leave everything to the last minute;
- *Do not* take on any new investment commitments just before leaving;

- *Do not* forget that most countries are happy to let money in but may impose restrictions on taking it out again—check the rules;
- *Do not* leave valuables at home;
- *Do not* expect to have a large cash surplus, at least in the first few months.

While overseas

Given that earning and saving money is a prime motive in working abroad, many expatriates are very disappointed to find that after six months they have yet to amass a fortune. In retrospect it is hardly surprising. Even the 'fully furnished' company house is usually missing much essential equipment, there can be a great deal of entertaining to be done either at home or at 'the club', the cost of living until experience of local produce and markets is gained is invariably high, and, after all, a new video and hi-fi are essential.

Usually after about six months, a regular savings or cash surplus pattern can be discerned and at that point some serious consideration can be given to investment.

- *Do* invest surplus cash initially in a readily realisable form such as a very short-term bank deposit;
- *Do* retain an adequate cash reserve;
- *Do* wait until a regular pattern of surplus appears before entering into any major investment commitments;
- *Do* examine all investment propositions very carefully;
- Do seek independent advice on all financial matters;
- *Do not* be tempted by tales of massive profits just waiting to be made, at least until a reasonably secure base has been built up;
- *Do not* sign any investment document or part with cash as a result of a brief meeting with a salesman of whose credentials you are not absolutely certain;
- *Do not* make any long-term commitments based on current earning capacity unless that capacity is extremely secure (for most expatriates, it is not);
- *Do not* attempt to beat currency or tax regulations, as the penalties can be extremely severe;
- *Do not* neglect to plan.

Coming home

One of the most vital occasions for tax and investment planning is in the months before returning to the UK. Much of what has been achieved in terms of savings and investment can be largely undone by a lack of forethought at this point. Amid the round of farewell parties, packing up and thinking of home, it is often very easy to forget to close a bank account or to realise accrued gains. The secret is to plan.

- *Do* seek professional advice at least three months before the return date (or if the overseas period is unlikely to last, or to have lasted for at least three years, get advice in the tax year prior to return);
- *Do* check any local requirements for tax clearance before the issue of exit visas;
- *Do* check current exchange control regulations;
- *Do* close all offshore deposit accounts (and in the tax year before return close any UK bank deposit accounts);
- *Do* consider CGT and UK income tax liabilities on existing investments;
- *Do* give notice to any tenants at home to quit;
- *Do* read Chapter 4 again.

Appendix I Inland Revenue booklet IR 20: Residents' and non-residents' liability to tax in the UK

Part I Introduction

Scope of booklet

1 In general terms, the United Kingdom tax system seeks to tax:

(a) all income arising in the United Kingdom, no matter to whom it belongs; and

(b) all income arising outside the United Kingdom which belongs to persons resident in the United Kingdom.

There are however a number of situations in which these general principles do not apply. In these situations a person's liability often depends on what is known as his 'residence status' or on his domicile. The purpose of this booklet is to explain the law and practice concerning an individual's 'residence status' for United Kingdom tax purposes, and how this, and his domicile, affect his liability to tax.

2 This booklet is concerned with the 'residence status', domicile, and consequent tax liability of individuals only. It does not deal with the tax position of companies or similar legal or artificial persons or bodies such as clubs, societies or trusts.

3 The normal rules of taxation of various types of income may be modified where a double taxation agreement applies. Brief particulars only are given in Part VII; more information on this subject may be obtained from the Board's booklet on Double Taxation Relief (see paragraph 57).

Definitions

4 Although the terms used in the booklet are intended to be read in their everyday sense, there are a few which, for convenience and brevity, are used in a particular sense, and should be read accordingly.

'Tax Year' means the United Kingdom income tax year, which is the 12 months ending on 5 April.

'Person' means an individual.

'United Kingdom' comprises only England and Wales, Scotland and Northern Ireland; it does *not* include the Channel Islands or the Isle of Man.

'Abroad' and 'overseas' mean outside the United Kingdom.

Address of Inland Revenue Offices

5 The booklet refers to various Inland Revenue offices which deal with different aspects of the subjects covered. The full addresses of these offices are:

Inland Revenue Headquarters,
Somerset House, Strand, London, England, WC2R 1LB
(Telephone number 01–438 6622)

Inland Revenue Claims Branch, Foreign Division,
1st Floor, St John's House, Merton Road, Bootle,
Merseyside, England, L69 9BL
(Telephone number 051–922 6363)

Inspector of Foreign Dividends,
Lynwood Road, Thames Ditton, Surrey, England, KT7 0DP
(Telephone number 01–398 4242)

Inland Revenue Head Office (Public Departments),
Foreign Section, Ty-Glas, Llanishen, Cardiff, Wales, CF4 5ZD
(Telephone number 0222 753271)

If it is necessary to contact the local Inspector of Taxes, his address may be obtained from the appropriate local telephone directory

Appendix I 183

(under the heading 'Inland Revenue') or from one of the offices mentioned above.

Part II Residence and ordinary residence for United Kingdom tax purposes

General

6 The terms 'resident' and 'ordinarily resident' are not defined in the United Kingdom Taxes Acts, but guidance as to the meaning of these words has been given in decisions by the Court. These show that both expressions are used in their everyday sense and do not have any special or technical meaning. The term 'domicile', on the other hand, is always used in its strictly legal sense (see paragraphs 31–35).

7 In the Taxes Acts, 'resident' and 'ordinarily resident' are always used to describe a situation arising in a tax year, and not in relation to some longer or shorter period. The question that generally has to be decided is whether or not a person is resident (or ordinarily resident) in the United Kingdom in a particular tax year. It is not practicable to do more in this booklet than set out the main principles which are followed in answering this question because each case depends on its particular facts.

8 If a person is to be regarded as resident in the United Kingdom for a given tax year he must normally be physically present in the country for at least part of that year. He will always be resident if he is here for six months or more in the year. **There are no exceptions to this rule**. Six months is regarded as equivalent to 183 days, whether or not the year is a leap year. For this purpose a count is made of the total number of days spent in the United Kingdom during the year whether the stay is one period only or a succession of visits. Under present practice days of arrival and days of departure are normally ignored. If the person is here for less than six months, the decision whether or not he is resident depends on other circumstances (see paragraphs 13–30).

9 'Ordinarily resident' is broadly equivalent to habitually resident; if a person is resident in the United Kingdom year after year, he is ordinarily resident here. It follows that a person may be resident but not ordinarily resident in the United Kingdom for a given tax year if, for instance, he normally lives outside the United

Kingdom but visits here in that year for six months or more. Or he may be ordinarily resident but not resident for a given tax year if, for instance, he usually lives in the United Kingdom but has gone abroad for a long holiday and does not set foot in the United Kingdom during that year.

10 A person may be resident (or ordinarily resident) in two or more countries at the same time. He cannot claim to be not resident (or not ordinarily resident) in the United Kingdom merely because in that tax year he is resident (or ordinarily resident) in another country. Where, however, a person is regarded as resident both in the United Kingdom and in a country with which the United Kingdom has a double taxation agreement there may be special provisions in the agreement for treating the person as a resident of only one of the countries for purposes of the agreement.

11 Strictly speaking, each tax year must be looked at as a whole, and a person is to be treated as either resident or not resident for the whole year; he cannot be regarded as resident for part of the year and not resident for the remainder. Thus a person who is ordinarily resident in the United Kingdom and who goes abroad for a period which does not include a complete tax year (eg, if he was abroad for the period from July 1981 to March 1983) is regarded as remaining resident and ordinarily resident throughout. But it is the practice, by concession, to split the year if the person:

(a) is a new permanent resident, provided that he has been not ordinarily resident in the United Kingdom; or

(b) has left the United Kingdom for permanent residence abroad, provided that he becomes not ordinarily resident in the United Kingdom; or

(c) subject to certain conditions (see paragraph 18) is taking full-time employment abroad.

Where the tax year is split in this way, the day of departure from, or arrival in, the United Kingdom falls into the period of residence and ordinary residence here.

Husband and wife

12 A wife's residence and ordinary residence status is not governed by her husband's status but is determined by her own circumstances. If, for example, a husband is employed abroad full-

Appendix I   185

time and his wife goes out to join him, but later returns to the United Kingdom without having been away for a complete tax year, she is regarded as remaining resident and ordinarily resident although he may be not resident and not ordinarily resident. If the residence status of husband and wife differ they may be treated as separate persons for tax purposes if it is to their advantage—see paragraph 83.

Leaving the United Kingdom

13 A person who has been ordinarily resident here is treated as remaining resident and ordinarily resident if he goes abroad for short periods only.

14 If a person goes abroad permanently but has accommodation (eg, a house or apartment) available for his use in the United Kingdom, he is regarded as resident here for any tax year in which he visits the United Kingdom, however short the visit may be; and he is regarded as remaining ordinarily resident if he comes here in most years. The circumstances in which accommodation is regarded as available are set out in paragraphs 28 to 30.

15 Even if a person who has taken up permanent residence abroad has no accommodation available in the United Kingdom he is regarded as continuing to be resident and ordinarily resident here if he returns here for periods which amount to an average of three months or more per tax year.

16 If a person claims that he has ceased to be resident and ordinarily resident in the United Kingdom, and can produce some evidence for this (for example that he has sold his house here and set up a permanent home abroad), his claim may be admitted provisionally with effect from the day following his departure. Normally this provisional ruling is confirmed after he has remained abroad for a period which includes a complete tax year and during which any visits to this country have not amounted to an average of three months or more a year.

17 If, however, he cannot produce sufficient evidence, a decision on his claim will be postponed for three years and will then be made by reference to what actually happened in that period. During the intervening tax years, his tax liability is computed provisionally on the basis that he remains resident in the United Kingdom. He therefore continues to receive the various income tax reliefs due to a resident of the United Kingdom (see paragraph 59), except for any tax year in which he does not set foot in the United Kingdom. His liability is adjusted, if necessary, when the final decision is made at the end of the three years.

18 If a person goes abroad for full-time service under a contract of employment and:

(a) all the duties of his employment are performed abroad or any duties he performs here are incidental to his duties abroad (see paragraphs 37 to 39); *and*

(b) his absence from the United Kingdom and the employment itself both extend over a period covering a complete tax year; *and*

(c) any interim visits to the United Kingdom during the period do not amount to

   (i) six months or more in any one tax year or

   (ii) an average of three months or more per tax year,

he is normally regarded as not resident and not ordinarily resident in the United Kingdom from the day following the date of his departure until the day preceding the date of his return. On his return he is regarded as a new permanent resident.

Coming to the United Kingdom

New permanent residents

19 A person whose home has previously been abroad and who comes to the United Kingdom to take up permanent residence here is regarded as resident and ordinarily resident from the date of his arrival.

Visitors—general

20 A person whose home is abroad and who comes to the United Kingdom only as a visitor will not be treated as resident or ordinarily resident here except in the circumstances described in the following paragraphs.

Appendix I 187

21 As mentioned in paragraph 8, a visitor who stays for six months in a tax year will always be regarded as resident here. A visitor who has accommodation available here will be regarded as resident for any year in which he comes to the United Kingdom, however short his visit may be (but see paragraphs 29 and 30 below): if he visits in four or more consecutive tax years, or intends to do so, he will be treated as ordinarily resident also. A visitor who has no accommodation available will be regarded as becoming resident and ordinarily resident after his visits for four consecutive tax years have averaged three months or more per tax year. If it is clear when he first comes that he proposes to make such visits, he may be treated as resident and ordinarily resident in the United Kingdom from the start. A person who only visits the United Kingdom occasionally will not become ordinarily resident, but he will be resident for any tax year in which his visits amount to six months or more in aggregate.

22 The general principles described above are applied in the case of all visitors to the United Kingdom. There are additional principles applicable to visitors in certain special categories, and these are set out in the following paragraphs.

Visits for education

23 A person who comes to the United Kingdom for a period of study or education which is expected to last for more than four years will be regarded as resident and ordinarily resident from the date of his arrival. If the period is not expected to exceed four years, he may be treated as not ordinarily resident, but this will depend on whether

(a) he has accommodation available here (see paragraph 28); or

(b) he intends to remain here at the end of his period of education; or

(c) he proposes to visit the United Kingdom in future years for average periods of three months or more per tax year.

If, despite the original expectation, he remains in the United Kingdom for more than four years, he will be treated in any event as ordinarily resident as from the beginning of the fifth tax year of his stay. His residence position will in any case be decided on the lines set out in paragraph 21.

24 If a parent or guardian of a child comes to the United Kingdom in connection with the child's education, the practice described in paragraph 23 is also applied to him.

Visits for temporary employment

25 A person who comes to the United Kingdom to work for a period of at least two years is treated as resident here for the whole period from the day of arrival to the day of departure. In general, any other person coming to this country for employment will not be treated as resident unless he spends six months or more here in a tax year, or unless he has accommodation available for his use (see paragraph 28). His ordinary residence status will normally follow the rules in paragraphs 26 and 27 below.

Visits for prolonged or indefinite residence

26 A person who comes to the United Kingdom, whether to work here or not, will be ordinarily resident from the date of his arrival if it is clear that he intends to remain here for three years or more. If he has no definite intention as to the length of his stay and does not have accommodation in the United Kingdom available for his use (see paragraph 27), he may be regarded as ordinarily resident from the beginning of the tax year in which the third anniversary of his arrival falls. A person who does not decide to stay here permanently until he has been here for a little while is normally regarded as ordinarily resident from the beginning of the tax year in which he takes that decision.

27 In addition it is the general practice to regard someone who comes to the United Kingdom as ordinarily resident for tax purposes;

(a) from the date of arrival if he has or acquires during the year of arrival, accommodation for his use in the United Kingdom which he occupies on a basis that implies a stay in this country of three years or more; or

(b) from the beginning of the tax year in which such accommodation becomes available.

If a person, who has been regarded as ordinarily resident solely because he has accommodation here, disposes of the accommodation and leaves the United Kingdom within 3 years of his arrival he

Appendix I 189

may be treated as not ordinarily resident for the duration of his stay if this is to his advantage.

Available accommodation

28 Where a person's residence or ordinary residence position turns on whether or not he has accommodation available for his use, the question is whether any accommodation is *in fact* available for his use. For this purpose ownership is immaterial—a person does not have to own or rent a house, apartment or other accommodation for it to be available for his use: contrariwise, a house he owns and lets out on a lease under the terms of which he has no right or permission to stay in it will be ignored. A house owned or rented by one spouse will usually be considered available for the use of the other. But any accommodation rented for use during a temporary stay here may be ignored if the period of renting is less than two years for furnished accommodation or one year for unfurnished accommodation.

29 Even if there is accommodation available for his use, it may be ignored if the person is working full-time in a business, profession or employment carried on wholly abroad. But such accommodation is *not* ignored where the person owns a business, or is a partner in a business, carried on mainly abroad but which has a branch or permanent establishment in the United Kingdom; and this is so even though he himself does not work here.

30 If a person is employed abroad and some of his duties are performed in the United Kingdom it may be possible to ignore available accommodation provided that his duties in the United Kingdom are merely incidental to his duties abroad; the circumstances in which duties are regarded as merely incidental to the main duties of the employment are outlined in paragraphs 37 to 39.

Part III Domicile

31 Domicile is a concept of general law and it is outside the scope of this booklet to do more than indicate its meaning briefly: it is not possible to list all the factors that are considered in determining whether or not a person is domiciled in a particular country.

32 Broadly speaking a person is domiciled in the country in which he has his permanent home. Domicile is distinct from nationality or residence. A person may be resident in more than one country but at any given time he can be domiciled in one only.

33 A person acquires a domicile of origin at birth: this is normally the domicile of his father and therefore not necessarily the country where he himself was born. He retains this domicile until he acquires a different domicile, either of dependency or choice. Normally the domicile of a minor (a pupil in Scotland—ie a girl under 12 or a boy under 14) follows that of the person on whom he is legally dependent. In Scotland a minor with legal capacity (ie a girl of 12 or over or a boy of 14 or over) is capable of acquiring an independent domicile; and since 1 January 1974 this legal capacity extends to the remainder of the United Kingdom as respects any person who is married or has attained 16 years of age.

34 A person with the necessary legal capacity can acquire a new domicile—a domicile of choice—at any time. To do so he must sever his ties with the country of his existing domicile and settle in another country with the clear intention of making his permanent home there. Long residence in another country is not enough in itself to prove that a person has acquired a domicile of choice there unless it can be regarded as indicating intention; there has to be evidence that he firmly intends to live there permanently.

35 Before 1974 a woman on marriage acquired the domicile of her husband. If he acquired a new domicile of choice she acquired it too. She retained this domicile not only so long as her husband was alive and she was legally married to him but also during widowhood or following divorce unless and until it was changed by the acquisition of another domicile.

As from 1 January 1974 however the domicile of a married woman is no longer necessarily the same as her husband's, but is decided by the same factors as in the case of any other individual capable of having an independent domicile; except that where immediately before 1 January 1974 a married woman had her husband's domicile by dependence she retains that domicile until it is changed by the acquisition of another domicile.

Part IV Tax on earnings from an office or employment

Basis of liability

36 Income tax on earnings from any office or employment is charged under one or more of three Cases—I, II or III—of Schedule E. The table on p 192 shows how the application of the various cases is affected by the residence status. In considering this table it should be noted that 'foreign emoluments' is the term used in the Taxes Acts to denote 'emoluments of a person not domiciled in the United Kingdom from an office or employment under or with any person, body of persons or partnership resident outside and not resident in the United Kingdom'. (This does not however include emoluments from an office or employment under or with a person, body of persons or partnership resident in the Republic of Ireland.)

Further and more detailed information, including the extent of the conditions for the special deductions mentioned in the table, is provided in the Board's pamphlet on the taxation of foreign earnings and foreign pensions (IR 25), obtainable from Inland Revenue Headquarters or from any Tax Office.

Place of performance of duties

37 The place where the duties of an office or employment are performed is a determining factor in liability to tax on the earnings. If the duties are normally performed abroad and any duties in the United Kingdom are merely incidental to the overseas duties, then the duties in the United Kingdom will be treated as though they had been performed abroad.

38 To determine whether duties in the United Kingdom are 'incidental' it is necessary to consider both the nature of the duties in the United Kingdom and their relation to the duties abroad. If the overseas representative of a United Kingdom employer comes to the United Kingdom merely to report to his employer or to receive fresh instructions, the duties so performed in the United Kingdom will usually be regarded as incidental to the duties carried out abroad. But there are many circumstances in which the duties in the United Kingdom are not incidental to the overseas duties: for instance, a company director who, though usually working abroad, attends directors' meetings in the United Kingdom; or a member of the crew of a ship or aircraft; or a courier or similar employee who visits many countries in the course of his work. Although it is primarily the nature of the duties, rather than the time spent on them, which determines whether or not they can be regarded as incidental to the overseas duties, duties performed in the United Kingdom for periods amounting to more than three months in a year are not so treated.

Scope of the liability to income tax under Schedule E*

Type of emoluments	UK residence status of employee in the year of assessment	Duties of employment performed wholly or partly in the UK		Duties of employment performed wholly outside the UK
		Emoluments for duties in the UK	Emoluments for duties outside the UK	
Foreign emoluments	Resident and ordinarily resident	Case I*	Case I*	Case III
	Resident but not ordinarily resident	Case II*	Case III	Case III
	Not resident	Case II*	No liability	No liability

*Less 25% deduction under TA 1988, s 192.

Scope of the liability to income tax under Schedule E*

Type of emoluments	UK residence status of employee in the year of assessment	Duties of employment performed wholly or partly in the UK		Duties of employment performed wholly outside the UK
		Emoluments for duties in the UK	Emoluments for duties outside the UK	
Other emoluments	Resident and ordinarily resident	Case I	Case I*	Case I*
	Resident but not ordinarily resident	Case II	Case III	Case III
	Not resident	Case II	No liability	No liability

*Less 25% deduction under TA 1988, Sched 12.

39 If an overseas employee visits the United Kingdom for periods of training which do not exceed three months in the year, such periods may be treated as incidental to his duties abroad if he does no productive work while he is here.

40 The duties of seafarers and members of aircraft crews are treated as performed in the United Kingdom if

(a) the voyage or flight does not extend to a place outside the United Kingdom; or

(b) the person concerned is resident in the United Kingdom and part of the voyage or flight begins or ends in this country.

Exemption under double taxation agreements

41 Under many double taxation agreements

(a) earnings from an employment, and

(b) profits or earnings in respect of independent personal or professional services,

performed within the United Kingdom by a person who for the purposes of the agreement is a resident of the overseas country, are, subject to certain conditions, exempt from United Kingdom tax. In the case of employments the usual conditions are that the employee should not be present in the United Kingdom for more than 183 days in the tax year, and that the employer should be neither a resident of the United Kingdom nor a foreign-owned branch business in the United Kingdom. In the case of independent personal or professional services the usual condition is that those services should not be performed from a fixed base in the United Kingdom.

42 Some double taxation agreements also provide that a professor or teacher who comes to the United Kingdom for a period of not more than two years to teach at a university, college, school or other educational institution is exempt from United Kingdom tax on his earnings from the teaching post. Temporary absences from the United Kingdom during this period are treated as part of the period. If the professor or teacher stays in the United Kingdom for longer than two years he is not entitled to exemption and is liable to tax on the whole of the earnings. Under some agreements exemption is conditional on the earnings being taxed in the home country.

Appendix I 195

43 Most agreements provide that a student or business apprentice from the overseas country who is visiting the United Kingdom solely to receive full-time education or training in the United Kingdom is exempt from United Kingdom tax on payments made to him from sources outside the United Kingdom for his maintenance, education and training.

Special classes of employees

44 The information in this booklet needs to be supplemented for the following special groups of people who are employed overseas:

(a) Those in the service of the Crown. They should write to the Inland Revenue Head Office (Public Departments), Foreign Section stating their precise circumstances and the information required in the light of these circumstances.

(b) Those ordinarily employed in this country but absent for a period from their employment (eg on leave). They should write to the Inspector of Taxes who normally deals with their tax affairs.

(c) Those working for the European Communities. They should write to the Inland Revenue Claims Branch, Foreign Division.

Part V Tax on income other than earnings

Income from sources within the United Kingdom

45 In general a person is liable to United Kingdom tax on income from sources within the United Kingdom whether or not he is resident here.

However:

(a) interest on a number of United Kingdom Government securities is not liable to United Kingdom income tax if the person who is the beneficial owner is not ordinarily resident in the United Kingdom, except where the interest forms part of the profits of a trade or business carried on in the United Kingdom or where the income is deemed under provisions for the prevention of tax avoidance to be that of some other person. A current list of such securities will be supplied on request by the Inspector of Foreign Dividends.

(b) by concession, where for any year of assessment, for the whole of which he is regarded as being not resident in the United Kingdom a person receives interest (eg Bank Interest) without deduction of income tax and is not chargeable in the name of an agent under S78 TMA 1970, or has not a branch in this country which has the management or control of the interest, no action is taken to pursue his liability to income tax except so far as it can be recovered by set off in a claim to relief (eg under S27 ICTA 1970) in respect of taxed income from United Kingdom sources.

Income arising outside the United Kingdom

46 A person is liable to United Kingdom tax on income from sources abroad only if he is resident in the United Kingdom. Normally the full amount of the overseas income arising to him is chargeable (after allowance of certain deductions where the source is an overseas pension or a trade, profession or vocation carried on wholly abroad: see the Board's pamphlet IR 25). Where, however, a person is resident but not domiciled in the United Kingdom, or a British subject or citizen of the Republic of Ireland resident but not ordinarily resident here, he is normally chargeable to tax in respect of income from abroad only on amounts remitted here whatever its nature. This remittance basis does not apply to income arising in the Republic of Ireland. Where the remittance basis applies, the deductions in respect of pension or trade etc income referred to above are not given. In determining the amounts of income remitted, income is regarded as remitted to the United Kingdom if it is paid here or is transmitted or brought to the United Kingdom in any way.

47 Special rules apply in respect of foreign dividends and interest paid through a paying agent in the United Kingdom, or obtained overseas by a banker or other United Kingdom agent. Such income is charged to tax on the paying or collecting agent and he recoups that tax by deducting an equivalent amount when he pays over the income. If the person entitled to the income is not resident in the United Kingdom he can reclaim the tax deducted (or in some circumstances arrange for the paying or collecting agent to pay the income over without deducting tax).

48 Where income from overseas sources is not received after deduction of tax (see paragraph 47), the amount to be assessed for any tax year is generally the amount arising or remitted (as is appropriate) in the *previous* tax year; but in certain circumstances the liability may be based on the amount arising or remitted in the tax year concerned.

Part VI   Capital gains tax

49   The Board of Inland Revenue have issued a booklet, CGT 8, on capital gains tax and reference should be made to that booklet for detailed information. Copies may be obtained from Inland Revenue Headquarters or from any Tax Office in the United Kingdom.

50   Put shortly, the tax applies to gains arising from the disposal of assets after 6 April 1965 whenever those assets were acquired. For assets owned on 6 April 1965, only the proportion of the gain attributable to the period since that date is chargeable. Gains are charged to the tax if they arise to a person who is resident or ordinarily resident in the United Kingdom wherever the assets concerned were situated. A person not resident and not ordinarily resident in the United Kingdom who carries on a trade through a branch or agency here is chargeable to the tax in respect of any gains on the disposal of assets in the United Kingdom which were used for the purpose of his trade or the branch or agency.

51   Capital gains tax for any tax year is normally assessed on the gains arising in the year. If however the assets are situated outside the United Kingdom and the person concerned is resident or ordinarily resident but not domiciled here he will be taxed on the gains remitted to the United Kingdom in the year. Gains are regarded as remitted to the United Kingdom if they are paid or used or enjoyed here or are transmitted or brought to the United Kingdom in any way.

52   Gains on United Kingdom Government securities and certain United Kingdom Government guaranteed securities disposed of after 15 April 1969 are exempted from capital gains tax provided that they are held for at least twelve months. The securities concerned are listed in booklet CGT 8. In addition the exemption from United Kingdom income tax in respect of certain United Kingdom Government securities (see paragraph 45(a)) extends also to capital gains tax on those securities if the beneficial owner is neither domiciled nor ordinarily resident in the United Kingdom, and in this case exemption is granted regardless of how long the securities have been held.

Part VII   Relief and exemption under double taxation agreements

Persons not resident in the United Kingdom

53   A person who is a resident of a country with which the United Kingdom has a double taxation agreement may be entitled to exemption or partial relief from United Kingdom income tax on certain kinds of income from United Kingdom sources and may also be exempt from United Kingdom tax on the disposal of assets. The conditions of exemption or relief vary from agreement to agreement and it is not possible to set them out in detail here. **Reference should therefore be made to the relevant agreement.** However, the agreements normally provide a measure of relief from United Kingdom tax on pensions (other than United Kingdom Government pensions), purchased annuities, alimony, maintenance payments, royalties, dividends (but see paragraph 56) and, in some cases, interest. In some agreements it is a condition of the relief that the income is subject to tax in the other country.

54   A pension in respect of governmental service paid by the Government of one country to a person resident in the other is usually to be taxed only by the paying Government.

55   Relief in respect of royalties, interest or dividends may not be due where the person is engaged in any trade or business through a permanent establishment in the United Kingdom.

56   Although a company resident in the United Kingdom does not deduct income tax from the dividends it pays, a resident shareholder is entitled to a tax credit in respect of any dividends he receives. He is liable to income tax on the sum of his dividends and the corresponding tax credit. He is able to use the tax credit to meet his liability, in full or in part, or if it exceeds his liability the balance will be paid to him. A non-resident shareholder is not normally entitled to a tax credit in respect of the dividends he receives, nor is he liable to United Kingdom income tax at the basic rate on those dividends. However, under some of the United Kingdom's more recent double taxation agreements many non-resident shareholders will be entitled to a tax credit in respect of dividends from United

Kingdom companies; where they are so entitled, they are liable to United Kingdom income tax on the sum of their dividends and the corresponding tax credit, in the same way as resident shareholders, at whatever rate of tax is laid down in the agreement. Those non-residents who are entitled to and claim the relief indicated in paragraphs 59–61 will also be entitled to a tax credit in respect of any dividends they receive from United Kingdom companies, in which case their tax credit will be taken into account as part of their United Kingdom income.

57 Detailed information about double taxation agreements can be found in the Board's booklet on Double Taxation Relief (IR 6) obtainable from the Inland Revenue Headquarters, from the Inspector of Foreign Dividends or from the office of any Inspector of Taxes. A list of the agreements at present in force is given in the Annex hereto.

Persons resident in the United Kingdom

58 Where income or gains are taxed in both the United Kingdom and the country of origin, relief may be allowable in the United Kingdom in respect of part or all of the overseas tax whether the United Kingdom has a double taxation agreement with that country or not. More information on this subject may be obtained from the Board's booklet on Double Taxation Relief (see paragraph 57).

Part VIII Personal allowances

59 A person who is resident in the United Kingdom is entitled to certain personal reliefs and allowances, based on personal and family circumstances. A person who is not resident and who is a British subject or who satisfies certain other requirements (see paragraph 60) may also claim a measure of relief. If he makes such a claim he will also be entitled to a tax credit in respect of any dividends he receives from United Kingdom companies (see paragraph 56). A similar claim may be made by residents or nationals of many of the countries with which the United Kingdom has concluded a double taxation agreement whether or not such persons will be entitled to a tax credit in respect of dividends will depend on the terms of the agreement. As regards the personal allowances and reliefs of married women see paragraphs 81 to 83.

60 To qualify for this relief a person resident abroad must show that he or she:

(a) is a British subject or a citizen of the Republic of Ireland; or

(b) is or has been employed in the service of the British Crown; or

(c) is employed in the service of a missionary society; or

(d) is employed in the service of any territory under the protection of Her Majesty; or

(e) is resident in the Isle of Man or the Channel Islands; or

(f) has previously resided within the United Kingdom and is resident abroad for the sake of his or her health, or the health of a member of his or her family resident with him or her; or

(g) is a widow whose husband was employed in the service of the British Crown; or

(h) is a resident of and/or a national of a country with which there is a double taxation agreement providing for such reliefs.

61 Where a claim for relief by a non-resident under the preceding paragraphs is to his advantage, it is given by:

(a) first calculating the tax that would be payable if the claimant's total income were chargeable to United Kingdom tax and if he were granted those personal allowances to which he would be entitled if he were resident in the United Kingdom, and then

(b) restricting the tax which otherwise would be payable by him to the proportion of the tax ascertained as in (a) which his liable income (ie that part of his total income which is liable to United Kingdom income tax) bears to his total income. However, the tax payable cannot be reduced below the amount which would be payable on the liable income were it the sole income of a United Kingdom resident.

'Total income' means total income from all sources including wife's income and interest on those United Kingdom government securities referred to in paragraph 45(a), whether liable to United Kingdom income tax or not. It also includes any tax credit to which he and/or his wife may be entitled in respect of dividends paid by United Kingdom companies. If United Kingdom tax has already been paid on the liable income, any excess over the tax payable as in (b) is refunded.

Appendix I 201

Part IX New permanent residents in the United Kingdom: special provisions

United Kingdom government securities

62 Interest on those United Kingdom government securities referred to in paragraph 45(a) will be liable to tax from the date on which ordinary residence in this country begins—that is, the date of arrival for permanent residence (see paragraph 19).

Gains on the disposal of assets

63 If the person has not been resident or ordinarily resident in the United Kingdom at any time in the preceding thirty-six months, gains are charged to tax (see paragrahs 49 to 52) only in so far as they are made on the disposal of assets on or after the date of arrival for permanent residence.

Earnings from an employment wholly abroad

64 Earnings from an employment wholly abroad for a tax year in which a person is not resident in the United Kingdom are not liable to United Kingdom tax. In the year in which permanent residence begins, earnings for the part of the year before arrival are not charged.

65 The taxation of earnings from employment abroad after permanent residence begins is governed by the rules explained in the Board's pamphlet IR 25.

Lump sums from Provident Funds, etc

66 Income tax is not charged on lump sums relating to service overseas and receivable by employees from Provident Funds (or under arrangements analogous to those of such a Fund) on termination of employment overseas.

Other income arising abroad

67 The normal basis of liability to tax on income, other than earnings, arising abroad is outlined in paragraphs 46 to 48. Investment income receivable under deduction of tax from a paying or collecting agent is liable to tax from the date of arrival for permanent residence.

68 Where the income is not received under deduction of tax and the liability is on the income arising, the normal basis of liability is modified as follows:

(a) No liability will arise in respect of a source which ceases before the date on which permanent residence begins.

(b) If the source ceases in the tax year in which permanent residence begins the charge to tax will be on the amount arising from the date of arrival for permanent residence to the date of cessation of the source.

(c) If the source is continuing, and the income first arose either in the tax year of arrival but before permanent residence began, or in the previous year, the charge will be on the proportion of the full amount of the income of the tax year of arrival which the period from the date of arrival to the following 5 April bears to a complete year.

Example

A person takes up permanent residence in the United Kingdom on 6 August 1982 and his investment income for the whole year (ending 5 April 1983) from an overseas source is £1,000. The income first arose on 1 January 1982. The period 6 August 1982 to 5 April 1983 amounts to 8 months, and the person is chargeable to United Kingdom tax for the tax year 1982/83 (year ending 5 April 1983) on £1,000 × $^{8}/_{12}$ = £666.

(d) If the source is continuing and the income first arose in some earlier year, then the charge is calculated in the same way as in (c) above, but by reference to the income of the year preceding the year of arrival.

Example

The investment income of the person described in (c) above first arose in 1970, and the income for the year ended 5 April 1982 was £1,600. The person will be chargeable on £1,600 × $^{8}/_{12}$ ie £1,066 for the year 1982/83.

(e) Where the income is from a trade, profession, vocation or pension the deductions referred to in paragraph 46 are equally applicable for this purpose.

69 Where the income is not received after deduction of tax and the 'remittance basis' applies (see paragraph 46) the normal basis of liability is modified as follows:

(a) If the source of the income ceases before permanent residence begins, there is no liability to tax in respect of remittances of income from that source.

(b) If the source ceases after the recipient takes up permanent residence in the United Kingdom but in the same tax year, the charge to tax will be on the lesser of:

   (i) the total remittances to the United Kingdom in the year, and

   (ii) the amount of income arising for the period from the date of arrival in this country to the date of cessation of the source.

(c) If the source ceases in the tax year following the year of arrival for permanent residence, there may be a charge to tax for both years. For the tax year of arrival the charge will be on:

   (i) the remittances to the United Kingdom in that year, or in certain circumstances, the preceding year; or

   (ii) if less than (i) the proportion of the full amount of the income of the tax year of arrival (or in certain circumstances the preceding year) which the period from the date of arrival to the following 5 April bears to a complete year.

For the year following the tax year of arrival the charge will be on the remittances in that year reduced if necessary so that the sum charged to tax for the two years does not exceed the total of (a) an amount computed in accordance with paragraph (c)(ii) for the tax year of arrival, and (b) the amount of the income arising from 6 April in the following year to the date of cessation of the source.

Personal allowances and reliefs

70 For the year of arrival for permanent residence in the United Kingdom full personal allowances and reliefs are granted.

Part X Persons leaving the United Kingdom for permanent residence abroad: special provisions

United Kingdom government securities

71 Interest on those United Kingdom government securities referred to in paragraph 45(a) is exempt from tax if it is payable after the date on which ordinary residence in this country ceases—that is, after the date of departure for permanent residence abroad (see paragraph 11).

Other United Kingdom investment income

72 In general, all other United Kingdom investment income remains liable to United Kingdom tax but relief or exemption may be due under a double taxation agreement (see paragraphs 53 to 57).

Income from property in the United Kingdom

73 Profits from lettings of property in the United Kingdom remain liable to United Kingdom tax. Further information can be found in the Board's booklet on taxation of income from real property (IR 27), obtainable from the Inland Revenue Headquarters or from any Tax Office in the United Kingdom.

Gains on the disposal of assets

74 In the year of a person's departure for permanent residence abroad tax is not charged on gains (see paragraphs 49 et seq) which accrue to him on the disposal of assets after the date on which ordinary residence ceases—that is, after the date of departure (see paragraph 11).

Earnings from an office or employment

75 The liability on the earnings from an office or employment is explained in the Board's pamphlet IR 25.

Other income arising abroad

76 The normal basis of liability to tax on income, other than earnings, arising abroad is outlined in paragraphs 46 to 48. A person who takes up permanent residence abroad is not liable on such income received through a paying or collecting agent after the date of departure, and any tax deducted can be reclaimed. For all other income where the liability is on the income arising the liability for the year of departure is based on the smaller of:

(a) the proportion of the full amount of the income of the year of departure (or of the income of the preceding year, if that is the basis of assessment) which the period from 6 April to the date of departure bears to a complete tax year; and

(b) the actual income arising for the period 6 April to the date of departure.

The deductions mentioned in paragraph 46 are applicable to income from trades, professions, vocations and pensions as appropriate.

77 Where the 'remittance basis' applies (see paragraph 46) the tax liability of a person who takes up permanent residence abroad is restricted for the tax year of departure to the smaller of the following amounts:

(a) the proportion of the remittances to the United Kingdom in the year of departure (or of the remittances in the preceding year if that is the basis of assessment) which the period from 6 April to the date of departure bears to a complete tax year; and

(b) the actual amount of the remittances to the United Kingdom in the period from 6 April to the date of departure for permanent residence abroad.

Personal allowances and reliefs

78 For the year of departure for permanent residence abroad full personal allowances and reliefs are granted.

Part XI   Claims to relief

General

79 In general, claims to relief from United Kingdom tax must be made within six years after the end of the year of assessment to which they relate.

Claims to personal allowances and reliefs

80 A claim to personal allowances and reliefs by a person resident in the United Kingdom should be submitted to the Inspector of Taxes responsible for the assessment of his earned income or for the district in which he resides.

Claims by persons resident abroad to the relief indicated in paragraphs 59 to 61 should be submitted to the Inland Revenue Claims Branch, Foreign Division.

Married women

81 Whether the income of a married woman is chargeable to income tax depends on her own residence status and domicile (see paragraphs 12 and 35). Income so chargeable of a married woman who is living with her husband (see paragraphs 82 and 83) is generally deemed to be income of her husband but this does not apply—except where the marriage takes place on 6 April—for the year in which they marry or in which they are reconciled after a period of being treated as separated for tax purposes. In addition if both husband and wife ask for such treatment, the wife's United Kingdom earnings may be taxed as if she were a single person with no other income. In either case, however, the wife's income should be included in her husband's return of income.

82 A wife is treated as living with her husband unless:

(a) they are separated under an Order of a Court or by a Deed of Separation; or

(b) they are in fact separated in such circumstances that the separation is likely to be permanent.

83 If for a tax year a married woman is living with her husband but one of them is resident in the United Kingdom either for part or the whole of the year and the other is not resident for the year, they are regarded for income tax purposes as if they were permanently separated, and entitled to make separate claims, if it is to their advantage.

Other claims

84 Claims to relief from United Kingdom income tax by a person who is not resident or not ordinarily resident in the United Kingdom in respect of:

(a) income arising from sources outside the United Kingdom,

(b) interest on the United Kingdom government securities referred to in paragraph 45(a), or

(c) income from United Kingdom sources covered by double taxation agreements (see paragraphs 53 to 57),

should be made to the Inspector of Foreign Dividends. In certain circumstances arrangements can be made for relief to be given at the time when the income is paid.

85 Where however any income of the nature described in paragraph 84 is included in a claim made to the Claims Branch, Foreign Division under paragraph 80, the repayment of United Kingdom income tax will normally be made in one sum. In certain circumstances, however, a separate claim must be made to the Inspector of Foreign Dividends in respect of items within (c) of paragraph 84; where this is necessary the claimant will be so advised.

86 A married woman living with her husband is entitled to claim the repayment referred to in paragraph 84 in her own name, but if her husband submits a claim under paragraph 80 to the Claims Branch Foreign Division, she does not need to lodge a separate claim except where necessary in respect of items within (c) of paragraph 84.

Part XII Appeals

87 In the great majority of cases, a person's residence, ordinary residence or domicile can be established, and any claim which he may make for relief from United Kingdom tax can be settled, by agreement between the person concerned (or his agents) and the Inland Revenue. If agreement cannot be reached, the law provides for the matter to be considered by an independent tribunal.

88 The procedure is, in general, for a formal decision in the case to be given by the Inland Revenue and for the person concerned to give notice of appeal against that decision. The law specifies the period within which the notice must be given; this period varies according to the issue which is in dispute. The appeal is heard by one of two bodies—either the General Commissioners or the Special Commissioners. In some cases the law directs which Commissioners shall hear the appeal but in others the person concerned may choose. If a formal decision is given, the Inland Revenue state the time within which any appeal must be made, and which Commissioners may hear the appeal.

89 Both the General Commissioners and Special Commissioners are independent of the Inland Revenue. The decision of either body of Commissioners on a question of fact is final, but an appeal against their decision may be made to the High Court on a question of law.

Appendix II Tax tables

Income tax rates for 1988–89 and the previous five years

For 1983–84:

Slice of income	Rate	Total income (after allowances)	Total tax
£14,600 (£0–14,600)	30%	£14,600	£4,830
2,600 (14,601–17,200)	40%	17,200	5,420
4,600 (17,201–21,800)	45%	21,800	7,490
7,100 (21,801–28,900)	50%	28,900	11,040
7,100 (28,901–36,000)	55%	36,000	14,945
Remainder	60%		

For 1984–85:

Slice of income	Rate	Total income (after allowances)	Total tax
£15,400 (0–15,400)	30%	£15,400	£4,620
2,800 (15,401–18,200)	40%	18,200	5,740
4,900 (18,201–23,100)	45%	23,100	7,945
7,500 (23,101–30,600)	50%	30,600	11,695
7,500 (30,601–38,100)	55%	38,100	15,820
Remainder	60%		

For 1985–86:

Slice of income	Rate	Total income (after allowances)	Total tax
£16,200 (0–16,200)	30%	£16,200	£4,860
3,000 (16,201–19,200)	40%	19,200	6,060
5,200 (19,201–24,400)	45%	24,400	8,400
7,900 (24,401–32,300)	50%	32,300	12,350
7,900 (32,301–40,200)	55%	40,200	16,695
Remainder	60%		

For 1986–87:

Slice of income	Rate	Total income (after allowances)	Total tax
£17,200 (0–17,200)	29%	£17,200	£4,988
3.000 (17,201–20,200)	40%	20,200	6,188
5,200 (20,201–25,400)	45%	25,400	8,528
7,900 (25,401–33,300)	50%	33,300	12,478
7,900 (33,301–41,200)	55%	41,200	16,823
Remainder	60%		

For 1987–88:

Slice of income	Rate	Total income (after allowances)	Total tax
£17,900 (0–17,900)	27%	£17,900	£4,833
2,500 (17,901–20,400)	40%	20,400	5,833
5,000 (20,401–25,400)	45%	25,400	8,083
7,900 (25,401–33,300)	50%	33,300	12,033
7,900 (33,301–41,200)	55%	41,200	16,378
Remainder	60%		

For 1988–89:

Slice of income	Rate	Total income (after allowances)	Total tax
First £19,300	25%	£19,300	£4,825
Remainder	40%		

Income tax basic rates and allowances for 1988–89 and the previous five years

	1983– 84	1984– 85	1985– 86	1986– 87	1987– 88	1988– 89
Income tax basic rate	30%	30%	30%	29%	27%	25%
Additional rate on certain trusts*	15%	15%	15%	16%	18%	10%
Single personal allowance (£)	1,785	2,005	2,205	2,335	2,425	2,605
Married personal allowance (£)	2,795	3,155	3,455	3,655	3,795	4,095
Wife's earned income allowance (max) (£)	1,785	2,005	2,205	2,335	2,425	2,605
Dependent relative relief (£) Female claimant	145	145	145	145	145	nil
Other	100	100	100	100	100	nil

* and investment income of individuals 1983/84

Appendix III Extra-statutory concessions and Revenue statements (IR1-1985)

The concessions described are of general application, but it must be borne in mind that in a particular case there may be special circumstances which will require to be taken into account in considering the application of the concession. A concession will not be given in any case where an attempt is made to use it for tax avoidance.

A. Individuals (income tax)

A10 Overseas provident fund balances

Income tax is not charged on lump sums referable to service overseas and receivable by employees from overseas provident funds (or under arrangements analogous to those of such a fund) on termination of employment overseas.

A11 Residence in the UK: year of commencement or cessation of residence

The Income and Corporation Taxes Acts make no provision for splitting a tax year in relation to residence and an individual who is resident in the United Kingdom for any year of assessment is chargeable on the basis that he is resident for the whole year.

But where an individual

- comes to the United Kingdom to take up permanent residence or to stay for at least three years; or
- comes to the United Kingdom to take up employment which is expected to last for a period of at least two years; or
- ceases to reside in the United Kingdom if he has left for permanent residence abroad,

liability to United Kingdom tax which is affected by residence is computed by reference to the period of his residence here during the year. It is a condition that the individual should satisfy the Board of Inland Revenue that prior to his arrival he was, or on his departure is, not ordinarily resident in the United Kingdom. The concession would not apply, for example, where an individual who had been ordinarily resident in the United Kingdom left for intended permanent residence abroad but returned to reside here before the end of the tax year following the tax year of departure.

The concession has only limited application to changes of permanent residence between the United Kingdom and the Irish Republic and to income arising in the Irish Republic.

A12 Double taxation relief: alimony, etc under UK court order or agreement: payer resident abroad

Where alimony or maintenance payments are paid under a United Kingdom court order or agreement, the income arises from a United Kingdom source regardless of the country of residence of the payer. Notwithstanding that the source is in law a United Kingdom source, relief by way of credit is, however, allowed where:

- the individual making the payments has left the United Kingdom and becomes resident in an overseas country;
- the payments are made out of that individual's income in that country and are subject to tax there;
- United Kingdom income tax if deducted from the payments is duly accounted for; and
- the payee is resident in the United Kingdom and effectively bears the overseas tax.

A24 Foreign social security benefits

United Kingdom residents are normally liable to United Kingdom income tax in respect of social security payments made to them by foreign governments. Payments made by foreign governments which correspond to those United Kingdom Government social security benefits for which exemption from income tax is provided under TA 1970, s 219(1) [TA 1988, s 617(1)] are, however, treated as exempt (for the tax years 1974–75 and subsequent years, so long as the corresponding exemption under s 219 [s 617] subsists). Similarly, payments made by foreign governments which correspond to United Kingdom Government child benefit for which exemption from income tax is provided under TA 1970, s 219(2) [TA 1988, s 617(2)] are treated as exempt with effect from 4 April 1977 for so long as the corresponding exemption under s 219 [s 617] subsists.

A25 Crown Servants engaged overseas

TA 1970, s 184(3) [TA 1988, s 132(4)] provides for the duties of an office or employment under the Crown, which is of a public nature and the emoluments of which are payable out of public revenue, to be treated as performed in the United Kingdom. The effect of this rule is that the emoluments of the office or employment are chargeable to United Kingdom tax irrespective of where the duties are actually performed or of the residence status of the person concerned.

In practice however United Kingdom tax is not charged in the case of locally engaged (as distinct from United Kingdom based), unestablished staff working abroad who are not resident in the United Kingdom, if the maximum rate of pay for their grade is less than that of an executive officer in the United Kingdom Civil Service working in Inner London.

A27 Mortgage interest relief: temporary absence from mortgaged property

Under the provisions of FA 1974, Sched 1, para 4, [TA 1988, s 355] tax relief for interest paid on a mortgage taken out after 26 March 1974 is given where the loan is applied for the purchase or improvement of a property which at the time the interest is paid is used as the only or main residence of the borrower, his divorced or separated spouse or a dependent relative. Relief is also allowed where the property is let at a commercial rent but only against the owner's income from letting.

Temporary absences of up to a year are in practice ignored in determining whether a property is used as an only or main residence. In addition where a person is required by reason of his employment to move from his home to another place, either in the United Kingdom or abroad for a period not expected to exceed four years, any property being purchased with the aid of a mortgage which was being used as his only or main residence before he went away, will still be treated as his only or main residence, provided it can reasonably be expected to be so used again on his return. Where a person has acquired an estate or interest in a property, for example by exchange of contracts, but is prevented by his move from occupying it as his home, he will nevertheless be regarded as having used the property as his home for the purposes of the concession. Relief will not be given beyond a period of four years but if there is a further temporary absence after the property has been reoccupied for a minimum period of three months the four year test will apply to the new absence without regard to the previous absence.

If an individual already on an overseas tour of duty purchases a property in the United Kingdom in the course of a leave period and uses that property as an only or main residence for a period of not less than three months before his return to the place of his overseas employment he will be regarded as satisfying the condition that the property was being used as his only or main residence before he went away.

If an individual lets his property whilst he is away at a commercial rent the benefit of the concession may be claimed, where appropriate if this is more favourable than a claim for relief against letting income.

A28 Mortgage interest relief: residents of the Republic of Ireland

Relief will be allowed from United Kingdom income tax to a resident of the Republic of Ireland for interest paid on a loan from an Irish Building Society or other lender in the Republic of Ireland, provided all the other requirements of the United Kingdom legislation on the allowance of interest on loans are met. These requirements are contained in FA 1972, s 75, Sched 9, as amended by FA 1974, s 19, Sched 1, and FA 1977, s 36 [TA 1988, ss 353–358].

A39 Exemption for Hong Kong officials: extension of TA 1970, s 372 [TA 1988, s 320] relief

Income tax is not charged on the salaries of certain Hong Kong officials who work in the United Kingdom. The relief corresponds to that provided for official agents for Commonwealth countries or self-governing colonies by TA 1970, s 372(2) [TA 1988, s 320(2), (3)].

The officials concerned are employees of the Hong Kong Government who would otherwise be liable to tax here because

- they have been posted to London, but only those who are based in and who will return to Hong Kong, eg those working at the

Hong Kong Government Office (and not including staff who work at the Hong Kong Trade Development Council), or

- they have undergone courses of training or study leave in the United Kingdom.

A55 Arrears of foreign pensions

When a foreign pension or increase thereof is granted retrospectively and that pension is chargeable to tax under Case V of Schedule D on the arising basis, the full amount of the award, including arrears, is assessable in one sum. But where it is to the advantage of the taxpayer, the tax on the pension is calculated as if the arrears (after making the appropriate deduction due under FA 1974, s 22 [TA 1988, s 65(2)]) arose in the years to which they relate.

B. Individuals and companies (income tax and corporation tax)

B13 Untaxed interest paid to non-residents

Where for any year of assessment for the whole of which he is regarded as being not resident in the UK, a person receives interest (eg bank or *building society* interest) without deduction of income tax and is not chargeable under TMA 1970, s 78, in the name of *a trustee etc mentioned in TMA 1970, s 72, or in the name of an agent or branch having management or control of the interest*, no action is taken to pursue his liability to income tax except so far as it can be recovered by set-off in a claim to relief (eg under TA 1988, s 278) in respect of taxed income from UK sources. This concession does not apply to the corporation tax chargeable on the income of the UK branch or agency of a non-resident company *or to income tax which is chargeable on the profits of a trade carried on in the UK. This concession also applies to discount, to profits on disposal of certificates of deposit, to dividends paid gross by a building society and to payments representing interest in respect of a general client account within the meaning of TA 1988, s 482(6).*

B22 Close companies: non-resident participators: apportionment

1. Where a close company, 90% or more of the ordinary share capital of which is beneficially owned by non-residents, wishes to

retain its surplus funds in this country, a request that the company should not be liable to apportionment of its income will be favourably considered.

2. A non-resident whose dividend income from United Kingdom resident companies is effectively relieved from United Kingdom tax at the higher rates under a double taxation agreement is normally exempted from the United Kingdom income tax charge on any close company income apportioned to him.

B24 Postponement of capital allowances to secure double taxation relief

TA 1970, s 515 as amended by FA 1971, s 54(1) [TA 1988, s 810] enables a person chargeable to tax in respect of a trade, profession or vocation and who is liable to overseas tax on the income to claim a postponement of all or part of certain capital allowances in order to secure double taxation relief where that relief would otherwise be restricted because of a difference in the basis on which depreciation allowances are given in each country. The Section applies to persons chargeable under Schedule D, Case I or II but by concession claims are accepted where the trade, etc is carried on wholly abroad and therefore within Schedule D, Case V.

B25 Schedule D Case V losses

Apart from TA 1970, s 177(1) [TA 1988, s 393] and FA 1974, s 23(2) [TA 1988, s 391] (trading losses), there is no statutory authority for relief of Schedule D Case V losses. By concession, deficiencies of income from lettings of overseas property, including caravans and houseboats, may be carried forward for set-off against future income from the same property.

D. Capital gains (individuals and companies)

D2 Residence in the United Kingdom: year of commencement or cessation of residence

A person who is treated as resident in the United Kingdom for any year of assessment from the date of his arrival here but who has not been regarded at any time during the period of 36 months immediately preceding the date of his arrival as resident or ordinarily resident here, is charged to capital gains tax only in respect of the chargeable gains accruing to him from disposals made after his arrival in the United Kingdom. When a person leaves the United Kingdom and is treated on his departure as not resident and not ordinarily resident in the United Kingdom he is not charged to capital gains tax on gains accruing to him from disposals made after the date of his departure.

This concession applies to changes of permanent residence between the United Kingdom and the Irish Republic for years ended 5 April 1976 and earlier notwithstanding that in such cases the person is treated as resident for the whole of the year of assessment in which the change takes place. *This concession does not apply to trustees of a settlement who commence or cease residence in the United Kingdom after 10 March 1981.* With effect from 1988–89 this concession does not extend to a settlor who commences or ceases residence during the year in relation to gains of a settlement to which FA 1984, s 109 and Sched 10 (now FA 1988) apply.

F. Concessions relating to inheritance tax

F6 Foreign assets

Where, because of restrictions imposed by the foreign government, executors cannot immediately transfer to this country sufficient of the deceased's foreign assets for the payment of the [IHT] attributable to them, they are given the option of deferring payment until the transfer can be effected. If the amount in sterling that the executors finally succeed in bringing to this country is less than this tax, the balance is waived.

F7 Foreign owned works of art

Where a work of art normally kept overseas becomes liable to [IHT] on the owner's death solely because it is physically situated in the United Kingdom at the relevant date, the liability will—by concession—be waived if the work was brought into the United Kingdom solely for public exhibition, cleaning or restoration. If the work of art is held by a discretionary trust (or is otherwise comprised in settled property in which there is no interest in possession), the charge to tax arising under IHTA 1984, s 64, will, similarly, be waived.

Income Tax: Reliefs for non-residents. Treatment of wife's income (SP 7/85)
[Relevant until 1989–90 only]

Introduction

1 This statement explains how the Board propose to deal with the tax liabilities of those non-residents affected by the High Court decision in *IRC* v *Addison* ([1984] STC 540).

Background

2 An individual who is resident in the UK is entitled, in computing his liability to UK income tax, to claim certain personal allowances and reliefs under TA 1970, Part I, Ch II [TA 1988, Part VI, Ch.I]. A person who is not resident and who is a British subject or satisfies certain other requirements may also claim a measure of relief. The amount of relief due is governed by TA 1970, s 27(2) [TA 1988, s 278(2)]. This gives a non-resident who satisfies the necessary requirements the benefit of the personal allowances and reliefs to which he would be entitled if he were resident in the UK, except that the relief due cannot reduce the tax payable by the individual to less than a specified amount. This amount is given by the formula—

$$\frac{A}{B} \times T$$

where A = the amount of the individuals's income subject to income tax charged in the UK;

B = the amount of his total income from all sources; and

T = the amount of tax which would be payable by the individual if UK income tax were chargeable on his total income from all sources.

The expression 'total income from all sources' includes income which is not subject to UK income tax.

3 For a married couple, TA 1970, s 37 [TA 1988, s 279] aggregates a wife's income with her husband's for tax purposes. In accordance with the Revenue's understanding of this provision the Department's practice, in calculating the liability of a married man under s 27(2) [TA 1988, s 278(2)], has been to include any income of his wife whether or not it was subject to UK income tax. In *IRC* v *Addison*, however, the High Court decided that the income of a wife which was *not* chargeable to UK tax was not to be aggregated with her husband's income under TA 1970, s 37 [TA 1988, s 279]

and should not be brought into the calculation of the relief due to him under TA 1970, s 27(2) [TA 1988, s 278(2)].

Effect of decision in *IRC* v *Addison*

4 The High Court judgment in *IRC* v *Addison* is now final and the Revenue have amended their practice in accordance with the decision of the Court. In calculating the amount of UK income tax payable by a non-resident who qualifies for relief under s 27(2) [TA 1988, s 278(2)] any relief due to a married man will be determined on a basis which excludes from the taxpayer's total income any income of his wife which is not chargeable to UK income tax. Any income of the wife which is chargeable to UK tax will continue to be aggregated with her husband's income for the purposes of s 27(2) [TA 1988, s 278(2)] in accordance with TA 1970, s 37 [TA 1988, s 279]. Claims for relief which were open at the date of the High Court decision (13 July 1984) have been settled on this basis.

Appendix IV Text of the 1977 OECD Model Agreement

Chapter I Scope of the Convention

Article 1 Personal scope

This Convention shall apply to persons who are residents of one or both of the Contracting States.

Article 2 Taxes covered

1 This Convention shall apply to taxes on income and on capital imposed on behalf of a Contracting State or of its political subdivisions or local authorities, irrespective of the manner in which they are levied.

2 There shall be regarded as taxes on income and on capital all taxes imposed on total income, on total capital, or on elements of income or of capital, including taxes on gains from the alienation of movable or immovable property, taxes on the total amounts of wages or salaries paid by enterprises, as well as taxes on capital appreciation.

3 The existing taxes on which the Convention shall apply are in particular:

(*a*) (in State A) ....
(*b*) (in state B) ....

4 The Convention shall apply also to any identical or substantially similar taxes which are imposed after the date of signature of the Convention in addition to, or in place of, the existing taxes. At the end of each year, the competent authorities of the Contracting States shall notify each other of changes which have been made in their respective taxation laws.

Chapter II Definitions

Article 3 General definitions

1   For the purposes of this Convention, unless the context otherwise requires:

(*a*)   the term "person" includes[1] an individual, a company and any other body of persons;
(*b*)   the term "company" means any body corporate or any entity which is treated as a body corporate for tax purposes;
(*c*)   the terms "enterprise of a Contracting State" and "enterprise of the other Contracting State" mean respectively an enterprise carried on by a resident of a Contracting State and an enterprise carried on by a resident of the other Contracting State;
(*d*)   the term "international traffic" means any transport by a ship or aircraft operated by an enterprise which has its place of effective management in a Contracting State, except when the ship or aircraft is operated solely between places in the other Contracting State;
(*e*)   the term "competent authority" means:
(i)   (in State A): ....
(ii) (in State B):....................................

2   As regards the application of the Convention by a Contracting State any term not defined therein shall, unless the context otherwise requires, have the meaning which it has under the law of that State concerning the taxes to which the Convention applies.[2]

[1] The word "includes" replaces "comprises" which appeared in the revised 1963 text.
[2] The definition of "nationals", contained in para 1(*d*) of the revised 1963 text, is now found in Art 24, para 2 of this model convention.

Article 4 Resident

1   For the purposes of this Convention, the term "resident of a Contracting State" means any person who, under the laws of that State, is liable to tax therein by reason of his domicile, residence, place of management or any other criterion of a similar nature. But this term does not include any person who is liable to tax in that State in respect only of income from sources in that State or capital situated therein.

2   Where by reason of the provisions of paragraph 1 an individual is a resident of both Contracting States, then his status shall be determined as follows:

(a) he shall be deemed to be a resident of the State in which he has a permanent home available to him; if he has a permanent home available to him in both States, he shall be deemed to be a resident of the State with which his personal and economic relations are closer (centre of vital interests);
(b) if the State in which he has his centre of vital interests cannot be determined, or if he has not a permanent home available to him in either State, he shall be deemed to be a resident of the State in which he has an habitual abode;
(c) if he has an habitual abode in both States or in neither of them, he shall be deemed to be a resident of the State of which he is a national;
(d) if he is a national of both States or of neither of them, the competent authorities of the Contracting States shall settle the question by mutual agreement.

3 Where by reason of the provisions of paragraph 1 a person other than an individual is a resident of both Contracting States, then it shall be deemed to be a resident of the State in which its place of effective management is situated.

Article 5 Permanent establishment

1 For the purposes of this Convention, the term "permanent establishment" means a fixed place of business through[1] which the business of an enterprise is wholly or partly carried on.

2 The term "permanent establishment" includes especially:

(a) a place of management;
(b) a branch;
(c) an office;
(d) a factory;
(e) a workshop, and
(f) a mine, an oil or gas well,[2] a quarry or any other place of extraction of natural resources.

3 A building site or construction or installation project constitutes a permanent establishment only if it lasts more than twelve months.[3]

4 Notwithstanding the preceding provisions of this Article, the term "permanent establishment" shall be deemed not to include:

(a)   the use of facilities solely for the purpose of storage, display or delivery of goods or merchandise belonging to the enterprise;
(b)   the maintenance of a stock of goods or merchandise belonging to the enterprise solely for the purpose of storage, display or delivery;
(c)   the maintenance of a stock of goods or merchandise belonging to the enterprise solely for the purpose of processing by another enterprise;
(d)   the maintenance of a fixed place of business solely for the purpose of purchasing goods or merchandise or of collecting information, for the enterprise;
(e)   the maintenance of a fixed place of business solely for the purpose of [carrying on, for the enterprise, any other activity of a preparatory or auxiliary character;]4
(f)   the maintenance of a fixed place of business solely for any combination of activities mentioned in sub-paragraphs (a) to (e), provided that the overall activity of the fixed place of business resulting from this combination is of a preparatory or auxiliary character.5

5   Notwithstanding the provisions of paragraphs 1 and 2, where a person—other than an agent of an independent status to whom paragraph 6 applies—is acting on behalf of an enterprise and has, and habitually exercises, in a Contracting State an authority to conclude contracts in the name of the enterprise, that enterprise shall be deemed to have a permanent establishment in that State in respect of any activities which that person undertakes for the enterprise, unless the activities of such person are limited to those mentioned in paragraph 4 which, if exercised through a fixed place of business, would not make this fixed place of business a permanent establishment under the provisions of that paragraph.6

6   An enterprise shall not be deemed to have a permanent establishment in a Contracting State merely because it carries on business in that State through a broker, general commission agent or any other agent of an independent status, provided that such persons are acting in the ordinary course of their business.

7   The fact that a company which is a resident of a Contracting State controls or is controlled by a company which is a resident of the other Contracting State, or which carries on business in that other State (whether through a permanent establishment or otherwise), shall not of itself constitute either company a permanent establishment of the other.

[1] The word "through" replaces "in" which appeared in the revised 1963 text.
[2] The words "an oil or gas well, a" did not appear in the revised 1963 text.
[3] This replaces para 2(*g*) of the revised 1963 text.
[4] The words in square brackets replace those in the revised 1963 text.
[5] This did not appear in the revised 1963 text.
[6] This replaces para 4 of the revised 1963 text.

Chapter III   Taxation of income

Article 6   Income from immovable property

1   Income derived by a resident of a Contracting State from immovable property (including income from agriculture or forestry) situated in the other Contracting State may be taxed in that other State.

2   The term "immovable property" shall have the meaning which it has under the law of the Contracting State in which the property in question is situated. The term shall in any case include property accessory to immovable property, livestock and equipment used in agriculture and forestry, rights to which the provisions of general law respecting landed property apply, usufruct of immovable property and rights to variable or fixed payments as consideration for the working of, or the right to work, mineral deposits, sources and other natural resources; ships, boats, and aircraft shall not be regarded as immovable property.

3   The provisions of paragraph 1 shall apply to income derived from the direct use, letting, or use in any other form of immovable property.

4   The provisions of paragraphs 1 and 3 shall also apply to the income from immovable property of an enterprise and to income from immovable property used for the performance of independent personal services.

"Independent personal services" includes other activities of an independent character, as well as "professional" services.

Article 7   Business profits

1   The profits of an enterprise of a Contracting State shall be taxable only in that State unless the enterprise carries on business in the other Contracting State through a permanent establishment situated therein. If the enterprise carries on business as aforesaid, the profits of the enterprise may be taxed in the other State but only so much of them as is attributable to that permanent establishment.

2 Subject to the provisions of paragraph 3, where an enterprise of a Contracting State carries on business in the other Contracting State through a permanent establishment situated therein, there shall in each Contracting State be attributed to that permanent establishment the profits which it might be expected to make if it were a distinct and separate enterprise engaged in the same or similar activities under the same or similar conditions and dealing wholly independently with the enterprise of which it is a permanent establishment.

3 In determining the profits of a permanent establishment, there shall be allowed as deductions expenses which are incurred for the purposes of the permanent establishment, including executive and general administrative expenses so incurred, whether in the State in which the permanent establishment is situated or elsewhere.

4 Insofar as it has been customary in a Contracting State to determine the profits to be attributed to a permanent establishment on the basis of an apportionment of the total profits of the enterprise to its various parts, nothing in paragraph 2 shall preclude that Contracting State from determining the profits to be taxed by such an apportionment as may be customary; the method of apportionment adopted shall, however, be such that the result shall be in accordance with the principles contained[1] in this Article.

5 No profits shall be attributed to a permanent establishment by reason of the mere purchase by that permanent establishment of goods or merchandise for the enterprise.

6 For the purposes of the preceding paragraphs, the profits to be attributed to the permanent establishment shall be determined by the same method year by year unless there is good and sufficient reason to the contrary.

7 Where profits include items of income which are dealt with separately in other Articles of this Convention, then the provisions of those Articles shall not be affected by the provisions of this Article.

---

[1] The word "contained" replaces "embodied" which appeared in the revised 1963 text.

Article 8 Shipping, inland waterways transport and air transport

1   Profits from the operation of ships or aircraft in international traffic shall be taxable only in the Contracting State in which the place of effective management of the enterprise is situated.

2   Profits from the operation of boats engaged in inland waterways transport shall be taxable only in the Contracting State in which the place of effective management of the enterprise is situated.

3   If the place of effective management of a shipping enterprise or of an inland waterways transport enterprise is aboard a ship or boat, then it shall be deemed to be situated in the Contracting State in which the home harbour of the ship or boat is situated, or, if there is no such home harbour, in the Contracting State of which the operator of the ship or boat is a resident.

4   The provisions of paragraph 1 shall also apply to profits from the participation in a pool, a joint business or an international operating agency.

Article 9   Associated enterprises

1   Where

   (a)   an enterprise of a Contracting State participates directly or indirectly in the management, control or capital of an enterprise of the other Contracting State, or
   (b)   the same persons participate directly or indirectly in the management, control or capital of an enterprise of a Contracting State and an enterprise of the other Contracting State,

and in either case conditions are made or imposed between the two enterprises in their commercial or financial relations which differ from those which would be made between independent enterprises, then any profits which would, but for those conditions, have accrued to one of the enterprises, but, by reason of those conditions, have not so accrued, may be included in the profits of that enterprise and taxed accordingly.

2   Where a Contracting State includes in the profits of an enterprise of that State—and taxes accordingly—profits on which an enterprise of the other Contracting State has been charged to tax in

that other State and the profits so included are profits which would have accrued to the enterprise of the first-mentioned State if the conditions made between the two enterprises had been those which would have been made between independent enterprises, then that other State shall make an appropriate adjustment to the amount of the tax charged therein on those profits. In determining such adjustment, due regard shall be had to the other provisions of this Convention and the competent authorities of the Contracting States shall if necessary consult each other.[1]

[1] The text of para 2 has been re-drafted.

Article 10   Dividends

1 Dividends paid by a company which is a resident of a Contracting State to a resident of the other Contracting State may be taxed in that other State.

2 However, such dividends may also be taxed in the Contracting State of which the company paying the dividends is a resident and according to the laws of that State, but if the recipient is the beneficial owner of the dividends the tax so charged shall not exceed:

>(*a*)   5 per cent of the gross amount of the dividends if the beneficial owner[1] is a company (other than a partnership) which holds directly at least 25 per cent of the capital of the company paying the dividends;
>(*b*)   15 per cent of the gross amount of the dividends in all other cases.

The competent authorities of the Contracting States shall by mutual agreement settle the mode of application of these limitations.

This paragraph shall not affect the taxation of the company in respect of the profits out of which the dividends are paid.

3 The term "dividends" as used in this Article means income from shares, "jouissance" shares or "jouissance" rights, mining shares, founders' shares or other rights, not being debt-claims, participating in profits, as well as income from other corporate rights which is subjected to the same taxation treatment as income from shares by the laws of the State of which the company making the distribution is a resident.

4 The provisions of paragraphs 1 and 2 shall not apply if the beneficial owner[2] of the dividends, being a resident of a Contracting State, carries on business in the other Contracting State of which the company paying the dividends is a resident through a permanent establishment situated therein, or performs in that other State independent personal services from a fixed base situated therein, and the holding in respect of which the dividends are paid is effectively connected with such permanent establishment or fixed base. In such a case the provisions of Article 7 or Article 14, as the case may be, shall apply.

5 Where a company which is a resident of a Contracting State derives profits or income from the other Contracting State, that other State may not impose any tax on the dividends paid by the company, except insofar as such dividends are paid to a resident of that other State or insofar as the holding in respect of which the dividends are paid is effectively connected with a permanent establishment or a fixed base situated in that other State, nor subject the company's undistributed profits to a tax on the company's undistributed profits, even if the dividends paid or the undistributed profits consist wholly or partly of profits or income arising in such other State.

[1]The words "beneficial owner" replace "recipient" which appeared in the revised 1963 text.
[2]The words "beneficial owner" replace "recipient" which appeared in the revised 1963 text.

Article 11   Interest

1 Interest arising in a Contracting State and paid to a resident of the other Contracting State may be taxed in that other State.

2 However, such interest may also be taxed in the Contracting State in which it arises and according to the laws of that State, but if the recipient is the beneficial owner of the interest the tax so charged shall not exceed 10 per cent of the gross amount of the interest. The competent authorities of the Contracting State shall by mutual agreement settle the mode of application of this limitation.

3 The term "interest" as used in this Article means income from debt-claims of every kind, whether or not secured by mortgage and whether or not carrying a right to participate in the debtor's profits, and in particular, income from government securities and income from bonds or debentures, including premiums and prizes attaching to such securities,[1] bonds or debentures. Penalty charges for late payment shall not be regarded as interest for the purpose of this Article.

4 The provisions of paragraphs 1 and 2 shall not apply if the beneficial owner[2] of the interest, being a resident of a Contracting State, carries on business in the other Contracting State in which the interest arises, through a permanent establishment situated therein, or performs in that other State independent personal services from a fixed base situated therein, and the debt-claim in respect of which the interest is paid is effectively connected with such permanent establishment or fixed base. In such a case the provisions of Article 7 or Article 14, as the case may be, shall apply.

5 Interest shall be deemed to arise in a Contracting State when the payer is that State itself, a political subdivision, a local authority or a resident of that State. Where, however, the person paying the interest, whether he is a resident of a Contracting State or not, has in a Contracting State a permanent establishment [or a fixed base] in connection with which the indebtedness on which the interest is paid was incurred, and such interest is borne by such permanent establishment [or fixed base], then such interest shall be deemed to arise in the State in which the permanent establishment [or fixed base] is situated. (The words in square brackets did not appear in the revised 1963 text.)

6 Where, by reason of a special relationship between the payer and the beneficial owner or between both of them and some other person, the amount of the interest, having regard to the debt-claim for which it is paid, exceeds the amount which would have been agreed upon by the payer and the beneficial owner[3] in the absence of such relationship, the provisions of this Article shall apply only to the last-mentioned amount. In such case, the excess of the payments shall remain taxable according to the laws of each Contracting State, due regard being had to the other provisions of this Convention.

[1]The words "such securities" did not appear in the revised 1963 text.
[2]The words "beneficial owner" replace "recipient" which appeared in the revised 1963 text.
[3]The words "beneficial owner" replace "recipient" which appeared in the revised 1963 text.

Article 12 Royalties

1 Royalties arising in a Contracting State and paid to a resident of the other Contracting State shall be taxable only in that other State if such resident is the beneficial owner of the royalties.

2   The term "royalties" as used in this Article means payments of any kind received as a consideration for the use of, or the right to use, any copyright of literary, artistic or scientific work including cinematograph films, any patent, trade mark, design or model, plan, secret formula or process, or for the use of, or the right to use, industrial, commercial, or scientific equipment, or for information concerning industrial, commercial or scientific experience.

3   The provisions of paragraph 1 shall not apply if the beneficial owner[1] of the royalties, being a resident of a Contracting State, carries on business in the other Contracting State in which the royalties arise, through a permanent establishment situated therein, or performs in that other State independent personal services from a fixed base situated therein, and the right or property in respect of which the royalties are paid is effectively connected with such permanent establishment or fixed base. In such a case the provisions of Article 7 or Article 14, as the case may be, shall apply.

4   Where, by reason of a special relationship between the payer and the beneficial owner or between both of them and some other person, the amount of the royalties, having regard to the use, right or information for which they are paid, exceeds the amount which would have been agreed upon by the payer and the beneficial owner in the absence of such relationship, the provisions of this Article shall apply only to the last-mentioned amount. In such case, the excess part of the payments shall remain taxable according to the laws of each Contracting State, due regard being had to the other provisions of this Convention.

[1]The words "beneficial owner" replace "recipient" which appeared in the revised 1963 text.

Article 13   Capital gains

1   Gains derived by a resident of a Contracting State from the alienation of immovable property referred to in Article 6 and situated in the other Contracting State may be taxed in that other State.

2   Gains from the alienation of movable property forming part of the business property of a permanent establishment which an enterprise of a Contracting State has in the other Contracting State or of

movable property pertaining to a fixed base available to a resident of a Contracting State in the other Contracting State for the purpose of performing independent personal services, including such gains from the alienation of such a permanent establishment (alone or with the whole enterprise) or of such fixed base, may be taxed in that other State.

3   Gains from the alienation of ships or aircraft operated in international traffic, boats engaged in inland waterways transport or movable property pertaining to the operation of such ships, aircraft or boats, shall be taxable only in the Contracting State in which the place of effective management of the enterprise is situated.

4   Gains from the alienation of any property other than that referred to in paragraphs 1, 2 and 3, shall be taxable only in the Contracting State of which the alienator is a resident.

Article 14   Independent personal services

1   Income derived by a resident of a Contracting State in respect of professional services or [other activities of an independent character] shall be taxable only in that State unless he has a fixed base regularly available to him in the other Contracting State for the purpose of performing his activities. If he has such a fixed base, the income may be taxed in the other State but only so much of it as is attributable to that fixed base.

2   The term "professional services" includes especially independent scientific, literary, artistic, educational or teaching activities as well as the independent activities of physicians, lawyers, engineers, architects, dentists and accountants.

Article 15   Dependent personal services

1   Subject to the provisions of Articles 16, 18 and 19, salaries, wages and other similar remuneration derived by a resident of a Contracting State in respect of an employment shall be taxable only in that State unless the employment is exercised in the other Contracting State. If the employment is so exercised, such remuneration as is derived therefrom may be taxed in that other State.

2   Notwithstanding the provisions of paragraph 1, remuneration derived by a resident of a Contracting State in respect of an employment exercised in the other contracting State shall be taxable only in the first-mentioned State if:

(*a*)   the recipient is present in the other State for a period or periods not exceeding in the aggregate 183 days in the fiscal year concerned, and
(*b*)   the remuneration is paid by, or on behalf of, an employer who is not a resident of the other State, and
(*c*)   the remuneration is not borne by a permanent establishment or a fixed base which the employer has in the other State.

3   Notwithstanding the preceding provisions of this Article, remuneration derived in respect of an employment exercised aboard a ship or aircraft operated in international traffic, or aboard a boat engaged in inland waterways transport, may be taxed in the Contracting State in which the place of effective management of the enterprise is situated.

Article 16   Directors' fees

Directors' fees and other similar payments derived by a resident of a Contracting State in his capacity as a member of the board of directors of a company which is a resident of the other Contracting State may be taxed in that other State.

Article 17   Artistes and athletes

1   Notwithstanding the provisions of Articles 14 and 15, income derived by a resident of a Contracting State as an entertainer, such as a theatre, motion picture, radio or television artiste, or a musician, or as an athlete, from his personal activities as such exercised in the other Contracting State, may be taxed in that other State.

2   Where income in respect of personal activities exercised by an entertainer or an athlete in his capacity as such accrues not to the entertainer or athlete himself but to another person, that income may, notwithstanding the provisions of Articles 7, 14 and 15, be taxed in the Contracting State in which the activities of the entertainer or athlete are exercised.

Article 18   Pensions

Subject to the provisions of paragraph 2 of Article 19, pensions and other similar remuneration paid to a resident of a Contracting State in consideration of past employment shall be taxable only in that State.

Article 19 Government service

1 (*a*) Remuneration, other than a pension, paid by a Contracting State or a political subdivision or a local authority thereof to an individual in respect of services rendered to that State or subdivision or authority shall be taxable only in that State.
(*b*) However, such remuneration shall be taxable only in the other Contracting State if the services are rendered in that State and the individual is a resident of that State who:
(i) is a national of that State; or
(ii) did not become a resident of that State solely for the purpose of rendering the services.

2 (*a*) Any pension paid by, or out of funds created by, a Contracting State or a political subdivision or a local authority thereof to an individual in respect of services rendered to that State or subdivision or authority shall be taxable only in that State.
(*b*) However, such pension shall be taxable only in the other Contracting State if the individual is a resident of, and a national of, that State.

3 The provisions of Articles 15, 16 and 18 shall apply to remuneration and pensions in respect of services rendered in connection with a business carried on by a Contracting State or a political subdivision or a local authority thereof.

Article 20 Students

Payments which a student or business apprentice who is or was immediately before visiting a Contracting State a resident of the other Contracting State and who is present in the first-mentioned State solely for the purpose of his education or training receives for the purpose of his maintenance, education or training shall not be taxed in that State, provided that such payments arise[1] from sources outside that State.

[1]The word "arise" replaces "are made to him" which appeared in the revised 1963 text.

Article 21 Other income

1 Items of income of a resident of a Contracting State, wherever

Appendix IV 237

arising, not dealt with in the foregoing Articles of this Convention shall be taxable only in that State.

2   The provisions of paragraph 1 shall apply [to income, other than income from immovable property as defined in paragraph 2 of Article 6,] if the recipient of such income, being a resident of a Contracting State, carries on business in the other Contracting State through a permanent establishment situated therein, or performs in that other State [independent personal] services from a fixed base situated therein, and the right or property in respect of which the income is paid is effectively connected with such permanent establishment or fixed base. In such case the provisions of Article 7 or Article 14, as the case may be, shall apply.

Note   The words enclosed by the square brackets did not appear in the revised 1963 text. This paragraph previously referred to "professional" services: "independent personal services" includes other activities of an independent character, see Art 14, para 1.

Chapter IV   Taxation of capital

Article 22   Capital

1.   Capital represented by immovable property referred to in Article 6, owned by a resident of a Contracting State and situated in the other Contracting State, may be taxed in that other State.

2   Capital represented by movable property forming part of the business property of a permanent establishment [which an enterprise of a Contracting State has in the other Contracting State or by movable property pertaining to a fixed base available to a resident of a Contracting State in the other Contracting State for the purpose of performing independent personal services, may be taxed in that other State.][1]

3   Capital represented by ships and aircraft operated in international traffic and by boats engaged in inland waterways transport, and by movable property pertaining to the operation of such ships, aircraft and boats, shall be taxable only in the Contracting State in which the place of effective management of the enterprise is situated.

4   All other elements of capital of a resident of a Contracting State shall be taxable only in that State.

Note The words enclosed by square brackets replace those of the revised 1963 text. The words "available . . . for the purpose of performing independent personal services" replace "used for the performance of professional services."

Chapter V Methods for elimination of double taxation

Article 23A Exemption method

1 Where a resident of a Contracting State derives income or owns capital which, in accordance with the provisions of this Convention, may be taxed in the other Contracting State, the first-mentioned State shall, subject to the provisions of paragraphs 2 and 3, exempt such income or capital from tax.

2 Where a resident of a Contracting State derives items of income which, in accordance with the provisions of Articles 10 and 11, may be taxed in the other Contracting State, the first-mentioned State shall allow as a deduction from the tax on the income of that resident an amount equal to the tax paid in that other State. Such deduction shall not, however, exceed that part of the tax, as computed before the deduction is given, which is attributable to such items[1] of income derived from that other State.

3 Where in accordance with any provisions of the Convention income derived or capital owned by a resident of a Contracting State is exempt from tax in that State, such State may nevertheless, in calculating the amount of tax on the remaining income or capital of such resident, take into account the exempted income or capital.

[1] The words "attributable to such items of" replace "appropriate to the" which appeared in the revised 1963 text.

Article 23B Credit method

1 Where a resident of a Contracting State derives income or owns capital which, in accordance with the provisions of this Convention, may be taxed in the other Contracting State, the first-mentioned State shall allow:

(*a*) as a deduction from the tax on the income of that resident, an amount equal to the income tax paid in that other State;
(*b*) as a deduction from the tax on the capital of that resident, an amount equal to the capital tax paid in that other State.

Such deduction in either case shall not, however, exceed that part of the income tax or capital tax, as computed before the deduction is given, which is attributable, as the case may be, to the income or the capital which may be taxed in that other State.

2[1] Where in accordance with any provision of the Convention income derived or capital owned by a resident of a Contracting State is exempt from tax in that State, such State may nevertheless, in calculating the amount of tax on the remaining income or capital of such resident, take into account the exempted income or capital.

[1]Para 2 is the same as Art 23A para 3.

Chapter VI Special provisions

Article 24 Non-discrimination

1 Nationals of a Contracting State shall not be subjected in the other Contracting State to any taxation or any requirement connected therewith, which is other or more burdensome than the taxation and connected requirements to which nationals of that other State in the same circumstances are or may be subjected. [This provision shall, notwithstanding the provisions of Article 1, also apply to persons who are not residents of one or both of the Contracting States.][1]

[2[2] The term "nationals" means:

(*a*) all individuals possessing the nationality of a Contracting State;
(*b*) all legal persons, partnerships and associations deriving their status as such from the laws in force in a Contracting State.]

3 Stateless persons who are residents of a Contracting State shall not be subjected in either Contracting State to any taxation or any requirement connected therewith, which is other or more burdensome than the taxation and connected requirements to which nationals of the State concerned in the same circumstances are or may be subjected.

4 The taxation on a permanent establishment which an enterprise of a Contracting State has in the other Contracting State shall not be less favourably levied in that other State than the taxation levied on enterprises of that other State carrying on the same activities. This provision shall not be construed as obliging a Contracting State to grant to residents of the other Contracting State any personal allowances, reliefs and reductions for taxation purposes on account of civil status or family responsibilities which it grants to its own residents.

5   Except where the provisions of paragraph 1 of Article 9, paragraph 6 of Article 11, or paragraph 4 of Article 12, apply, interest, royalties and other disbursements paid by an enterprise of a Contracting State to a resident of the other Contracting State shall, for the purpose of determining the taxable profits of such enterprise, be deductible under the same conditions as if they had been paid to a resident of the first-mentioned State. Similarly, any debts of an enterprise of a Contracting State to a resident of the other Contracting State shall, for the purpose of determining the taxable capital of such enterprise, be deductible under the same conditions as if they had been contracted to a resident of the first-mentioned State.

6   Enterprises of a Contracting State, the capital of which is wholly or partly owned or controlled, directly or indirectly, by one or more residents of the other Contracting State, shall not be subjected in the first-mentioned State to any taxation or any requirement connected therewith which is other or more burdensome than the taxation and connected requirements to which other similar enterprises of [the] first-mentioned State are or may be subjected.

7   The provisions of this Article shall, notwithstanding the provisions of Article 2, apply to taxes of every kind and description.

[1]The words enclosed by square brackets did not appear in the revised 1963 text.
[2]This has been added to the revised 1963 text.

Article 25   Mutual agreement procedure

1   Where a person considers that the actions of one or both of the Contracting States result or will result for him in taxation not in accordance with the provisions of this Convention, he may, irrespective of the remedies provided by the domestic law[1] of those States, present his case to the competent authority of the Contracting State of which he is a resident or, if his case comes under paragraph 1 of Article 24, to that of the Contracting State of which he is a national. The case must be presented within three years from

the first notification of the action resulting in taxation not in accordance with the provisions of the Convention.

2   The competent authority shall endeavour, if the objection appears to it to be justified and if it is not itself able to arrive at a satisfactory solution, to resolve the case by mutual agreement with the competent authority of the other Contracting State, with a view to the avoidance of taxation [which is] not in accordance with the Convention. Any agreement reached shall be implemented notwithstanding any time limits in the domestic law of the Contracting States.

3   The competent authorities of the Contracting States shall endeavour to resolve by mutual agreement any difficulties or doubts arising as to the interpretation or application of the Convention. They may also consult together for the elimination of double taxation in cases not provided for in the Convention.

4   The competent authorities of the Contracting States may communicate with each other directly for the purpose of reaching an agreement in the sense of the preceding paragraphs. When it seems advisable in order to reach agreement to have an oral exchange of opinions, such exchange may take place through a Commission consisting of representatives of the competent authorities of the Contracting States.

[1]The words "domestic law" replace "national laws" which appeared in the revised 1963 text.

Article 26   Exchange of information

1   The competent authorities of the Contracting States shall exchange such information as is necessary for carrying out the provisions of this Convention or of the domestic laws of the Contracting States concerning taxes covered by the Convention insofar as the taxation thereunder is not contrary to the Convention. The exchange of information is not restricted by Article 1. Any information received by a Contracting State shall be treated as secret in the same manner as information obtained under the domestic laws of that State and shall be disclosed only to persons or authorities (including courts and administrative bodies) involved in the assessment or collection of, the enforcement or prosecution in respect of, or the determination of appeals in relation to, the taxes covered by the Convention. Such persons or authorities shall use the information only for such purposes. They may disclose the information in public court proceedings or in judicial decisions.

2 In no case shall the provisions of paragraph 1 be construed so as to impose on a Contracting State the obligation:

(*a*) to carry out administrative measures at variance with the laws and administrative practice of that or of the other Contracting State;
(*b*) to supply information which is not obtainable under the laws or in the normal course of the administration of that or of the other Contracting State;
(*c*) to supply information which would disclose any trade, business, industrial, commercial or professional secret or trade process, or information, the disclosure of which would be contrary to public policy (*ordre public*).

Article 27[1]   Diplomatic agents and consular officers

Nothing in this Convention shall affect the fiscal privileges of diplomatic agents or consular officers under the general rules of international law or under the provisions of special agreements.

[1] The title of Article 27 appeared as "Diplomatic and Consular Officials" in the revised 1963 text.

Article 28   Territorial extension

1 This Convention may be extended, either in its entirety or with any necessary modifications to any part of the territory of (State A) or of (State B) which is specifically excluded from the application of the Convention or, to any State or territory for whose international relations (State A) or (State B) is responsible, which imposes taxes substantially similar in character to those to which the Convention applies. Any such extension shall take effect from such date and subject to any such modifications and conditions, including conditions as to termination, as may be specified and agreed between the Contracting States in notes to be exchanged through diplomatic channels or in any other manner in accordance with their constitutional procedures.

2 Unless otherwise agreed by both Contracting States, the termination of the Convention by one of them under Article 30 shall also terminate, in the manner provided for in that Article, the application of the Convention [to any part of the territory of (State A) or of (State B) or] to any State or territory to which it has been extended under this Article.

Appendix IV 243

Note The words between square brackets are of relevance when, by special provision, a part of the territory of a Contracting State is excluded from the application of the Convention.

Chapter VII   Final provisions

Article 29   Entry into force

1   This Convention shall be ratified and the instruments of ratification shall be exchanged at .... as soon as possible.

2   The Convention shall enter into force upon the exchange of instruments of ratification and its provisions shall have effect:

(*a*)   (in State A):.....................................
(*b*)   (in State B):.....................................

Article 30   Termination

This Convention shall remain in force until terminated by a Contracting State. Either Contracting State may terminate the Convention, through diplomatic channels, by giving notice of termination at least six months before the end of any calendar year after the year .... In such event, the Convention shall cease to have effect:

(*a*)   (in State A):.....................................

(*b*)   (in State B):.....................................

Terminal clause

Note The terminal clause concerning the signing shall be drafted in accordance with the constitutional procedure of both Contracting States.

Appendix V
Guide to domicile and residence

To use the guide

Important Notes

- The guide leads to general conclusions and strategies and is intended to point in the right direction. **It is not a rule-book**
- If married couple, **check each spouse separately** to identify category.

Step 1

Establish domicile

Use Domicile Chart as guide;

For IHT purposes **only**, it is possible for the Revenue to **deem** an individual UK-domiciled (such action does not disturb the legal domicile).

Step 2

Establish where resident for tax purposes

Use:

Resident Chart 1 for non-UK domiciled client
Resident Chart 2 for working UK expatriates
Resident Chart 3 for non-working UK expatriates.

Step 3

Check tax and investment considerations

Having decided domicile and residence category, use:

UK Taxation Chart to check planned actions for tax effectiveness

UK Taxation—Effect on Investment etc to check overall financial strategy*

*The symbols on this chart can be regarded as:

☺ Usually 'harmless', or even good!

❓ May well be harmless, but take care to double check

❗ Check—there could be disadvantages

🛑 Check carefully—there will usually be major disadvantages

Ensure no conflict with sensible tax and investment planning.

Category: A

Applies to:

Non-UK Domicile
Non-UK Resident
Non-UK Ordinarily Resident

Basic Strategy:

Can invest in UK provided local legal and exchange controls permit. To minimise risk of IHT on UK assets, should:

- restrict UK assets below IHT zero-rated band

- take advantage of UK Government exempt stocks

- ensure any 'portable' assets are held outside UK

Also, of IHT advantage and effective in reducing UK withholding tax, are the investments offered by offshore subsidiaries of UK institutions, which can offer UK investment qualities without UK taxation.

Appendix V 247

Category: B

Applies to:

Non-UK Domicile
UK Resident
UK Ordinarily Resident

Basic Strategy:

To minimise UK tax liabilities should keep all assets and accumulated gains/income outside the UK, remitting to UK **only** the absolute minimum. If remittance, to cover living expenses, is unavoidable, client should create separate accounts to contain and identify.

(1) Income arising outside UK.

(2) Gain-laden capital from asset disposal

(3) Capital untainted by income or gain.

Remittance could be from (2) up to limit of CGT exemptions in any one year; if more cash is required, remittance could be made from (3); only in the direst straits should cash be remitted from (1).

Category: C

Applies to:

UK Domicile
Non-UK Resident
Non-UK Ordinarily Resident

Basic Strategy:

Invest in offshore subsidiaries of UK institutions, to retain investment qualities without unnecessary UK tax implications. Ensure spare capital is working for capital growth as well as income, and realise all accumulated capital gains while still non-UK ordinarily resident.

Take care to maintain a realistic level of health insurance and life cover and keep equal cover for a spouse running the UK family base, if appropriate.

If one spouse remains UK resident, take care to avoid **joint** assets, as the income/gain on the asset will be assessable to UK taxes.

Category: D

Applies to:

UK Domicile (but claiming new domicile of choice)
Non-UK Resident
Non-UK Ordinarily Resident

Basic Strategy:

As part of exercise to replace UK domicile with new domicile of choice, client must show that all formal ties with UK have been severed. Single 'ties' eg a banking service, an investment in a UK equity, etc, will not individually prevent a successful claim to non-UK domicile, but together could convince the UK authorities that the client retains British roots.
Should, therefore, move everything possible offshore and use UK facilities only if quite sure it will not damage non-domicile claim.
It may be a wise precaution to plan for eventual IHT liability, on the assumption that the claim may eventually fail.

Note: Client will be treated as deemed domiciled (for IHT purposes only) for first three years following departure.

Appendix V

DOMICILE CHART
UK domiciled or Non-UK Domiciled?

Note: If 'domicile of choice' not **actively** established, domicile will be either 'domicile of origin' or 'domicile of dependence'.

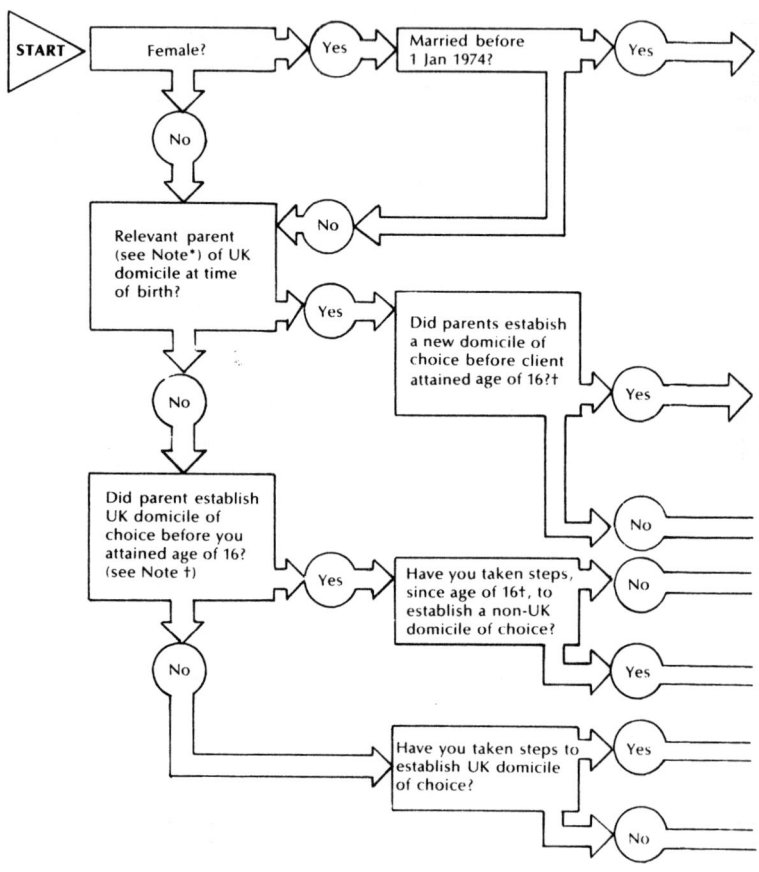

Appendix V   251

Note*: If parents were married (to each other!) at time of birth, take father as relevant parent: otherwise, take mother as relevant parent.

Note†: Except in Scotland, where the relevant age is 14 for males and 12 for females.

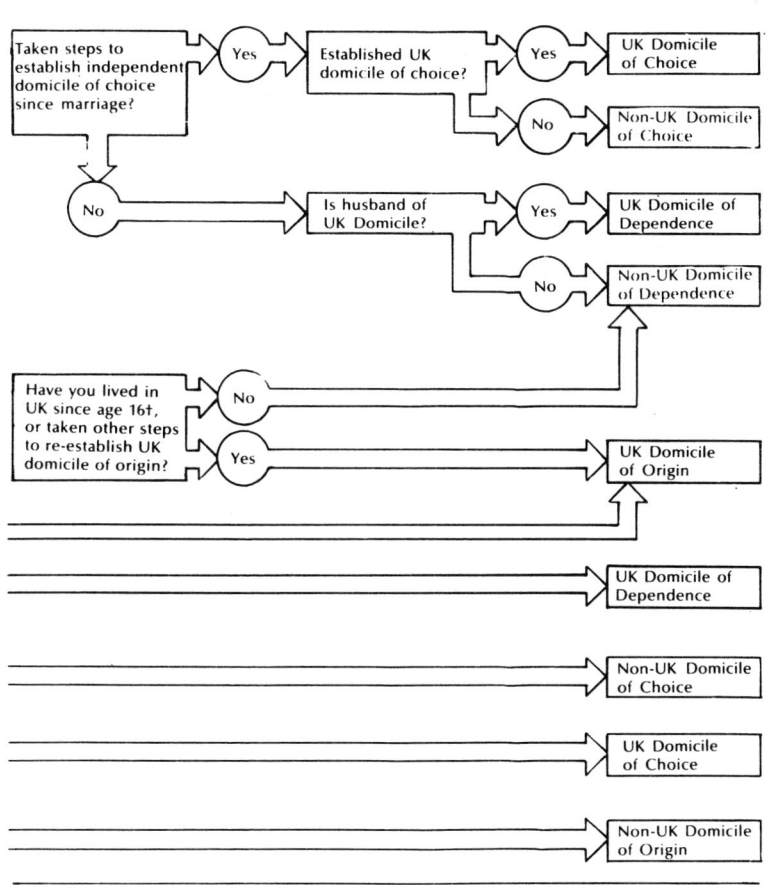

RESIDENCE CHART-1 (NON-UK DOMICILE)
Non-UK Domiciled ie

Roots, parentage etc outside UK

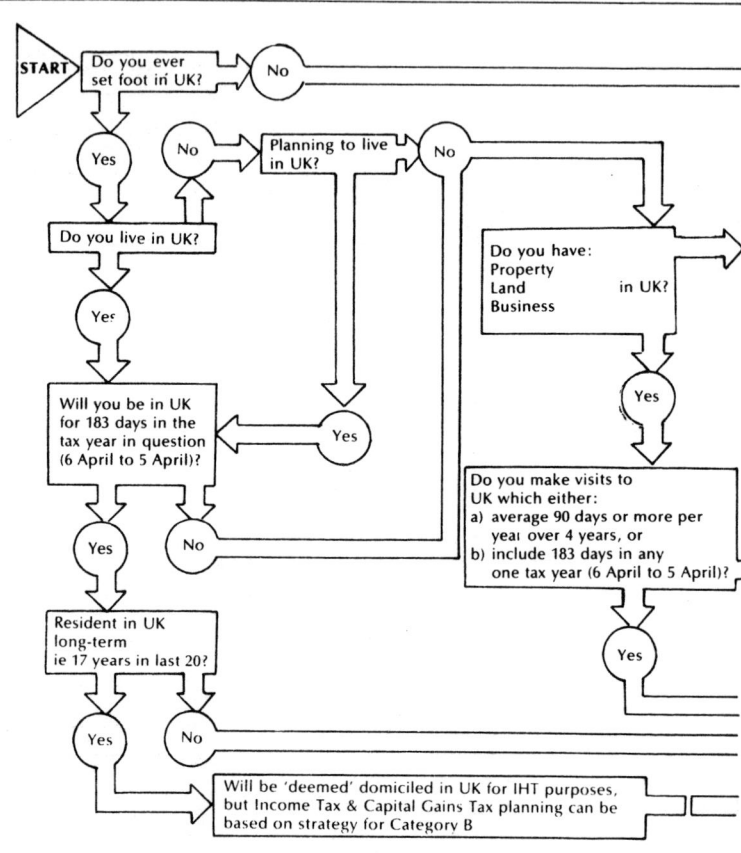

Appendix V 253

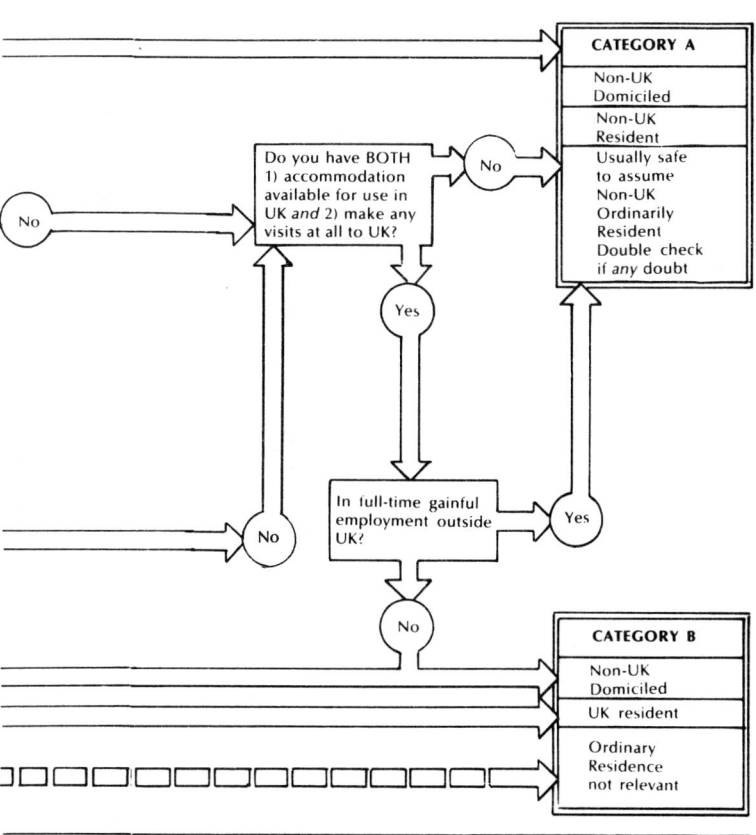

RESIDENCE CHART-2 (UK DOMICILE EMPLOYED)
Non-UK Domiciled working abroad ie

Roots, parentage etc (domicile) in UK, and in full-time gainful occupation outside UK.

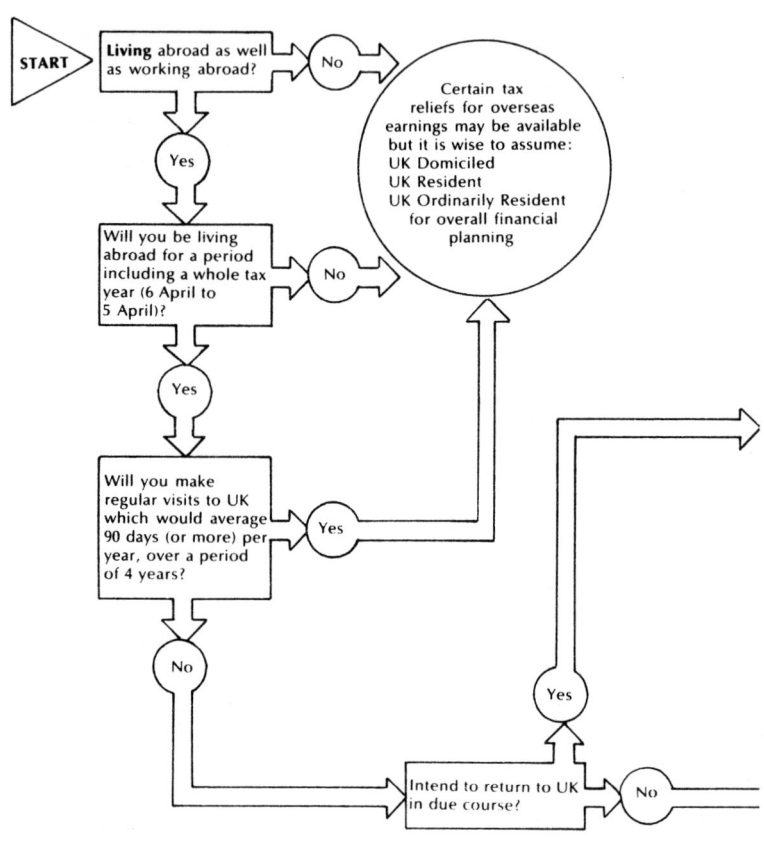

Appendix V 255

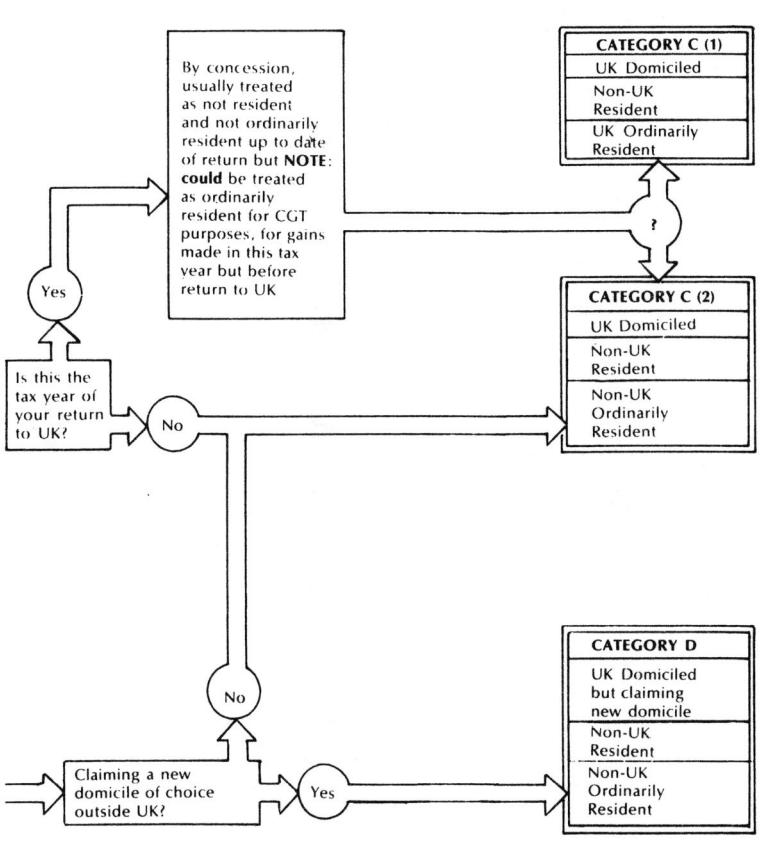

RESIDENCE CHART-3 (UK DOMICILE-NOT EMPLOYED)

UK-Domiciled living abroad ie

Roots, parentage etc (domicile) in UK, living outside UK, but not in full-time gainful occupation.

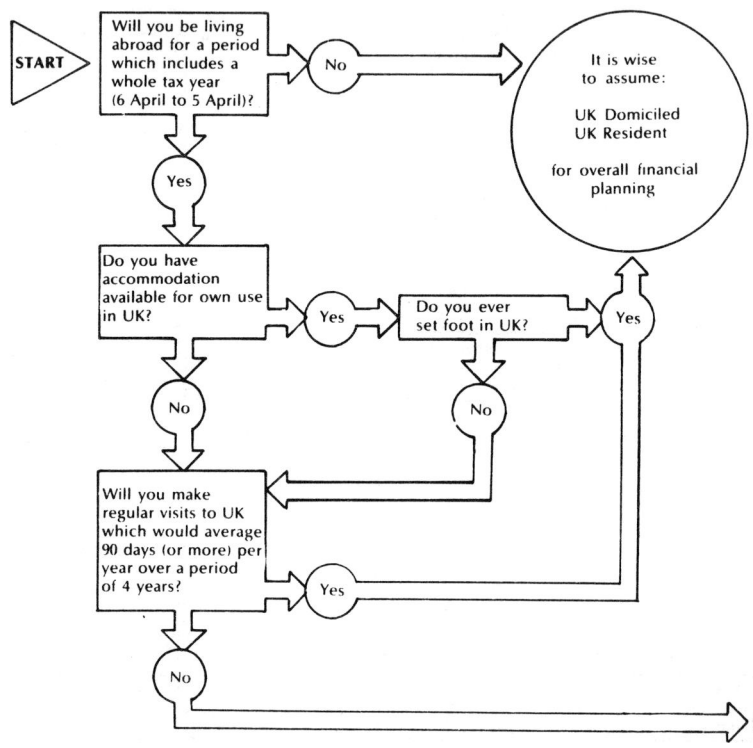

Appendix V

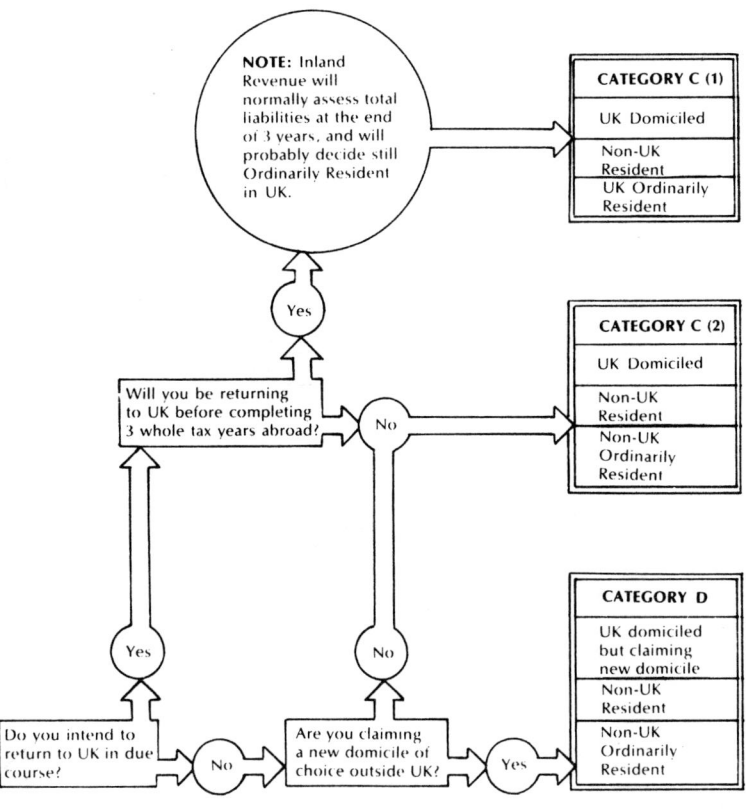

Client Category	UK Income Tax	
	Income arising in UK	Income arising Abroad
A Non-UK Domicile Non-UK Resident	• UK withholding tax deducted on dividends etc arising in UK • Overseas dividends collected in UK can be passed on gross of UK tax to non-residents • Some UK Government Stocks (exempt Gilts): interest and Bank and Building Society interest can be paid gross if non-UK ordinarily resident	No liability
B Non-UK Domicile UK Resident	Liable on all income arising in UK Able to claim normal UK Personal reliefs and exemptions	Liable on any income remitted to the UK (Income arising and retained outside UK is not assessed unless and until remitted to UK)
C1 UK Domicile Non-UK Resident UK Ordinarily Resident	As for Category A (but gilt exemptions do not apply while still ordinarily resident in UK also Bank and Building Society interest liable to deduction of CRT—composite rate tax not repayable	No liability
C2 UK Domicile Non-UK Resident Non-UK Ordinarily Resident	As for Category A	No liability
D Claiming Non-UK Domicile of Choice Non-UK Resident Non-UK Ordinarily Resident	As for Category A	No liability

Appendix V   259

UK Capital Gains Tax		UK Inheritance Tax	
Assets in UK	Assets Abroad	Assets in UK	Assets abroad
No liability (except perhaps on disposal of business property in UK CGTA. 1979 s 12)	No liability	Liability can arise on assets held in UK (Some Gilts exempt under IHTA 1984 s 602)	No liability (but may incur IHT liability if ever becomes 'deemed' UK domiciled)
Liable on gains realised in UK while UK resident and/or ordinarily resident	Liable on any Gain remitted to the UK (gains realised and retained outside UK are not assessed unless and until remitted to UK)	As for Category A	No liability (but may incur IHT liability in due course if 'deemed' UK domiciled)
Liable on Worldwide gains while still ordinarily UK Resident		Liable on Worldwide assets	
As for Category A			
As for Catgegory A		Liable on Worldwide assets (if client successfully establishes a non-UK domicile of choice, liability will be as for Category A)	

260 Allied Dunbar Expatriate Tax and Investment Guide

Client Category	UK Taxation—effect on investments		
	UK Equities UK Loan Stocks UK Unit Trusts etc	UK exempt Government Stocks	Other UK Government Stocks (excluding exempt Gilts)
A Non-UK Domicile Non-UK Resident Not Ordinarily Resident in UK	Beware IHT and UK withholding tax—although investment advantages may outweigh tax disadvantages	Can claim interest gross of UK withholding tax, and asset is exempt from IHT	Beware IHT and UK withholding tax—prefer UK Exempt Government Stocks if possible
B Non-UK Domicile UK Resident	Beware IHT and CGT, plus: Income will be paid in UK net of withholding tax or CRT (composite rate tax) Prefer offshore alternatives, with income paid gross, and assets outside UK for CGT and IHT purposes		
C1 UK Domicile Non-UK Resident UK Ordinarily Resident	Beware UK withholding tax—prefer offshore alternatives with less, or no, withholding taxes on Income distribution (Offshore funds are usually cheaper to invest in than dealing directly with foreign markets)	Strictly, cannot claim interest gross of UK withholding tax until no longer ordinarily UK resident (will receive any income net in interim)	Beware UK withholding tax—prefer offshore alternatives with similar security: for example Allied Dunbar Sterling Fixed Interest Fund
C2 UK Domicile Non-UK Resident Non-UK Ordinarily Resident		Can claim interest gross of UK withholding tax as not ordinarily UK resident (CARE if making claim to UK personal reliefs under TA 1988, s 278	
D Claiming Non-UK Domicile of Choice Non-UK Resident Non-UK Ordinarily Resident	Apart from the tax disadvantages as described in **C** above the investment will form a UK connection which may damage the domicile claim prefer offshore alternatives	If non-UK domicile is established, will be as for **A** above but in the interim a UK asset and a UK connection	The same considerations apply as for UK equities for **D** prefer offshore alternatives eg Allied Dunbar Sterling Fixed Interest Fund

Appendix V

UK Taxation—effect on investments		UK Taxation—effect on money movement		
UK Bank and Building Society Deposits	Joint holdings with spouse who is UK resident for tax purposes	Overseas Income remitted to UK	Capital Gains arising in UK	Overseas Capital Gains remitted to UK
Can request Interest paid gross of CRT as UK non-resident—but Beware IHT	Could expose income and gains to UK tax liability	No tax implications to prevent free movement of money into UK (CARE if increasing UK assets—Beware IHT)		
	No immediate disadvantage while both UK resident	Will incur UK income tax if remitted to UK—Retain offshore	Delay realisation of any UK gains until after leaving UK if possible Gains realised while resident will incur CGT	Will incur CGT if remitted Retain offshore and only remit to limit of annual CGT exemption
Strictly, cannot claim interest gross of CRT until no longer ordinarily UK resident (will receive any income net in interim)	Any assets held jointly with resident spouse are assessable to UK taxes. (each spouse should maintain separate bank account, investments and other assets in own sole name)	Remitting to UK will not incur a tax liability in itself—but it usually makes more practical sense to send all 'spare' income direct to offshore investment to save time, postage and paper	Will incur CGT liability if realised while still ordinarily UK resident—delay realisation until no longer UK ordinarily resident	Will incur CGT liability if realised while still ordinarily UK resident **whether remitted to UK or not**—delay until not ordinarily resident
Can claim interest gross of CRT as not ordinarily UK resident. Care if making claim to UK personal reliefs under TA 1988, s 278 —prefer offshore alternatives			An ideal time to ensure that all UK gains already accrued are realised **do not delay** until after return to UK!	An ideal time to realise gains but more practical to remit proceeds to offshore bank than to UK—**do not delay** until after return to UK!
UK Banking could be regarded as a strong remaining tie with UK and taken together with other UK links, invalidate non-domicile claim—prefer offshore Bank Services	Non-domicile claim would be rare if spouse remains in UK—joint assets with resident spouse would almost certainly defeat any non-UK domicile claim	Remittance of Income to UK may serve to reinforce UK links and increase UK assets	This would mark a disposal of UK assets and therefore severing of UK ties. Helpful in decreasing UK assets in event of non-domicile claim being successful	Remittance of capital to UK may serve to reinforce UK links and increase UK assets

Index

Absence
  long 16–19
  qualifying period 16–18
Academic exchange programmes 93
Accommodation rule 9–10
Administration of tax 68–9
Agricultural property relief 108–9
Airmen 26–7
Anti-avoidance provisions 135
Armed forces 26, 92
Artistes 80
Assets, location of 109–10
Athletes 80

Bank
  deposits 49–51, 150–1
  non-sterling accounts 102
Bonds
  exchange rates and 174
Building society
  deposits 49–51, 151–2
Business
  double taxation agreement 78–9
  gains 97–100
  property relief 107–9
  sale of 97–100

Capital gains tax
  business gains 97–100
  distributions 102
  double taxation agreement 79
  emigration 96
  foreign taxes 100
  general rules 35
  gifts 102
  husband and wife 95
  immigration 96
  non-sterling accounts 102
  non-UK domiciled 101
  offshore funds 101–2
  principal private residence 72–4
  property 71–4, 96–7

Capital gains tax—*contd*
  residence *see* Residence
  returning expatriate 44–5
  trusts 101, 124–5
Capital transfer tax *see* Inheritance tax
Car
  benefit 89–91
  tax 141
Cash
  exchange rates and 175–6
Checklists
  coming home 178–9
  going abroad 177–8
  while overseas 178
Children 27–9
Collection of tax 68–9
Companies
  anti-avoidance provisions 135
  controlled foreign 136–7
  dual resident 132
  investing in UK 133
  non-resident Irish 137–8
  offshore funds 135–6
  pre-return planning 137
  property development in UK 133–4
  residence 131–2
  trading in UK 132–3
  treaty shopping 134–5
Corporate stocks 53
Crown servants 25–6

Distributions 102
Dividends
  double taxation agreement 76–7
  income 53–4
Domicile
  acquisition on marriage 2–3
  change of 3–4
  concept of 1–5
  deemed 4
  forms 2
  in UK 4

Domicile—*contd*
  meaning 1
  of choice 3
  of dependence 2–3
  of origin 2
  possible changes in law 4–5
  see also Residence
Double taxation agreements
  artists 80
  athletes 80
  businesses 78–9
  capital gains 79
  dependent personal services 79–80
  dividends 76–7
  exchange of information 83
  fiscal residence 75–6
  income from real property 78
  independent personal services 79
  inheritance tax 36, 83–4
  interest 53, 77
  mutual agreement procedure 82
  non-discrimination 82
  other income 82
  pensions 80–1
  royalties 77–8
  students 82
  teachers 82
  treaty shopping 84
  unilateral relief 84

Emigration 96
Emoluments, foreign 19–20
Employment
  income 57–8
Equity investment 173
Estate
  income 61
Eurobonds 155
Evasion
  returning expatriate 45–6
Exchange controls 167–8
Exchange rates *see* Floating exchange rates
Excise duties 141
Expatriate
  family 27–9
  meaning 15
  permanent emigration 33–7
  resident *see* Resident expatriate
  retiring abroad 33–7
  returning *see* Returning expatriate
  semi 15
  working *see* Working expatriate

Family
  dispositions for maintenance of 107
  home 114–15
  of expatriate 27–9
Floating exchange rates
  bonds 174
  cash 175–6
  equity investment 173
  introduction 171
  movements 71–3
Foreign
  diplomats 92
  emoluments 19–20
  taxes 100
  trusts 127–30
Full-time employee
  residence, 9
Furnished holiday lettings 70

Gift
  capital gains tax 102
  in consideration of marriage 106–7
Government
  securities 154–5
  stocks 52, 153–4

Higher rate liability 61–2
Holiday lettings 70
Husband and wife
  annual allowances 105
  capital gains tax 95
  expatriate wife 28–9
  non-UK domiciled 110–11
  transfers between 105

Immigration 96
Income
  avoidance of higher rate liability 61–2
  bank deposits 49–51
  building society deposits 49–51
  dividends 53–4
  employment 57–8
  estate 61
  interest—
    bank and other deposits 49–51
    corporate stocks 53
    double taxation agreements 53, 77
    government stocks 52
    local authority stocks 52–3
    mortgage interest relief at source 70–1
    other 53
  investment 29–30, 34–5

264 Index

Income—*contd*
  life assurance policies 54–5
  Lloyd's Underwriters 62–3
  maintenance payments 59–60
  National Savings 56
  non-UK investment 29–30
  patents 59
  pensions 56–7
  professions 58–9
  rental 67–8
  royalties 59
  trades 58–9
  trust 61
  unremittable 46–7, 92
Income tax
  mortgage interest relief at
    source 70–1
  personal allowances 63–5
  rental income 67–8
  residence *see* Residence
  Schedule D—
    relief 24
    remittance basis 86–8
  Schedule E relief 24
  trusts 121–4
Inheritance tax
  agricultural property relief 108
  annual allowances 105–6
  avoidance 35–6
  business property relief 107–9
  chargeable transfers 104
  charge to 103
  criteria for 35
  dispositions for maintenance of
    family 107
  double taxation agreement 36,
    83–4
  exemptions 104–5
  family home 114–15
  gifts in consideration of
    marriage 106
  incidence 116–17
  Inland Revenue powers 36
  insurance policies 113–14
  introduction 103
  liability 103
  location of assets 109–10
  non-UK domiciled spouse 110–11
  normal expenditure out of
    income 106
  other exempt transfers 107
  persons not domiciled in UK 109
  planning 112–13
  potentially exempt transfers 105
  reliefs 104–5

Inheritance tax—*contd*
  returning expatriate 36–7
  settled property 111–12
  transfers between spouses 105
  trusts 116, 125–7
  wills 115–116
  will trusts 116
  written variations 117–18
Insurance policies 113–14
Interest *see* Income
Investment
  banking and deposits 150–1
  building society deposit 151–2
  collective investments media 155–7
  construction of portfolio 147–50
  equity 173
  establishing the objective 146–7
  Eurobonds 155
  exchange controls 167–8
  floating exchange rates 171–6
  income *see* Income
  introduction 145
  methods of holding 168–9
  miscellaneous 167
  National Savings 152–3
  principal media 150–55
  selection 169–70
  trusts 157–8
Ireland
  non-resident companies 137–8

Lettings, furnished holiday 70
Life assurance policies 54–5, 113–14,
  160–3
Lloyd's Underwriters 62–3
Local authority stocks 52–3

Maintenance 59–60, 88–9, 107
Marriage
  gift in consideration of 106–7
Mortgage interest relief at
  source 70–1

National insurance 30–1, 47, 92
National savings 56, 152–3
Non-residence, claim to 6
Non-resident trusts 127–30

Occupational pension schemes 31, 81
Offshore funds 101–2, 135–6, 158–60
Oil rig workers 27
Overseas visitors to UK
  armed forces 92
  foreign diplomats 92

Overseas visitors to UK—*contd*
  long stays 85–6
  maintenance 88–9
  national insurance 92
  non UK-domiciled visitor 86
  ordinary residence 92
  remittance basis 86–8
  remuneration 89–91
  short visits 85
  teaching and other academic exchange programs 93
  unremittable income 92

Patents 59
Pensions
  double taxation agreements 80–1
  income 56–7
  investment in 163–7
  occupational schemes 31, 81
  self-employed 81
  state 81
Permanent emigration 33–7
Personal
  allowances 63–5
  belongings 141–2
  services 79–80
Potentially exempt transfers 105
Principal private residence 72–4
Professions 58–9
Profits, business 78–9
Property
  administration of tax 68–9
  agricultural property relief 108
  business property relief 107–9
  capital gains tax 71–4, 96–7
  collection of tax 68–9
  companies 133–4
  furnished holiday lettings 70
  mortgage interest relief at source 70–1
  principal private residence 72–4
  real, income from 78
  rental income 67–8
  settled 111–12
  tenancy arrangements 67
  value added tax 140–1

Qualifying
  period 17–18

Relief
  claims for 24
  inheritance tax 104–5
  mortgage interest, at source 70–1
  non-resident's entitlement 63–5

Relief—*contd*
  personal allowances 63–5
  unilateral 84
Remuneration
  overseas visitors 89–91
Rental income 67–8
Residence
  accommodation rule 9–10
  capital gains tax 95
  companies 131–2
  dual 6–7
  fiscal 5–6, 75–6
  full-time employees abroad 9
  in year of departure 12–13
  in year of return 13–14
  meaning 1, 7
  months 7–8
  ordinarily resident 6
  ordinary 1, 7, 12–13, 91
  physical presence 5–6
  principal private 72–4
  question of fact 6
  rules 7
  six-month rule 7–8
  summary 11
  three-month rule 8–9
  trusts 119–20
  see also Domicile
Resident expatriate
  airmen 26–7
  armed forces 26
  claims for relief 24
  Crown servants 25–6
  long absences 16–19
  meaning 15
  national insurance contributions 30–1
  non-UK investment income 29–30
  occupational pension schemes 31
  oil rig workers 27
  other reliefs 20–3
  overseas earnings of non-resident 24–5
  seafarers 26–7
  self-employed 23–4
Retiring abroad 33–7
Returning expatriate
  capital gains tax 44–5
  checklist 176–7
  evasion 45–6
  inheritance tax 36–7
  legal matters 47–8
  miscellaneous investments 46
  national insurance 47
  tax liabilities on return 39–44

Returning expatriate—*contd*
  tax planning 39
  unremittable overseas income 46–7
Royalties
  double taxation agreement 77–8
  income 59

Seafarers 26–7
Self-employed expatriate
  pensions 81
  profits from trade or
    profession 23–4
  residence 13
  resident 23–4
Semi-expatriate 15
Settlements *see* Trusts
Spouse *see* Husband and wife
Stamp duty 142–3
State retirement pension 81
Students 82

Teachers 82, 93
Tenancy arrangements 67
Trades 58–9
Treaty shopping 84, 134–5
Trusts
  capital gains tax 101, 124–5
  created *inter vivos* 121
  foreign 127–30
  income 61

Trusts—*contd*
  income tax 121–4
  inheritance tax 116, 125–7
  investment 157–8
  non-resident 127–30
  residence 119–20
  resident 120–1
  unit 157–8
  will 116

UK income *see* Income
Unit trusts 157–8
United Nations Organisation 64–5

Value added tax
  cars 141
  exemptions 139–40
  importation 139
  property 140–1
  registration 139
  zero-rating 139–40
Visitors *see* Overseas visitors to UK

Wife *see* Husband and wife
Will
  inheritance tax 115–16
  returning expatriate 48
  trusts 116
Working expatriate *see* Resident
  expatriate